Lecture Notes of the Institute for Computer Sciences, Social Informatics and Telecommunications Engineering 364

Ana Lúcia Martins · João C. Ferreira ·
Alexander Kocian · Vera Costa (Eds.)

Intelligent Transport Systems, From Research and Development to the Market Uptake

4th EAI International Conference, INTSYS 2020
Virtual Event, December 3, 2020
Proceedings

 Springer

Editors
Ana Lúcia Martins (iD)
University Institute of Lisbon
Lisbon, Portugal

João C. Ferreira (iD)
University Institute of Lisbon
Lisbon, Portugal

Alexander Kocian (iD)
University of Pisa
Pisa, Italy

Vera Costa (iD)
University of Porto
Porto, Portugal

ISSN 1867-8211   ISSN 1867-822X (electronic)
Lecture Notes of the Institute for Computer Sciences, Social Informatics
and Telecommunications Engineering
ISBN 978-3-030-71453-6   ISBN 978-3-030-71454-3 (eBook)
https://doi.org/10.1007/978-3-030-71454-3

This Springer imprint is published by the registered company Springer Nature Switzerland AG
The registered company address is: Gewerbestrasse 11, 6330 Cham, Switzerland

Preface

We are delighted to introduce the proceedings of the fourth edition of the International Conference on Intelligent Transport Systems (INTSYS 2020) from the European Alliance for Innovation (EAI). This conference brought together researchers, developers, and practitioners from around the world who are leveraging and developing Intelligent Transportation Systems (ITS) to increase efficiency, safety, mobility, and tackle Europe's growing emission and congestion problems.

The theme of INTSYS 2020 was "Intelligent Transportation Systems: Challenges for 2030". This edition received 38 submissions from which the technical program of INTSYS 2020 was developed and consisted of 16 full papers accepted. Of these, 15 papers were presented in oral sessions at the main conference tracks. All of the accepted papers were subjected to a double-blind peer-review process with a minimum of three reviews for each paper.

Concerning the committees, it was a great pleasure to work with the excellent organizing team of the EAI, which was essential for the success of the INTSYS 2020 conference. In particular, we would like to express our gratitude to Karolina Marcinova for all the support she provided in all subjects. We would like also to express our gratitude to all the members of the Technical Program Committee, who have helped in the peer-review process of the technical papers, as well as ensured a high-quality technical program. We would like to thank the extensive list of external reviewers from several areas of expertise and from numerous countries around the world. A special acknowledgement has to be addressed to all the authors for their effort producing such good-quality papers and also for the extremely rich and positive feedback shared at the conference.

We strongly believe that the INTSYS conference provides a good forum for all researchers, developers, and practitioners to discuss all scientific and technological aspects that are relevant to ITS. It is becoming a privileged space for knowledge sharing and networking. We also expect that the future INTSYS conferences will be as successful and stimulating, as indicated by the contributions presented in this volume.

December 2020

Ana Lúcia Martins
João C. Ferreira
Alexander Kocian
Vera Costa

Conference Organization

Steering Committee

Imrich Chlamtac	Bruno Kessler Professor, University of Trento, Italy
Ana Lúcia Martins	Iscte-Instituto Universitário de Lisboa, Portugal
João C. Ferreira	Iscte-Instituto Universitário de Lisboa, Portugal
Alexander Kocian	Pisa University, Italy

Organizing Committee

General Chair

Ana Lúcia Martins	Iscte-Instituto Universitário de Lisboa, Portugal

General Co-chairs

João C. Ferreira	Iscte-Instituto Universitário de Lisboa, Portugal
Alexander Kocian	Pisa University, Italy

TPC Chair and Co-chair

Ana Lúcia Martins	Iscte-Instituto Universitário de Lisboa, Portugal
João C. Ferreira	Iscte-Instituto Universitário de Lisboa, Portugal
Alexander Kocian	Pisa University - Italy

Sponsorship and Exhibit Chair

Márcia Batista	INOV, Portugal

Local Chair

Teresa Galvão	FEUP and INESC TEC - Portugal

Workshops Chair

Maria C. Pereira	Iscte-Instituto Universitário de Lisboa, Portugal

Publicity and Social Media Chair

Carlos M. P. Sousa	Molde University College, Norway

Publications Chair

Vera Costa	FEUP - Portugal

Web Chair

Bruno Mataloto	Iscte-Instituto Universitário de Lisboa, Portugal

Posters and PhD Track Chair

Rosaldo Rossetti   FEUP, Portugal

Panels Chair

Luis Elvas   Inov, Portugal

Demos Chair

Frederica Gonçalves   University of Madeira, Portugal

Tutorials Chair

Ana Madureira   ISEP - Portugal

Technical Program Committee

Adriano Del Lino	Federal University of Western Pará, Brazil
Alexander Kocian	Pisa University, Italy
Ana Lúcia Martins	Iscte-Instituto Universitário de Lisboa, Portugal
Ana Madureira	ISEP, Portugal
Bruno Mataloto	Iscte-Instituto Universitário de Lisboa, Portugal
Carlos M. P. Sousa	Molde Colegue, Norway
Dagmar Caganova	Slovak University of Technology in Bratislava, Slovakia
Diana Mendes	Iscte-Instituto Universitário de Lisboa, Portugal
Frederica Gonçalves	University of Madeira, ITI/LARSys Portugal
Gabriel Pestana	Inov, Portugal
Ghadir Pourhashem	Slovak University of Technology in Bratislava, Slovakia
Giuseppe Lugano	University of Žilina, Slovakia
João C. Ferreira	Iscte-Instituto Universitário de Lisboa, Portugal
Lia Oliveira	ESCE - Escola Superior de Ciências Empresariais, Portugal
Lorna Uden	Staffordshire University, UK
Ľuboš Buzna	University of Žilina, Slovakia
Luis Elvas	Inov, Portugal
Marek Kvet	University of Žilina, Slovakia
Maria C. Pereira	Iscte-Instituto Universitário de Lisboa, Portugal
Michal Koháni	University of Žilina, Slovakia
Michal Kvet	University of Žilina, Slovakia
Miroslav Svítek	Czech Technical University in Prague, Czech Republic
Pavan Kumar Mishra	National Institute of Technology Raipur, India
Peter Brida	University of Žilina, Slovakia
Peter Holečko	University of Žilina, Slovakia
Peter Jankovič	University of Žilina, Slovakia
Peter Počta	University of Žilina, Slovakia

Porfírio Filipe	ISEL, Portugal
Rahul Sharma	TECMIC, Portugal
Rosaldo Rossetti	FEUP, Portugal
Sofia Kalakou	Iscte-Instituto Universitário de Lisboa, Portugal
Tatiana Kováčiková	University of Žilina, Slovakia
Teresa Grilo	Iscte-Instituto Universitário de Lisboa, Portugal
Tomás Brandão	Iscte-Instituto Universitário de Lisboa, Portugal
Ulpan Tokkozhina	Iscte-Instituto Universitário de Lisboa, Portugal
Veronika Šramová	University of Žilina, Slovakia
Vitor Monteiro	University of Minho, Portugal
Vitoria Albuquerque	Universidade Nova de Lisboa, Portugal

Conference Manager

Karolina Marcinova	EAI - European Alliance for Innovation, n.o., Belgium

Contents

Simulation and Prediction

Mobility

Mobile Ticketing Customers: How to Attract Them and Keep Them Loyal

Marta Campos Ferreira[1,2(✉)], Catarina Ferreira[1],
and Teresa Galvão Dias[1,2]

[1] Faculty of Engineering, University of Porto,
Rua Dr. Roberto Frias, 4200-465 Porto, Portugal
{mferreira, tgalvao}@fe.up.pt,
catarinassferr@gmail.com
[2] INESC-TEC, Faculty of Engineering, University of Porto,
Rua Dr. Roberto Frias, 4200-465 Porto, Portugal

Abstract. Technological advances and the use of mobile solutions to make smartphone users' daily life easier is a mindset that has revolutionized the society lifestyle in the past years. In the public transport sector, mobile ticketing is an example of the applicability of mobile solutions in a real context. Using one smartphone to purchase and validate tickets is a revolutionary idea that has acquired fans around the world. The convenience of use and time savings throughout the process are positive aspects, however, the success of the adoption of such services is limited.

Based on the case of Porto, Portugal and particularly of the mobile app And, this study intends to understand customer churn factors of mobile ticketing services by analysing data from customer complaints and from usage history. Thus, an analysis of the complaints, the complainers and the effects of complaints is presented. A strategy for capturing and retaining users is also proposed considering four stages of mobile ticketing apps lifecycle: user onboarding, user engagement, user retention and user reinstall.

Keywords: Mobile ticketing · Urban passenger transport · Customer loyalty · Customer churn

1   Introduction

As the world becomes increasingly interconnected, technology adoption is one of the most influential factors in human progress. Accessing internet right away or owning a smartphone is now assumed as granted in the many advanced economies. It permeates commerce, social interactions, politics, culture and daily life [1]. Furthermore, while high-income economies keep using more internet and owning more high-tech gadgets, in the past years, there has been a tendency for the emerging countries to follow and copy these behaviors. These patterns are now global, regardless of how fast they grow in each type of economy. In 2018, more than 3.5 billion people, 47% of the world population, was connected to mobile internet [2].

A. L. Martins et al. (Eds.): INTSYS 2020, LNICST 364, pp. 3–15, 2021.
https://doi.org/10.1007/978-3-030-71454-3_1

Internet access and innovative services facilitate the access to modern public health services, free education services and financial services, including mobile payments. Accordingly, mobile has become a fundamental gateway to the digital economy. The general adoption of mobile devices to pay for goods and services is a wide-spreading reality [3–5]. Mobile payments were designed to provide a secure, convenient, consistent, efficient and trusted payment experience to the users [6]. Although, security and privacy issues, as well as interaction and reliability of the service, might be sometimes concerns that users share [7].

Mobile payments can be applied to several sectors such as public transport. There, mobile payment comprises both pay-as-you-go options - in which the mobile phones serves as a wallet and actual ticketing - where passengers buy and authenticate tickets on their mobile phone. The last feature is only possible due to an emerging technology based service called mobile ticketing.

Similarly, to what happens in mobile payment services, mobile ticketing is a process whereby customers can order, pay for, obtain and validate tickets using only mobile devices and without needing the physical ticket. A mobile ticket contains a unique ticket verification varying according to the technology used. While some mobile ticketing systems require the validation through SMS text, a QR or barcode, others require Near Field Communication (NFC) [6]. Mobile ticketing service solutions take advantage of wireless communication and thus intend to free customers from difficult purchase decisions, allowing easier access to other services.

The convenience of this technology makes it totally suitable to address the problems of urban congestion and stress of metropolitan areas. As public transportation improves the mobility of passengers, by means that are safe of high-quality, it can be seen as the required solution to urban sustainability. Although, the complexity of the transport networks and the lack of seamless options reduce the attractiveness of the sector. Long waiting times in queues for purchasing and validating tickets make people drop this solution and choose to use their own vehicle instead. Mobile ticketing in the public transport sector can deliver an innovative, ubiquitous and engaging service [8].

Although some cities implemented mobile ticketing solutions on their public transport network, the adoption of such services seems to achieve limited success [9]. The causes that lead to such a low rate of utilization of the service are so far unknown. However, researchers affirm that the churn factors are somehow related to the acquisition phase or to the user experience [10]. Others claim that usage rates are still low because mobile payments require customers to change their behaviors towards tightly ingrained payment habits [11].

In an attempt to understand the phenomenon, the authors [11] studied the failure of three mobile payment cases in Switzerland: m-Maestro project, European initiative compliant with Visa, and mobile payments by PostFinance. PostFinance initiative, for instance, failed to provide additional value for customers and local merchants. They faced significant difficulties in finding a workable balance between interoperability and the ease of use for customers, resulting in a clumsy solution that did suit the physical environment and the behaviors associated with payments in local stores. At the end of the study, the authors recognize that further research is needed to formulate a more complete framework grounded in the richer process data of mobile payment diffusion trajectories.

On the other hand, despite recognizing that despite the growing number of mobile payment apps, very few solutions have turned to be successful, the authors [12] selected some of those few successful platforms to study the success factors. The authors conclude that the success of mobile payment platforms lies with the ability of the platform to balance the reach (number of participants) and the range (features and functionalities) of the platform.

In the city of Porto, Portugal, a mobile ticketing application, called Anda was deployed in June 2018 [13]. An analysis of the level of service utilization allowed to conclude that there are many customers who have never used the application, even though they have downloaded it, and others who, despite having already use it, preferred to give up the application and continue to use the traditional ticketing system. This reality happens with a number of similar mobile ticketing applications existent in the market and literature fails in explaining this phenomenon.

Therefore, this paper aims to identify and analyze the customer churn factors of mobile ticketing services and to propose strategies for customer acquisition and retention. This work is based on an in-depth analysis of the case of Porto, Portugal. Half a year of Anda complaints and usage data was analyzed. These, comprise data from interaction between the users and the customer support - made by phone, email and social networks - as well as data from the app usage history of those who complain. Thus, it is possible to establish the causal relationship between all the data extracted and then identify the reasons behind the churn factors. Based on that, a mobile ticketing customers' lifecycle can be defined from customer onboarding to customer acquisition, customer retention and customer re-engagement. For each of those stages, the critical success factors are identified and a set of useful strategies is set to attract and delight customers.

In the next sections the paper methodology is described, followed by the results of the analysis of complaints and user validation data. The discussion of the results is presented together with a proposal of service improvement in each of its stages. The final section presents the conclusions.

2 Methodology

In the city of Porto, Portugal, the public transport system is comprised of three subsystems: buses, light rail, and suburban trains. The three are all integrated into a multimodal public transport ticketing system, Andante. This system was originally designed for the use of a smartcard with RFID contactless technology. Users can purchase a monthly subscription pass, a metropolitan subscription, an Andante 24 pass – available for only 24 h, a tourist card or an occasional card - if they only need it for a limited number of travels.

In June 2018, a new mobile ticketing solution, called Anda, was deployed in Porto as a complement to the Andante system. By using the app the Andante card is dispensable because all action required to travel in Porto public transportation, from tickets purchasing to validation, can be done with a mobile device [14].

The launch of Anda was widely reported in the media, having been accompanied by a massive communication plan. The objective was not only to disseminate the new service, but also to explain how it works. It involved news in TV channels, newspapers and social networks, placing outdoors and stands at stations, decorate vehicles, distribute flyers and informational leaflets, and having promoters presenting the service and helping customers.

To have a better understanding of how to capture and retain customers, it is crucial to first evaluate and then become entirely informed of current users' behavior. By identifying patterns of usage, as well as their tendency, it becomes easier to perceive the indicators of customers who are about to churn.

For instance, customer feedback might be a valuable tool to understand how the service has been communicated to current and potential users. Complaints analysis enables the understanding of how users perceive the app and what are their expectations and needs about it. By that, it is easier to recognize the vital areas for customer communication improvement and therefore the service improvement as well.

Since its full deployment, customers using the Anda application interact daily with the customer support service, through several channels, such as telephone, email, Facebook, Google play and physical stores. This interaction can have several purposes, such as asking questions, reporting errors, or making suggestions for improvement. The information from the various channels is collected in a single platform, to be further processed and analyzed.

The object of this study is the complaints received by the Intermodal Transports of Porto (TIP) over 6 months of use of Anda - from September 2019 to February 2020. The choice of this time interval is related to the fact that it is intended to study a normal period of use, with only regular updates to the app, but without major changes that would imply a greater influx of complaints.

The analysis included three main aspects: the complaints, the complainers, and the effects of the complaints on the usage of Anda. First, data on the complaints include the date when the statements were presented, the reasons which motivated them, the responsible transport operators, and the media through which they were submitted. Second, regarding the complainers, it is gathered information about their social profile – whether they belong to a specific age group or benefit from aids because of their social status – and about the type of ticket they most use. The information on the distribution of complainers over the different months was also collected. Finally, to assess the impact of the complaints on usage, data from app's validation history are considered.

To perform a descriptive analysis of the data gathered, MS Excel and Rapid Miner Software were required.

3   Results

This section includes the results of the analysis performed. In the first moment, the data of the complaints is presented. This is followed by the presentation of complainers' characterization and in the end, the results focus on the cross of data from the history of usage of Anda app and the complaints data.

3.1   The Complaints

During the period of time under analysis, the total of complaints Anda app received is at total 1223. Of those, only 68% (832 complaints) were submitted by different users, which means that 32% of the users complained at least more than once. To the date, the majority of those records (95,5%) are resolved and closed, but those which are still open require action by a third party – for example, external technical teams.

The problems that can arise in the use of Anda are several and can be categorized by the reasons that caused them. The main reasons are related to travel validation, login and register in the app, the correct completion of trips, the consultation of personal information, the associated tariff, and the disregarding of intermediate travel stops. Figure 1 shows the distribution of the main complaint reasons. Additionally, there are other reasons that can lead to a complaint - beacons, payment methods, questions, enroll, data change, improvement suggestions, inspection, and account deletion - but the total number of records with these reasons is not relevant to be considered in this study.

The Intermodal Transports of Porto (TIP) is constituted of 11 public transport operators and Anda can be used in all of them. Besides that, it is important to mention that 76,3% of the complaints is not related to travel itself and to the operators, but to issues related to the app or billing. The complaints to the transport operators are 23,7% of the total.

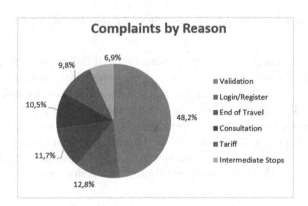

Fig. 1. Distribution of complaints by reason.

Anda's complaints can be submitted through the most varied means of communication, but two of them stand o-ut for their great use: the app's crash report (64%) and email (32,5%). Among the rest are phone calls (3%), the official Facebook page (0,4%) and the Google Play Store (0,2%).

3.2   The Complainers

The total number of Anda users from September 2019 to February 2020 is 5759 and 14% of them are complainers of the service. Usage data allows to know that, on average, about 3103 people use the app to travel on Porto's transport services per month. Likewise, it is also known that approximately 203 complaints are submitted per month. In Fig. 2, it is verified that, over the studied period, the relationship between the number of users and the total number of complaints received remained practically constant.

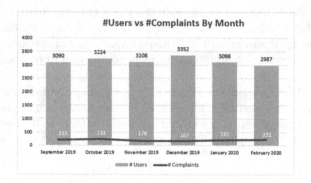

Fig. 2. Number of users vs number of complaints, per month.

Based on validation data, it is known what types of tickets were purchased by the complainers. The majority of people who complain buy single tickets (69.9%), ie for occasional trips. In Fig. 3a, it's seen the percentage distribution by different types of tickets. Additionally, TIP groups users by social profile according to their age group or social status. Through the analysis of these data, it can be seen in Fig. 3b that most of the complainers belong to the "Normal" social profile - which means they are adults who do not benefit from any type of discount. Among the remaining profiles are people who have lower rates (Social+), university students, students - under 18 - and seniors - over 65.

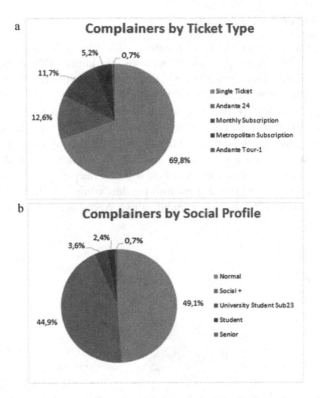

Fig. 3. a. Distribution of complainers by ticket type; b. Distribution of complaints by social profile.

The distribution of users by social profile also allows knowing that the users who most complain are the "Normal" and "Social+". Also, Fig. 4 shows that in all groups, the number of complaints is higher than the number of complainers, which, once again, reaffirms that there are users complaining more than once.

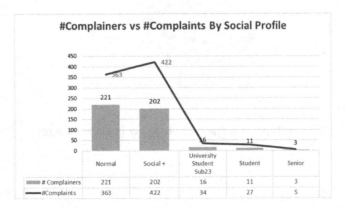

Fig. 4. Number of complainer vs number of complaints, by social profile.

3.3 The Effects of the Complaints

Finally, to understand the effect of complaints on the use of Anda, it is necessary to cross the data of both – complaints and validations. By knowing the complainers, it is noticeable their influence on the use of the application. Likewise, it is interesting to find out whether the use-complaint relationship is uni or bilateral.

When categorizing by type of users, as seen in Fig. 5a, it is possible to confirm that 78.7% of the complainers are people who use the app to make trips. However, 17.6% of app users complained without ever having used it - 9.9% complained before using it and 7.7% complained without ever having used it. In addition, 3.7% of complainers submit their statement at the time of their first trip. To deepen this connection, it was also assessed the use of the app on trips after the last complaint. In Fig. 5b, it can be seen that the majority (79%) have continued to use Anda, but 21% have not done so again.

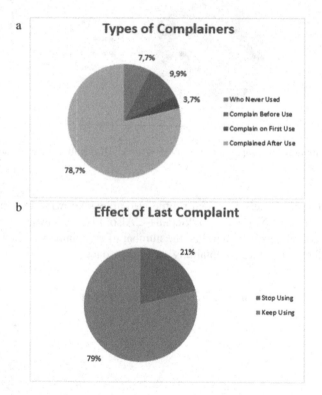

Fig. 5. a. Types of complainers; b. Effect of the last complaint.

4   Discussion

The analysis of the complaints and historical usage data opens the ground for several reflections and sets the path for the future development of the mobile ticketing services. In this sense, four fundamental stages were identified in the process of using this type of applications: user onboarding, user engagement, user retention and user reinstall. For each stage of the lifecycle, the main aspects to be taken into account - according to the results obtained - are identified and a series of tactics are established to increase the value of the service for the customers. The different user segments, as well as the appropriate channels to reach them, are also considered in the proposal presented.

4.1   User Onboarding

The data regarding to users who complain without having ever used the app are indicators that their first interactions with the service are not meeting their expectations. For technical or usability reasons, some users do not initially find the type of experience they were looking for and give up on the app before actually using it.

In order to counter this trend, Table 1 lists a series of tactics that can be put into practice. Regardless of the user segment, the application must present a welcoming message on first use, encourage users to register by emphasizing the benefits of the service and display a brief demonstration of the app and its main features.

Table 1.   Strategy to improve user onboarding for different types of user segments.

User segment	Tactics	Channels
Installed but not registered	• Welcome users on the app and introduce the main features of the app • Encourage the register in the first 24 h • Incentivize registration with rewards on the app (cashback, ticket discount)	• In-app Notifications • Push Notifications
Registered but not activated	• Welcome app users after the register. Incentivize them to complete the payment information • Stimulate users to make their first travel using the app, with rewards (cashback, ticket discount)	• In-app Notifications • Push Notifications • SMS • Email • Reminders
Registered and activated	• Encourage greater use of the app with rewards (cashback, ticket discount)	• In-app Notifications • Push Notifications • SMS • Email • Reminders

4.2   User Engagement

Once familiar with the service, users need to be converted and start using it consistently and frequently. The data collected shows that 9.9% of the complainers are people who complained before traveling with the app. Furthermore 3.7% are users who complained right after using the app for the first time. If these values aren't taken into account and if these users are not motivated to give the service a new chance, it is very likely that they will churn it.

At this stage of the cycle, the service should encourage consumers to complete the actions on the app – whether they are completing payment information or making a trip - stimulating the commitment already established. Notifications with special offers are also useful to promote constant use and encourage repeated interactions - for example, trips of the same type or with similar routes. Table 2 shows the different strategies to be targeted at the different users in the engagement stage.

Table 2. Strategy to improve user engagement for different types of user segments.

User segment	Tactics	Channels
Onboarded but non-converted	• Urge users to make their first travel using the app – push different use cases at different times • Create custom campaigns offering rewards for first users (cashback or travel discount)	• In-app Notifications • Push Notifications
First-time converted	• Confirm completion of first travel. Thank the choice of service, up to 5 min after it finishes • Encourage users to keep using the app	• Push Notifications • SMS • Email
Repeat converted	• Encourage continuous use through targeted personalized campaigns based on usage patterns • Promote different services with rewards (cashback or travel discount)	• In-app Notifications • Push Notifications • SMS • Email
Users not completing actions (abandonment)	• Notify users 1 h and 24 h after they abandon a task	• Push Notifications • SMS • Email • Reminders
No activity	• Remind users that have no activity in the app in the last 30 days	• Push Notifications • SMS • Email

4.3   User Retention

Mobile ticketing applications services tend to have difficulty retaining users. A consistent and constant customer base is the main foundation for the sustainable growth of any service.

At this stage, attention is drawn to data on the number of complaints and the number of complainers for each social profile. While in the "Normal" profile the number of complaints per complainer is approximately 3/2, in the rest the values increase by about two times. This information can become relevant in the sense that users dissatisfied with the service tend not only to abandon it but to negatively influence potential new users. The more complaints a person has submitted, the greater their dissatisfaction with the service and the greater the likelihood of churning it.

In order to optimize retention, users can be motivated to repeat the same interactions with the application in exchange for discounts on regular trips or cashback of the amount to be paid at the end of each month. A careful and attentive analysis to control the retention rates of current and potential users must be carried out, as well as personalized promotional campaigns and reminder of available offers. In Table 3 are some tactics to be implemented.

Table 3. Strategy to improve user retention for different types of user segments.

User segment	Tactics	Channels
Engaged but not loyal (hibernating)	• Communicate with the user and understand what's their perception of the app. Send messages to obtain an assessment of the service • Send customized campaigns with "We miss you" messages	• In-app Notifications • Push Notifications • Email
Engaged and loyal	• Ensure app rating and reviews • Reward loyalty with travel discounts or cashback	• In-app Notifications • Push Notifications • Email

4.4   User Reinstall

The reasons for uninstalling a mobile application can be of the most varied types, from problems with interaction with the interface, inefficiency of features, poor performance or disastrous user experience.

At this stage it is important to consider the data regarding the effect of the last complaint. That is, 21% of complainers have stopped using Anda since they made their last complaint. This aspect means that the reasons that motivated the complaint or the resolution obtained in the complaint became a reason to stop using the app. Thus, the likelihood of uninstalling the app increases, the more time has passed since the last time it was used.

In order to recover inactive or discontinued customers, conducting an analysis of user behavior, as well as requesting feedback from former customers, can be useful in understanding the points of friction between them and the application and possibly eliminating them. For regain lost users targeted promotional offers can be put into action. Table 4 presents some strategies to be put into action.

Table 4. Strategy to improve user reinstall for different types of user segments.

User segment	Tactics	Channels
Converted but disengaged	• Run customized campaigns with the latest offers • Update users' preferences. Suggestion on discounts based on new preferred routes • Send reminding messages about the advantages of the service	• Email
Churned	• Run personalized email survey seeking feedback to understand the reasons for app uninstall • Run "We miss you" or "Check what your missing" campaigns, highlighting new promotions and cashback offers • Run "We're just a click away" campaigns, following the suspension policy between 43rd to 50th days after uninstalling the app	• Email
Re-acquired	• Run personalizes "Welcome back" campaigns, highlighting new promotions and cashback offers	• In-app Notifications • Email

5 Conclusions

Complaints are statements submitted by customers of service and result from their dissatisfaction when what is provided does not meet their expectations. Realizing the degree of customers' dissatisfaction and assessing the impact this may have on current and/or new potential customers is an advantage. Thus, a strategy can be preventively defined to optimize the quality of service of mobile ticketing applications in each of its four stages of use.

Through this study, it is clear that in the context of the Anda app, not only does the use of the app lead to complaints, but complaints negatively influence the use of the application. The bilateral connection between these two aspects is the basis for a series of reasons that lead customers to churn it.

In order to understand this causal relationship more deeply, future work in this area should include Anda usability tests with current, potential and lost users. Interviews and focus group sessions with these same stakeholders can also be useful to understand their perspectives.

References

1. Poushter, J.: Smartphone ownership and internet usage continues to climb in emerging economies. Pew Res. Cent. **22**, 1–44 (2016)
2. GSMA: The State of Mobile Internet Connectivity 2020. GSMA Reports (2020)
3. Garrett, J.L., Rodermund, R., Anderson, N., Berkowitz, S., Robb, C.A.: Adoption of mobile payment technology by consumers. Fam. Consum. Sci. Res. J. **42**, 358–368 (2014). https://doi.org/10.1111/fcsr.12069
4. de Sena Abrahão, R., Moriguchi, S.N., Andrade, D.F.: Intention of adoption of mobile payment: an analysis in the light of the Unified Theory of Acceptance and Use of Technology (UTAUT). RAI Rev. Adm. e Inovação (2016). https://doi.org/10.1016/j.rai.2016.06.003

5. Fontes, T., Costa, V., Ferreira, M.C., Shengxiao, L., Zhao, P., Dias, T.G.: Mobile payments adoption in public transport. Transp. Res. Procedia **24**, 410–417 (2017). https://doi.org/10.1016/j.trpro.2017.05.093
6. Ferreira, M.C., Dias, T.G., e Cunha, J.F.: An in-depth study of mobile ticketing services in urban passenger transport: state of the art and future perspectives. In: Smart Systems Design, Applications, and Challenges, pp. 145–165. IGI Global (2020). https://doi.org/10.4018/978-1-7998-2112-0.ch008
7. Rodrigues, H., et al.: MobiPag: integrated mobile payment, ticketing and couponing solution based on NFC. Sensors **14**, 13389–13415 (2014). https://doi.org/10.3390/s140813389
8. Ferreira, M.C., Nóvoa, H., Dias, T.G., e Cunha, J.F.: A proposal for a public transport ticketing solution based on customers' mobile devices. Procedia – Soc. Behav. Sci. **111**, 232–241 (2014)
9. Dahlberg, T., Guo, J., Ondrus, J.: A critical review of mobile payment research. Electron. Commer. Res. Appl. **14**, 265–284 (2015). https://doi.org/10.1016/j.elerap.2015.07.006
10. Cheng, S.K.: Exploring Mobile Ticketing in Public Transport An analysis of enablers for successful adoption in The Netherlands Expertise Centre for E-ticketing in Public Transport (2017)
11. Ondrus, J., Lyytinen, K., Pigneur, Y.: Why mobile payments fail? Towards a dynamic and multi-perspective explanation. In: Proceedings of the 42nd Annual Hawaii International Conference on System Science, HICSS (2009). https://doi.org/10.1109/HICSS.2009.510
12. Staykova, K.S., Damsgaard, J.: Adoption of mobile payment platforms: managing reach and range. J. Theor. Appl. Electron. Commer. Res. **11**, 65–84 (2016). https://doi.org/10.4067/S0718-18762016000300006
13. Ferreira, M.C., Dias, T.G., Falcão, J.: Is Bluetooth Low Energy feasible for mobile ticketing in urban passenger transport? Transp. Res. Interdiscip. Perspect. **5**, 100120 (2020). https://doi.org/10.1016/j.trip.2020.100120
14. Ferreira, M.C., Dias, T.G., e Cunha, J.F.: Codesign of a mobile ticketing service solution based on BLE. J. Traffic Logist. Eng. **7**, 10–17 (2019). https://doi.org/10.18178/jtle.7.1.10-17

Understanding Spatiotemporal Station and Trip Activity Patterns in the Lisbon Bike-Sharing System

Vitória Albuquerque[1] , Francisco Andrade[2] ,
João Carlos Ferreira[2(✉)] , and Miguel Sales Dias[1,2]

[1] NOVA Information Management School (NOVA IMS),
Universidade Nova de Lisboa, Campus de Campolide,
1070-312 Lisboa, Portugal
{d20190115, jmdias}@novaims.unl.pt
[2] Instituto Universitário de Lisboa (ISCTE-IUL), ISTAR,
1649-026 Lisbon, Portugal
{fafaell, jcafa}@iscte-iul.pt

Abstract. The development of the Internet of Things and mobile technology is connecting people and cities and generating large volumes of geolocated and space-time data. This paper identifies patterns in the Lisbon GIRA bike-sharing system (BSS), by analyzing the spatiotemporal distribution of travel distance, speed and duration, and correlating with environmental factors, such as weather conditions. Through cluster analysis the paper finds novel insights in origin-destination BSS stations, regarding spatial patterns and usage frequency. Such findings can inform decision makers and BSS operators towards service optimization, aiming at improving the Lisbon GIRA network planning in the framework of multimodal urban mobility.

Keywords: Bike-sharing system · Mobility patterns · Statistical analysis · Cluster analysis · K-means · Urban mobility

1 Introduction

Cities are becoming more predominant in modern societies, and citizens mobility is a raising problem concerning pollution and traffic. To overcome such challenges, shared mobility approaches have been developed. In this domain, bike-sharing is a rising soft and active transportation modality, showing large growth rates around the world. In face of such demand, the number of bike-share companies operating in the world has increased also, becoming more effective and available in most developed cities. Therefore, citizens are shifting towards more sustainable urban transportation where bike-sharing is increasingly being adopted. Understanding how people use the bike and when, is thus mandatory, towards improving system efficiency.

In 2017, Lisbon implemented a fourth-generation Bike-Sharing System (BSS), which is currently expanding, under currently enforced development plans by the City Hall. Taking Lisbon as a use case, we have adopted a data mining approach to understand station and trip patterns in its GIRA bike-sharing system. To this aim, we

A. L. Martins et al. (Eds.): INTSYS 2020, LNICST 364, pp. 16–34, 2021.
https://doi.org/10.1007/978-3-030-71454-3_2

have analyzed GIRA bike data and environmental data, to derive the spatiotemporal distribution of travel distances, speed and durations and their relationship with environmental conditions, such as weather.

1.1   Historical Background

In 2017 Lisbon implemented its first bike-sharing system, GIRA. Over a year, it expanded and in 2018 there were already 140 bike stations across the city, among which 92 in the central area of the city, 27 downtown and riverfront, 15 at Parque das Nações and 6 at Avenida Fontes Pereira de Melo and Avenida da Liberdade. At that time the total available bikes were 1,410, with 940 electric. Currently, the GIRA bike-sharing system has future expansion plans, since bike-sharing is one an important strategy in the context of urban mobility policies approved by the city hall, towards achieving intelligent and sustainable mobility in Lisbon.

The deployed system includes a data collection feature, allowing to monitor spatiotemporal users' behavior and trip patterns. By analyzing such collected data, we can gain new insights about mobility in the urban fabric, specifically on real-world bicycle-sharing system usage behaviors. Additionally, monitoring and analyzing user behavior changes, provides a broader scenario of the Lisbon public transportation network, giving new opportunities and patterns for prediction and usability improvement.

1.2   Our Research Approach

Our approach started by posing the following research question: "What are the spatiotemporal station and trip activity patterns of GIRA, the Lisbon BSS, in 2018?" This question statement leads us to derive the following sub-questions: "What are the average figures of monthly and daily BSS use?"; "What is the bike trip relation to weather conditions, specifically to precipitation and temperature?"; "How can we group the BSS origin and destination stations, into clusters across the city?

To address these questions, we have applied statistical and machine learning methods, based in our literature review of the state of the art. We have looked at historical data of bike trips (approximately 700,000 records), Portuguese Institute of Sea and Weather – Instituto Português do Mar e Atmosfera (IPMA) data, and cycling network data of 2018, with a focus on finding usage patterns, towards service optimization.

The paper is structured as follows: Sect. 2 presents our survey of State of the Art. In Sect. 3, we introduce our methodology, which adopted state of the art methods. In Sect. 4, Major Findings, we discuss our results, with a comparative analysis with other cities and identify a few research gaps and limitations of our research. Finally, Sect. 5, we raise some conclusions and draw lines for further research.

2   State of the Art of Bike-Sharing Systems

The community agrees that BSS improve urban accessibility and sustainability, and thus more cities in the world are implementing BSS to tackle urban mobility and pollution problems. Since 2016 over 1000 BSS are running in 60 countries [1].

From its third-generation, BSS start using smart card technology [2], producing station-based and trip-level data, and facilitating studies that enable the adoption of these systems into urban transportation networks [3]. Evolving fourth-generation BSS provides key data on users' behavior and trip patterns.

Monitoring makes possible the identification of system performance and data analysis provides insights into users' behavior [4] enabling to balance bike demand and improve bike network resilience and response.

The latest bike-sharing systems technology [5] uses two configurations: a fixed number of bike stations to hire and return bikes and a free placement scheme. Bike stations can be monitored in real-time on online maps. Application Programming Interfaces (API), accessing the network usage data are supplied by operators and specified to be used by external software developers. In Europe, such access is governed by the GDPR – General Data Protection Regulation [6], enforced since 2018, which includes provisions for personal data privacy and protection, including data anonymization. This scheme produces usage datasets, of critical importance in transport research [5].

O'Brien [5] first analyzed 38 bike-sharing systems in Europe, the Middle East, Asia, Australasia and the Americas, identifying behavior patterns. Metrics were applied to classify bicycle sharing systems, based on non-spatial and spatial location attributes and temporal usage statistics, plus a qualitative classification. The study proposed applications such as demographic analysis and the role of operator redistribution activity.

BSSs have been studied over time by other authors, with important insights about station and bike trip patterns analysis.

One of the most sophisticated BSS in the world is deployed in Copenhagen, reaching a ratio of 557,920 inhabitants for 650,000 bikes, with 48,000 bike stations and 429 km of cycle lanes [7]. It is estimated that overall, 1,27 million km are travelled daily with 5 times more bicycles entering the city than cars, resulting in 4/5 access to bicycles.

Vélov, Lyon (France) bike-sharing system, studied by Jensen [8], analyzed 11,6 million journeys and visualized bike flows on map. Characteristics, such as peak usage in a strike as well as different work speeds, highest peak hours, where analyzed. The authors observed that the highest speed occurred in the morning peak.

The London BSS network (Santander Cycles) is also expanding. In 2016 it reached 11,000 bicycles for 8,416,535 inhabitants, with 750 bike stations, 402,199 km travelled daily and 131,000 bicycle trips. London BSS station data, analyzed by Lathia [9] and Jensen [8], observed usage peaks and significant weekday and weekend differences. Spatial clusters with distinctive structures were found grouping intra-day usage patterns.

Studies show that longer BSS trips are observed in larger cities such as Chicago [10] and New York, although the latter differs between weekday and weekend usage [11].

Caulfield [12] findings showed that the majority of trips of BSS in medium size cities were short and frequent trips. Weather conditions also had an important impact, meaning that good weather conditions corresponded to an increase of trips.

El-Assi [13] analyzed the variation of trip activity along the season, month, week and hour, establishing correlations between these variables. The authors found a positive correlation with temperature calculated for each season.

Other studies showed that morning and afternoon peak patterns are different in BSS.

Han study [14] on San Francisco spatial-temporal bike trip patterns showed that in the hourly metrics analysis, most of the trips were between 8:00–9:00 am and 5:00–6:00 pm, meaning that most users use bikes to commute to work. El-Assi [13] found similar results in Toronto BSS regarding day peaks.

On the other hand, in Montreal BIXI BSS [15], peaks occurs in the evening and weekends.

Clustering algorithms studies on BSS data are applied by combining temporal and spatial attributes variables. More specifically, three clustering algorithms, namely, hierarchical clustering [10, 16, 17], community detection clustering [10, 18], and K-means clustering, [18–21], are the most common.

According to Caggiani [18], who analyzed the performance of the three clustering algorithms, K-means has been proven to be the best clustering algorithm to detect and rebalance bike-sharing usage patterns.

3   Data Mining Methodology

Our data analysis and visualization were performed in Python [22] using Jupyter Notebook platform [23]. Data cleaning, preprocessing, analysis and visualization were performed using different libraries according to the purpose of the application. "Numpy" [24], "Pandas" [25], "Matplotlib" [26], "Seaborn" [27] were used for statistical analysis and visualization. "GDAL" [28], "Shapely" [29], "Folium" [30], "Fiona" [31] were used to visualize spatial analysis. Our data science algorithms used "Scikit-learn" [32] to perform K-Means, Naïve Bayes, Train-test split and Accuracy Score.

In our approach, we have adopted the Cross-Industry Standard Process for Data Mining (CRISP-DM) methodology (see Fig. 1). This method is structured in three phases that are organized in a sequence: firstly, data collection, secondly data cleaning and thirdly data mining. Chapman [33] is convinced that CRISP-DM ensures the quality of knowledge discovery in the project results, requires reduced skills for such knowledge discovery, and with reduced costs and time. Data collection consists in collecting and perceiving the characteristics of the collected data, to meet the users and business needs, understanding where the data comes from and what type of analysis can be done with it. With Data Cleaning, we remove noise in the data, so that further analysis cannot be affected by the data itself. Data Mining allows the application of statistical and/or machine learning techniques enabling discovery of behaviors that could not be possible to observe before. It also includes data visualization, with diagrams, plots and other graphical depictions, that show us visually, the found patterns and behaviors.

Our datasets included bike trip data with trip characteristics, and bike stations data holding information about the network of bike stations throughout the city. To investigate the built environment correlation with trips, we've used precipitation and temperature datasets for this analysis.

Two datasets were generated for our analysis: one combining precipitation and temperature data and bike trips data (see schemas in Table 2 and Table 3), and another combining bike trips data and bike station data (see schemas in Table 1 and Table 2), with the goal to generate bike paths in the city and to visualize the stations chosen by the users. The first dataset was joined through a temporal basis and the second one was joined via the stations field. To generate these datasets, we've developed an Extract, Transform and Load process (ETL), to load the external databases, transform them by creating common columns and joining the datasets, and finally by loading them into our project. I've performed an adaptation of the ETL methodology proposed in CRISP-DM. Our ETL was used in the Data Cleaning phase, as it performs some cleaning and conforming processes in the incoming data, to obtain data which is correct, complete, consistent, accurate and unambiguous [34].

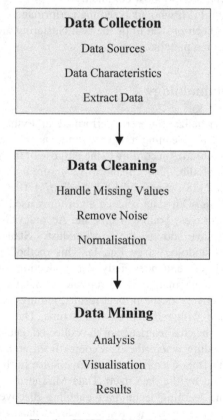

Fig. 1. CRISP-DM Methodology.

3.1 Data Sources and Data Characteristics

Three different sources of data provided by the Lisbon City Hall and the Portuguese Institute of Sea and Weather – Instituto Português do Mar e Atmosfera (IPMA), were used in our research: bike station data of 2018, bike trip data (from 25th January 2018 to 15th October 2018) and IPMA data of 2018.

Bike station data schema includes information about the stations, such as commercial designation ID (desigcomercial), entity ID (entity_id), planning ID (id_planeamento), latitude, longitude and the station capacity (capacidade_docas). This data was collected in 76 bicycle stations around Lisbon.

Table 1. Bike station data schema

Characteristics	Description
desigcomercial	Commercial designation
entity_id	Entity ID
id_planeamento	Planning ID
latitude	Latitude
longitude	Longitude
capacidade_docas	Station capacity

Table 2. Bike trip data schema

Characteristics	Description
id	Column ID
date_start	Start date and time
date_end	End date and time
distance	distance
station_start	Start station ID
station_end	End station ID
Bike_rfid	Bike ID
geom	Travel trajectory geometry
num_vertices	Number of nodes
Tipo_bicicleta	Bike type (conventional or electric)

Bike trip data of 2018, is characterized by origin-destination (O-D) trip that includes id (column ID), date_start (start date and time), date_end (end date and time), distance (distance in metres), station_start (start station ID), station_end (end station ID), bike_rfid (bike ID), geom (geometry), num_vertices (number of nodes), and tipo_bicicleta (bike_type).

The IPMA weather data of 2018 consists in the total precipitation in 2018, and its schema includes the fields ANO (Year), MS (Month), DI (Day), HR (Hour), "1200535", "1200579" and "1210762". These 3 last fields represent the reference (ID) of the 3 weather stations located in Lisbon, giving information about the precipitation, where "1200535" is Lisboa Geofísica (Lisbon centre), "1200579" is Lisboa Avenida Gago Coutinho and "1210762" is Lisboa Tapada da Ajuda.

Table 3. IPMA data schema

Characteristics	Description
ANO	Year
MS	Month
DI	Day
HR	Hour
1200535	Lisboa Geofísica Weather Station #1
1200579	Lisboa Avenida Gago Coutinho Weather Station #2
1210762	Lisboa Tapada da Ajuda Weather Station #3

From the 3 data sources whose schemas where presented in Tables 1, 2 and 3, we derived, via an ETL process, 2 datasets, namely, the "bike temporal analysis dataset" and the "bike trips-stations dataset", used in our data mining approach.

3.2 Data Cleaning

EMEL GIRA data, a fourth generation BSS, provides broad and extensive information. Data extraction methods have not yet been extensively explored [35], therefore there are limitations in the collected data, which needs to be evaluated on its limitations and cleaned, if appropriate. Data cleaning involves processes of handling missing data and noise removal, to generate datasets with accurate and validated data. In the GIRA dataset, we have found incoherent data, namely sparse, discontinuities and nonuniformities of data. On the contrary, bike station data and IPMA data did not require data cleaning and were ready to use.

The following data cleaning methods, where applied to bike trip data:

- We have removed the not assigned (NA) values of the bike type (1% of the dataset).
- We have removed the geometry and number of nodes which had NA values, corresponding to 50% of the data.
- The variable speed was removed due to the trips that were shorter than 1 min.
- The missing values in the distance were filled by computing the average speed times the duration.

After data cleaning, the total number of trips using the GIRA BSS in 2018 was 684,471. In that year, the average number of trips per month, ranging from January to October, was 68,447. In terms of stations, the average number of trips was 9,126 throughout year. Per day, there was an average number of trips of 2,602, starting from January 25th until October 15th.

3.3 Data Mining

Literature studies have tried to understand user's profile and travel behavior [36–38], activity patterns of bike stations [9] and the impact of the built environment in the BSS [39].

The methods applied are statistical methods to analyze data and visualization techniques. To understand bike trip patterns in the urban mobility network and trip models, studies have shown the importance to correlate transport mode and trip choices and built environment characteristics [40, 41].

Many methods are applied to perform data mining namely, to examine the relations between bike stations, bike trips and built environment. The evaluation of BSS success depends in these relationships, most of them leading to users' access to the bike stations [42].

Clustering algorithms combining temporal and spatial attributes variables are also data mining methods used for this analysis purpose. More specifically K-means clustering [18–21], used by McKenzie [43] and Zhong [44] to measure regularity at different scales and to measure spatiotemporal variation and cluster interaction.

3.3.1 Bike Usage Analysis

To investigate the monthly bicycle usage frequency, we have merged the "bike trip dataset" with the "bike temporal basis dataset" and got a new relation with columns ANO (Year), MÊS (Month), DIA (Day), FERIADO (Holiday), SEMANA (Week), SEMESTRE (Semester), TRIMESTRE (Trimester), DIA_DE_SEMANA (Weekday) and MÊS_DSC (Month description). This was our trips schema, with data spanning from January to October from 2018. In the Summer months (June, July, August and September), there were a total of 439,176 trips being the more concentrated period (64% of all trips), as depicted in Fig. 2.

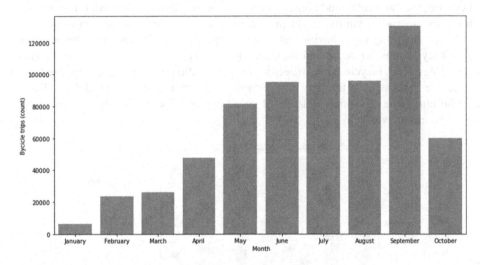

Fig. 2. Bicycle usage frequency per month.

The weekday and weekend usage were also analyzed to understand the preferences of using the bike-sharing service during the week. Results are presented in Fig. 3, where weekdays are ordered from 1 to 7. The weekend is represented by 1 (Sunday) and 7 (Saturday). Our results show that most users (82%) prefer to use the service during the week, rather than during the weekend.

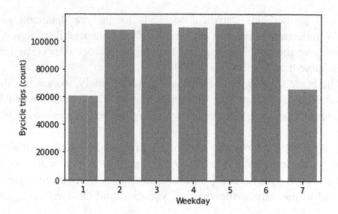

Fig. 3. Bicycle usage per weekday.

The distribution of trips throughout the different time periods of the day was analyzed too. The column date_starts was transformed into a time format and the hour was extracted in order to create the column Periodo_dia (Day period). The day was broken down into three-hour groups: Morning: 7:00am to 12:00am; Afternoon: 12:00am– 20:00 pm and Overnight: 20:00 pm–7:00am. Our analysis shows that most of the trips (56%) occur during the afternoon, when comparing with the morning and overnight periods (see Fig. 4). Additionally, during working weekdays, after the afternoon, the morning period comes second. In the weekends, users still prefer to ride during the afternoon, but overnight rides come second, rather than morning ones.

When analyzing the behavior and patterns regarding the distance and the duration of the bicycle trips, we addressed the differences between the weekdays versus bicycle type. Regarding bicycle type (Electric or Conventional), we have observed no noticeable differences in terms of trip distance and duration, during weekdays. There also no noticeable difference, in terms of speed and duration, across the different days of the week, in average.

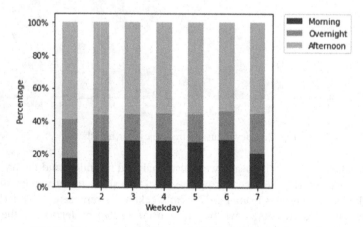

Fig. 4. Bicycle usage (%) per weekday within the day period.

3.3.2 Station Usage Analysis

Our analysis shows that the most used start stations are located in the main axis of the city. The top 6 start stations (see Fig. 5) are 105 (CC Vasco da Gama), 307 (Marquês de Pombal), 417 (Avenida Duque de Ávila), 421 (Alameda D. Afonso Henriques), 446 (Avenida da República/Interface de Entrecampos) and 481 (Campo Grande/Museu da Cidade).

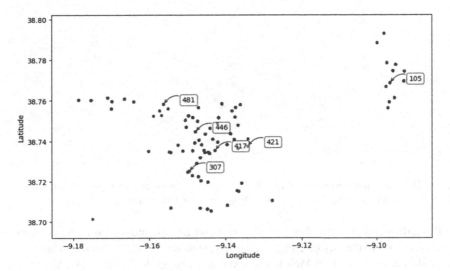

Fig. 5. Bike trip start stations (top 6)

A heatmap was created with "Folium" [30] Python package with built-in Open-StreetMap [45] tileset to visualize patterns of bike trip most used start stations (see Fig. 6). A bike dataset with the latitude and longitude start of each station was used for this purpose. As observed in Fig. 6, the major concentration of start stations demand is located in the Lisbon center.

Fig. 6. Bike trip start station heatmap. The red color corresponds to a higher concentration of bike trip start stations, whereas purple, to a lower. (Color figure online)

Regarding end stations of bike trips, we found that the most used ones, are located in the main axis of the city (see Fig. 7), namely, stations 105 (CC Vasco da Gama), 403 (Avenida Fontes Pereira de Melo), 417 (Avenida Duque de Ávila), 421 (Alameda D. Afonso Henriques), 446 (Avenida da República/Interface de Entrecampos) and 481 (Campo Grande/Museu da Cidade).

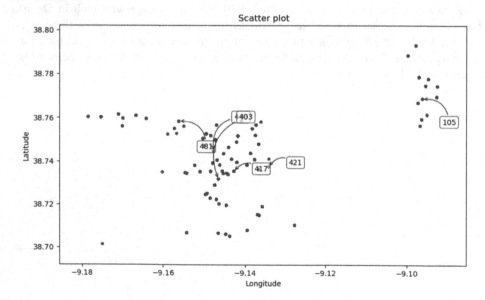

Fig. 7. Bike trip end stations (top 6)

3.3.3   Bike Trip Weather Analysis

We conducted an additional analysis aiming at finding behavior patterns between the users of BSS and the built environment variables, particularly, weather variables such as atmospheric precipitation and temperature. For the analysis in terms of atmospheric precipitation, we created a Boolean variable "rain" indicating if it was raining or not, in any of the three weather stations. To join the two datasets, we created a new date_key field from the date_start field of the bicycle trips. From our analysis, we can conclude that the trips are mostly done when there is no precipitation (97%) (see Fig. 8.). Regarding temperature analysis, the negative values were removed, and we calculated the average values of the three stations. Then, we divided the dataset into four

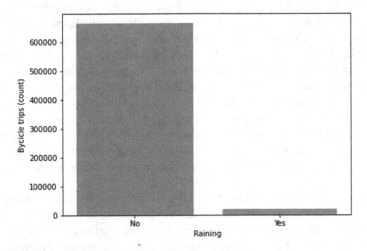

Fig. 8. Bicycle usage frequency relation to atmospheric precipitation.

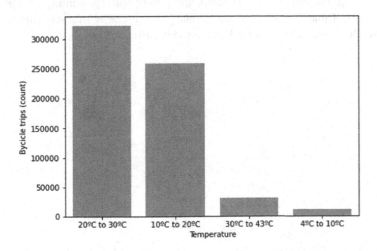

Fig. 9. Bicycle usage frequency relation to temperature.

categories: 0° to 10°, 10° to 20°, 20° to 30 and 30° to 42°, being 42° the maximum observed temperature value (see Fig. 9).

The trip speed was also analyzed in order to check if there was any observed change when raining, concluding that users are faster in their trips when it was not raining.

3.3.4   Spatial Cluster Analysis

In our research we seek to understand the behaviors of BSS users, particularly the movement of the bicycles in terms of the starting and ending of a trip, in each station, as well as and the frequency of usage of each station, across the available data. For that purpose, we performed a clustering analysis on the "bike trips dataset". Initially our study focused in identifying geographical (WGS84) patterns throughout the city of Lisbon in terms of trips starting and ending in each station. K-means was used to produce geographic clustering. An additional data pre-processing step was needed, before applying K-means. To get the clusters of trips and stations, we found the need to get all the trips from all the stations, irrespectively if a given station is a trip start or trip end station. To this aim, we split the original "bike trips dataset" in two, one having the station_start variable and the other having the station_end variable. Then, the variables name station_start and station_end are changed to "station" in the corresponding datasets. Both datasets are afterwards concatenated within the variable station. After, we computed the count of the trips in each station. The final result was a dataset with six variables: station, number of trips, station designation, latitude, longitude and dock capacity.

When applying K-means, we used the Elbow algorithm [46] to find the optimal K number through the calculation of the SSE (Sum of Squared Errors). The algorithm found four spatial clusters of the stations where bike trips start and end (see Fig. 8): one representing the center of Lisbon going from Alvalade to Saldanha (Purple), a second one representing the east side of Lisbon with just a few stations going from Telheiras to Cidade Universitária (Yellow), a third one representing the lower part of Lisbon going from Marquês de Pombal to Baixa (Green), and a forth one representing the Parque das Nações (Blue). Table 4 shows the coordinates of the center of each cluster for the geographic clustering generated by K-means (Fig. 10).

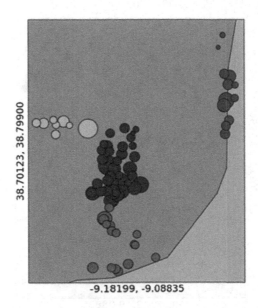

Fig. 10. Spatial clustering of stations where bike trips start and/or end (Yellow: Telheiras-Campo Grande (Museu da Cidade); Purple: Alvalade-Saldanha; Green: Marquês de Pombal-Baixa; Blue: Parque das Nações) (Color figure online)

Table 4. Cluster centroids

Latitude	Longitude
38.743263	−9.144271
38.772288	−9.095947
38.715984	−9.143659
38.759463	−9.168919

A second analysis was focused on station usage clustering. For that purpose, a pre-processing step required the creation of a new field n_trips (Number of trips per station), representing how many trips occurred on that specific station. Then we applied also K-means, with the same type of approach to find the optimal K number, as in the prior geographical cluster analysis. This time K-means was applied to find the main spatial clusters across the city, in terms of the number of trips that start and/or end in each station. We found four of such clusters (see Fig. 11). We can observe also that four of the most frequently used stations (labeled in green) are located in the center of the city, while a fifth one lies in the east side.

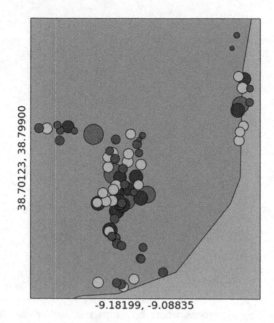

Fig. 11. Stations clustering by the number of trips that start and/or end on a given station (Green: 1st most used stations; Purple: 2nd most used stations; Yellow: 3rd most used stations; Blue: 4th most used stations) (Color figure online)

4   Major Findings

Our analysis shows that the total number of trips of EMEL GIRA BSS, from January 15th to October 25th, 2018 was 684,471. The average number of trips per month was 68,447, while the average station number of trips figure was 9,126. Moreover, we found that the daily average number of trips was 2,602.

The analysis shows also that the months of June, July, August and September had the most concentration of trips during 2018, with 439,176 trips, representing 64% of all trips. Regarding the day of the week, we have observed that users choose working weekdays to travel in the city (82%) compared to the weekend. Also, it is possible to affirm that the users prefer to use the service on working weekdays than during weekends.

Our findings also show that most of the trips happen, during 2018, in the afternoon (56%), followed by the morning period. We have also observed that during weekdays, the users prefer to ride during the afternoon but in the weekend, users mostly bike overnight.

Most used O-D stations were observed in two axis: one from Campo Grande to Marquês de Pombal and another in Parque das Nações, showing that bike demand start and end stations are located in Lisbon office areas. There are four major concentrations in the city for the number of trips. The main areas where users unlock GIRA bikes belong to Parque das Nações, the city center – Alvalade, Avenidas Novas, Santa Maria Maior - meaning that the center of Lisbon is where the most bike trips happen. There is also a close relation of the number of trips with the station capacity, and the station cluster with more trips is associated with the stations with the greater capacity.

We have also found that built environment factors such as precipitation, affect GIRA BSS usage, showing that almost 97% of trips take place when there is no rain. This observation was complemented by a correlation with speed analysis showing that higher speed is reached when there is no precipitation. Regarding temperature, it is possible to observe that most users prefer to travel when temperatures are between 20° and 30° (52%). There is also a significant number of users cycling when the temperature is between 10° and 20° (42%).

Finally, we also found that there was no significant difference, in terms of speed and duration of bike trips across the different days of the week, in average, nor of bicycle type (Electric or Conventional). Therefore, our research suggest that the type of bike is not a decisive factor when it comes to analyze bike trips.

5 Conclusions

This paper provides new insights on the recent implemented GIRA BSS in Lisbon. Overall, it was interesting to observe a strong use of BSS in a city that did not have a cycling culture, until recently.

Major findings show that most GIRA BSS trips take place on working weekdays, in the afternoon, which suggest a usage pattern that correlates well with working-home commute practices. We have also observed that weather conditions [12, 13] had an important impact on travel behavior. No rain was consistent with an increase of ridership, and temperatures between 10° to 30° were consistent with such behaviors too.

Lisbon GIRA BSS trip patterns are thus similar to other observed BSS mobility patterns of medium-size cities [12] discussed in the State of the Art section, such as patterns found in short and frequent trips and ride peak observed, observed in a case study in the city of Cork (Ireland) [12].

Parallels with larger cities can be established as well. In Canada, for instance, Montreal's BIXI BSS [15] is mostly used in weekdays evenings and weekends. In Toronto, bike trips are shorter in the weekdays mornings [13].

Large American cities BSS studies [10, 11, 14] show a frequent bike use in the morning and afternoon peaks [10] and different usage patterns between weekdays and weekends, identifying longer trips in the weekend [10].

In European large cities, weekday morning trips in the peak hour [8, 44] reach higher speed than trips over the weekdays and weekends.

As for the Lisbon GIRA BSS there is a strong possibility of overtime change, as future BSS network expansion plans are implemented in the city in the coming years.

Further work needs to be conducted regarding GIRA BSS in the scope of urban analytics [47] and literature discussion and parallel comparison with other BSS implemented nationally and internationally.

Future work needs to be conducted regarding bike station managing models, prediction of potential network demand to improve network planning, optimization of stations and locations, bikes rebalancing operation overtime and integration of BSS with multimodal transport systems, in the context of the first and last mile.

Acknowledgements. This study was performed in the scope of Lisboa Inteligente LxDataLab [48] – Lisbon City Council Data Centre – challenges to the academia. Vitória Albuquerque and Francisco Andrade work were partially supported by Fundação para a Ciência e a Tecnologia (FCT), under the project "IoT for Smart Cities and R&D Projects on Smart {Cities, Buildings, Education and Health} Summer School 2019/2020", with a Research Grant supporting the following projects: UIDB/04466/2020 and UIDP/04466/2020 [49].

References

1. Meddin, R., DeMaio, P.: The Meddin Bike-sharing World Map. Google Maps. https://bikesharingworldmap.com/#/all/2.3/-1.57/33.92/. Accessed 04 Oct 2020
2. DeMaio, P.: Bike-sharing: history, impacts, models of provision, and future. J. Public Transp. **12**(4), 41–56 (2009)
3. Zhang, J., Pan, X., Li, M., Yu, P.: Bicycle-sharing system analysis and trip prediction. In: 2016 IEEE International Conference on Mobile Data Management, pp. 174–179. IEEE (2016)
4. Padgham, M.: Human movement is both diffusive and directed. PLoS ONE **7**, e37754 (2012)
5. O'Brien, O., Cheshire, J., Batty, M.: Mining bicycle sharing data for generating insights into sustainable transport systems. J. Transp. Geogr. **34**, 262–273 (2014)
6. General Data Protection Regulation. https://gdpr-info.eu/. Accessed 04 Oct 2020
7. Kaplan, S., Manca, F., Nielsen, T., Prato, C.: Intentions to use bike-sharing for holiday cycling: an application of the Theory of Planned Behavior. Tour. Manag. **47**, 34–46 (2015)
8. Jensen, P., Rouquier, J.-B., Ovtracht, N., Robardet, C.: Characterizing the speed and paths of shared bicycle use in Lyon. Transp. Res. Part D Transp. Environ. **15**, 522–524 (2010)
9. Lathia, N., Ahmed, S., Capra, L.: Measuring the impact of opening the London shared bicycle scheme to casual users. Transp. Res. Part C Emerg. Technol. **22**, 88–102 (2012)
10. Zhou, X.: Understanding spatiotemporal patterns of biking behavior by analyzing massive bike sharing data in Chicago. PLoS ONE **10**, e0137922 (2015)
11. Nolan, R., Smart, M., Guo, Z.: Bikeshare trip generation in New York City. Transp. Res. Part A Policy Pract. **94**, 164–181 (2016)
12. Caulfield, B., O'Mahony, M., Brazil, W., Weldon, P.: Examining usage patterns of a bike-sharing scheme in a medium sized city. Transp. Res. Part A Policy Pract. **100**, 152–161 (2017)
13. El-Assi, W., Salah Mahmoud, M., Nurul Habib, K.: Effects of built environment and weather on bike sharing demand: a station level analysis of commercial bike sharing in Toronto. Transportation **44**(3), 589–613 (2017). https://doi.org/10.1007/s11116-015-9669-z
14. Han, X., Wang, P., Gao, J., Shah, M., Ambulgekar, R., Jarandikar, A., Dhar, S.: Bike sharing data analytics for silicon valley in USA. In: 2017 IEEE SmartWorld Ubiquitous Intelligence and Computing, Advanced and Trusted Computed, Scalable Computing and Communications, Cloud and Big Data Computing, Internet of People and Smart City Innovation, SmartWorld/SCALCOM/UIC/ATC/CBDCom/IOP/SCI, pp. 1–9. IEEE (2018)
15. Faghih-Imani, A., Eluru, N., El-Geneidy, A., Rabbat, M., Haq, U.: How land-use and urban form impact bicycle flows: evidence from the bycicle sharing system (BIXI) in Montreal. Transp. Geogr. **41**, 306–314 (2014)
16. Sarkar, A., Lathia, N., Mascolo, C.: Comparing cities' cycling patterns using online shared bicycle maps. Transportation **42**(4), 541–559 (2015). https://doi.org/10.1007/s11116-015-9599-9

17. Du, Y., Deng, F., Liao, F.: A model framework for discovering the spatio-temporal usage patterns of public free-floating bike-sharing system. Transp. Res. Part C Emerg. Technol. **103**, 39–55 (2019)
18. Caggiani, L., Camporeale, R., Ottomanelli, M., Szeto, W.: A modeling framework for the dynamic management of free-floating bike-sharing systems. Transp. Res. Part C Emerg. Technol. **87**, 159–182 (2018)
19. Zhao, Y., Dai, L., Peng, L., Song, Y., Zhou, Z.: Analysis of spatial distribution of China's station-free bike-sharing by clustering algorithms. In: ACM International Conference Proceeding Series, pp. 15–19. ACM Press (2019)
20. Li, D., Zhao, Y., Li, Y.: Time-series representation and clustering approaches for sharing bike usage mining. IEEE Access **7**, 177856–177863 (2019)
21. Guo, Y., Shen, X., Ge, Q., Wang, L.: Station function discovery: exploring trip records in urban public bike-sharing system. IEEE Access **6**, 71060–71068 (2018)
22. Python. https://www.python.org/. Accessed 04 Oct 2020
23. Jupyter. https://jupyter.org/. Accessed 04 Oct 2020
24. Numpy. https://numpy.org/. Accessed 04 Oct 2020
25. Pandas. https://pandas.pydata.org/. Accessed 04 Oct 2020
26. Matplotlib. https://matplotlib.org/. Accessed 04 Oct 2020
27. Seaborn. https://seaborn.pydata.org/. Accessed 04 Oct 2020
28. GDAL. https://pypi.org/project/GDAL/. Accessed 04 Oct 2020
29. Shapely. https://pypi.org/project/Shapely/. Accessed 04 Oct 2020
30. Folium. https://pypi.org/project/folium/. Accessed 04 Oct 2020
31. Fiona. https://pypi.org/project/Fiona/. Accessed 04 Oct 2020
32. Scikit-learn. https://scikit-learn.org/stable/. Accessed 04 Oct 2020
33. Chapman, P., Clinton, J., Kerber, R., Khabaza, T., Reinartz, T., Wirth, R.: CRISP-DM 1.0: Step-by-step data mining guide. Computer Science (2000)
34. El-Sappagh, S., Hendawi, A., Bastawassy, A.: A proposed model for data warehouse ETL processes. In: J. King Saud Univ. Comput. Inf. Sci. **23**, 91–104 (2011)
35. Zhang, Y., Thomas, T., Brussel, M., Van Maarseveen, M.: Expanding bicycle-sharing systems: lessons learnt from an analysis of usage. PLoS ONE **11**, e0168604 (2016)
36. Fuller, D., et al.: Use of a new public bicycle share program in Montreal Canada. Am. J. Prev. Med. **41**, 80–83 (2011)
37. Shaheen, S., Zhang, H., Martin, E., Guzman, S.: China's Hangzhou public bicycle. Transp. Res. Rec. J. Transp. Res. Board **2247**, 33–41 (2011)
38. Shaheen, S., Cohen, A., Martin, E.: Public bikesharing in North America: early operator understanding and emerging trends. Transp. Res. Rec. J. Transp. Res. Board **2387**, 83–92 (2013)
39. Buck, D., Buehler, R.: Bike lanes and other determinants of capital bikeshare trips. In: 91st Transportation Research Board Annual Meeting, pp. 703–706 (2012)
40. Ewing, R., Cervero, R.: Travel and the built environment. J. Am. Plann. Assoc. **76**, 265–294 (2010)
41. Kemperman, A., Timmermans, H., Timmerman, H.: Influences of built environment on walking and cycling by latent segments of aging population. Transp. Res. Rec. J. Transp. Res. Board **2134**, 1–9 (2009)
42. Liu, Z., Jia, X., Cheng, W.: Solving the last mile problem: ensure the success of public bicycle system in Beijing. Procedia Soc. Behav. Sci. **43**, 73–78 (2012)
43. McKenzie, G.: Docked vs. Dockless bike-sharing: contrasting spatiotemporal patterns. In: Leibniz International Proceedings in Informatics, vol. 114 (2018)

44. Zhong, C., Batty, M., Manley, E., Wang, J., Chen, F., Schmitt, G.: Variability in regularity: mining temporal mobility patterns in London, Singapore and Beijing using smart-card data. PLoS ONE **11**, e0149222 (2016)
45. OpenStreetMap. https://wiki.openstreetmap.org/wiki/Main_Page/. Accessed 04 Oct 2020
46. Yuan, C., Yang, H.: Research on K-value selection method of K-means clustering algorithm. J. Multidiscip. Sci. **2**, 226–235 (2019)
47. Batty, M.: Urban analytics defined. Environ. Plan. B Urban Anal. City Sci. **46**, 403–405 (2019)
48. LxDataLab – Laboratório de Dados Urbanos de Lisboa. https://lisboainteligente.cm-lisboa.pt/lxdatalab/. Accessed 03 Aug 2020
49. Summer School 2020 – IoT for Smart Cities. https://istar.iscte-iul.pt/summerschool2020/. Accessed 03 Aug 2020

A Context-Sensitive Cloud-Based Data Analytic Mobile Alert and Optimal Route Discovery System for Rural and Urban ITS Penetration

Victor Balogun[1], Oluwafemi A. Sarumi[2(✉)], and Olumide O. Obe[2]

[1] University of Winnipeg, Winnipeg, MB, Canada
vi.balogun@uwinnipeg.ca
[2] The Federal University of Technology, Akure, Nigeria
{oasarumi,ooobe}@futa.edu.ng

Abstract. The rapid growth in the number of road users and poor road management have been deemed responsible for the upsurge in road congestions and fatalities in recent times. Many of the lives lost was due to inadequate or inefficient public-accessible alerts system and rerouting mechanisms during emergencies. The Intelligent Transportation System (ITS) was anticipated as a solution to the numerous road networks usage problems. Recently, some developed countries have implemented some forms of ITS initiatives. But the transition of the road networks to a fully integrated ITS has been slow and daunting due to the huge cost of implementation. The use of mobile devices as backbone infrastructure for ITS networks during public emergencies has been proposed. Despite the advantage of being a cheap alternative, low computing power of mobile devices limit their potentials to support the expected Big Data ITS traffic. In this paper, we propose a cloud-based context-sensitive ITS infrastructure that uses the cloud as a primary aggregator of traffic messages plus a hybrid Data Analytics algorithm. The algorithm combines the enhanced features of Apache-Spark and Kafka frameworks blended with collaborative filtering using the ensemble machine learning classifier. The novelty of our approach stems from its ability to provide load balancing routing services based on the users' profiles, and avoid congestion-using the Dynamic Round Robin scheduling algorithm to reroute users with similar profiles.

Keywords: Context-sensitive · ITS · Mobile alert · Road incidences · Cloud · Data analytics

1 Introduction

The report in [1] stated that about 1.2 million people around the world are killed while about 50 million people are injured every year as a result of traffic related accidents. The World Health Organization (WHO) reported that due to

© ICST Institute for Computer Sciences, Social Informatics and Telecommunications Engineering 2021
Published by Springer Nature Switzerland AG 2021. All Rights Reserved
A. L. Martins et al. (Eds.): INTSYS 2020, LNICST 364, pp. 35–51, 2021.
https://doi.org/10.1007/978-3-030-71454-3_3

this massive loss of lives, the world economy declines by up to $500 billion every year [2]. Many of these lives that are lost within the road networks have been attributed to inadequate or inefficient traffic management systems to alert and provide alternative routes to users when there are traffic incidents and emergencies. The Intelligent Transportation System (ITS) was anticipated as a solution to the numerous problems that are associated with the use of the road networks. ITS has been defined by the U.S. Department of Transportation (US DOT) as the integration of advanced communication technologies into the transportation technologies and vehicles, including a broad range of wireless and wireline communications-based information and electronics technologies; and all transportation modes, from pedestrian activities to freight movement [3]. The report by US DOT in [4] also reiterated that the mobility and accessibility of a region can be enhanced when ITS technologies are efficiently implemented thereby helping road users to go to wherever they want and whenever they want, in a safe and reliable manner.

In the past few years, many developed countries of the world including Japan, South Korea, Singapore and the United States have taken the lead to embark on some forms of ITS initiatives. Japan being the world leader in the deployment of ITS began with the use of the Vehicle Information and Communication System (VICS) in 1996, and the use of probes to capture real-time information in 2003 [5]. ITS initiatives started in the United States after the development of the Electronic Route Guidance System (ERGS) in 1970. The ERGS was meant to provide road users with route guidance information via on-board and roadside equipment [6]. Singapore installed real-time bus arrival panels in January 2008 at bus stops to make public transportation a more attractive option for commuters [5]. As a result of the need for ITS, South Korea built legal and institutional support for ITS by creating a master plan in 1997 which led to the development of an ITS technical architecture and a regional and supra-regional implementation plan [7]. Despite the progress recorded in recent times as a result of all these initiatives, the transition of the road networks to a fully integrated ITS network have been slow and seemed to be a daunting endeavor. One of the major setbacks to ITS penetrations in our rural and urban communities can be traced to the huge cost of implementation, especially in terms of infrastructural procurement, installations and management. The need for accurate and real-time traffic information is critical to successful ITS deployment. ITS data comes from heterogeneous sources and are in different formats. Big Data analytic has been advantageous in predicting traffic flow in ITS [8]. Despite the potentials of the analysis of ITS Big data for pattern detection, dimension reduction and complex predictions, the heterogeneous nature of the ITS data still constitutes a major challenge to the integration of ITS data analytic system [9].

2   Challenges of Big Data Analytic in Intelligent Transportation System

ITS applications have been described by [10] as complex and data-intensive applications that exhibit the 5Vs of Big Data in terms of volume, variety, velocity, veracity, and value. Due to the unforeseen explosion in the amount of heterogeneous data generated by the ITS in the range of several Petabytes (PB) of data, the conventional data analytic approaches have been discovered to be inefficient in handling the complexities involved [11]. Therefore, there is a need for data analytic systems that can transform the heterogeneous and complex ITS data from a conventional technology-driven system to a complex data-driven system.

A major challenge of using Big Data analytic in ITS is determining how data is collected within an ITS infrastructure [12]. ITS users including vehicles and pedestrians are in regular motion within the road networks making the traffic data collected to be incomplete or inaccurate. As a result, such data can not be a reliable source for implementing an efficient Big Data analytic system. Therefore, there is a need to develop data collection systems that are automatic and with minimal human intervention so as to reduce data errors introduced by humans and to improve the quality of ITS data collected. A viable solution to the automatic data capturing need is to develop a user profiling system that can automatically capture traffic data from ITS users.

Another related challenge to using Big Data analytic in ITS is determining how to store the massive data that are captured within the ITS networks. According to [12], ITS data level has jumped from the range of Terabyte (TB) level to PB level thereby making the growth in data storage capacity to lag behind the ITS data growth. The implication of this is that the conventional approaches to data storage and database tools will no longer be adequate to handle the massive ITS data. Though several integrated Big Data capable, and multi-cloud storage and hybrid storage are emerging as solutions to Big Data storage, there is a need for smart management tools that can provide integrated analytic within storage devices. The authors in [13] stated that simply integrating and standardizing data systems does not remove the requirement for such systems to be capable of editing raw data so that it can yield useful results. In addition, there is a need to develop efficient data analytic algorithms that can leverage machine learning and predictive data analytic to support real-time data forecasting requirements of ITS applications.

The timeliness of processing ITS massive data to support Big Data applications is another major challenge. Heterogeneous and complex traffic data from diverse sources need to be compared with historical data and processed at an instant [14]. According to [8], several generic and dedicated Big Data analytic frameworks including Apache Storm, Apache Flink, Apache Spark and Kafka streams have been developed. Despite the successes of some of these frameworks, there is a need to investigate cloud-based context-sensitive hybrid Big Data analytic frameworks that can combine the advantages of existing frameworks to deliver faster real-time data processing for current and near future ITS networks.

3 Related Work

There have been several initiatives to provide traffic services to road users using mobile applications. The Waze Apps [15] currently operated by Google provide location-based traffic information services to travelers using their cell phones. The problem with this application is that traffic data are obtained from road users through their social media platform like Twitter. Such data are semi-structured and unreliable because the application does not enforce the user to activate their geolocation functionality so as to provide the actual location information of a specific traffic incident [16,17].

INRIX Traffic [18] is a next-generation navigation and traffic app that uses smartphones and vehicle GPS data to provide road users with real time traffic information. The App automatically profiles users to provide routing and other traffic related information especially as it concerns changing road conditions. Despite the automatic user profiling and sending of alerts provided by the App, there is no evidence of reduction in congestion when users are rerouted to a new route during road incidents. This is because a new route can drastically become congested as many road users within close proximity of the incident are rerouted to the same route.

Moovit App [19] is an example of mobile applications that provide road users with real-time public transportation journey planning by combining public transportation data with users' cell phones data. Gaode App [20] allows road users to plan their trips that involve the transition between different means of transportation including trains to buses and buses to cars or bicycles. There is no evidence of Big Data analytic of these mobile applications as next-generation mobile applications must be able to process the anticipated near future massive data that are generated by ITS users in order to support road users with real-time and reliable traffic information.

As a summary to issues with related work, most route discovery and routing approaches provide similar routing information to users on similar routes and such road users are directed to the same route within the ITS infrastructure. This can lead to congestion of a newly discovered alternative route and can even cause new incidents of accidents. Therefore, there is a need for an approach that reroutes users based on the particular situation of a user and that also considers load balancing of alternative routes. In addition, there is no evidence of Big Data analytic of these approaches for efficient processing of the near future ITS Big Data so as to support road users with real-time and reliable traffic information including road incident alerts. We therefore propose a context-sensitive mobile alert system that uses two-layer Aggregator design to provide road incident alerts to subscribers. In addition, the system uses an optimal route discovery and load balancing techniques to provide alternative routes to road users during traffic incidents. Users with similar profiles are distributed over discovered alternative routes based on the real-time traffic condition of each route, thereby reducing incidents of congestion and road accidents. The two-layer alerts/traffic data Aggregator also introduces redundancy by using the cloud as a primary Aggregator while still maintaining a secondary land-based Aggregator.

4 Context-Sensitive Cloud-Based Mobile Alert and Route Discovery System

4.1 General Description

The proposed mobile system allows the subscribers to undergo an initial registration process before using the system. This registration process acts as a security mechanism to ensure that users are authenticated before they can actively
contribute to ITS data. During this process, users detailed data are collected
so as to create an initial profile for each user. Next, the system through crowd-
sourcing prompts the user to take a survey so as to gather some vital information
related to the user's traffic experiences and preferences. These information will
be used to determine and refine the Traveling Model (TM) parameters. The
TM parameters include factors that influence choice of route taken by different
road users including pedestrians, drivers, and bikers. Specifically, the information collected will be used to assign weight to traffic parameters that will be
used when calculating the cost and the subsequent rating of a route. After the
registration process, authenticated users will be able to send alert and traffic
messages including: road condition (e.g. wet, slippery), weather conditions (e.g.
snowy, rainy), emergency incidences (e.g. accident, explosion, road close) to the
system. These traffic alerts can be sent automatically, periodically or on-demand
by the users' mobile devices.

Alert messages are classified based on type of alerts (e.g. road condition,
weather condition, emergency incidents), location of alerts, and the level of severity. These alert messages are aggregated using the Cloud-Based Alerts Aggregator (CBAA) and analyzed by the Big Data analytic component of the system.
Authenticated users can be provided with either a proactive service or a reactive
service. The proactive service involves users automatically sending and receiving alerts based on their locations to incidence of emergencies and the system
subsequently providing alternative routes based on our proposed optimal route
discovery and rating algorithm. With the reactive service, which is an on-demand
service is when authenticated users request for the shortest route to a Point of
Interest (POI) at any moment during traffic incidents. Alerts are sent to subscribers based on the 5W of user profiling including Who, Where, When, What
and Why. The Who profile involves identifying the current user, while the Where
addresses the location of the subscriber. The When profile deals with temporal
aspects of past, present and future i.e. the time of an incident, while the What
profile deals with identifying activities of the user on object, for instance biking,
driving, or walking. Lastly, the Why profile addresses the subtle content such as
the user's need and emotion, e.g. a user in need of routing assistance. The system
will profile the user before providing either the proactive or reactive services so
as to accurately meet the specific need of the user.

4.2 The Architecture

The proposed Context-Sensitive Cloud-Based Mobile Alert and Route Discovery
System architecture presented in Fig. 1 is an improvement over the architecture

proposed in [21]. It is essentially the integration of the existing Mobile Alert System with Context-Sensitive sub component and a cloud-based Big Data analytic technology. This is to provide real-time traffic alerts and optimal route discovery services to ITS users during traffic incidents including accidents and natural disasters. The idea is that the cloud and Big Data-based Mobile Alert system will use the cloud as a primary alerts Aggregator where traffic data can be analyzed using a proposed Big Data analytic algorithm, and the result sent as alerts to users. In this architecture, we still maintain a secondary Land-Based Aggregator (LBA) that will contain real-time results of data analytic from the cloud system. The LBA serves as a redundant mechanism to ensure that the Mobile Alert system continues to operate in the presence of unanticipated faults and failures.

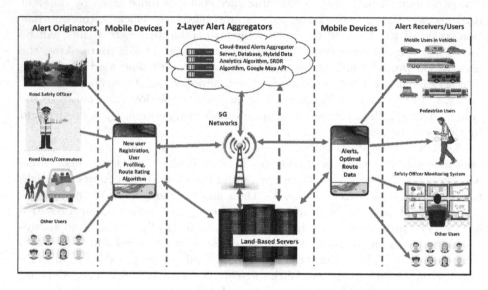

Fig. 1. The proposed architecture for context-sensitive cloud-based mobile alert and optimal route discovery ITS system

4.3   User Profiling (Context-Sensitive) Subsystem

The User Profiling subsystem illustrated in Fig. 2 uses the in-built mobile phones sensors to profile users so as to provide services that best meet the traffic needs of each user. The User Profiling subsystem consists of 10-tuple (decuple) attributes $(u_1, u_2, \ldots, u_{10})$ which are determined by four general travel model preferences including travelling preference, user location preference, weather condition and POI preference. We represented the travelling preference component with u_1 and u_2, where u1 captures the user's **travelling mode** (e.g. walking, riding, driving), and u_2 represents the **traffic condition** (congestion rate). The user location preference is set as u_3. This is an attribute which identifies the **user location at the moment** (the coordinate). We depicted the weather condition component with u_4 and u_5. Where u_4 is an attribute that captures the **weather condition of the user's current location** (e.g. snowy, rainy, clear, windy, cloudy), and u_5 is the attribute that describes the **weather condition of the user's destination**. We depicted the user's POI component with u_6 and u_7, where u_6 represents the user's destination and u_7 is an attribute that describes the user's perceived **fastest route to the POI**. We also consider some other factors that are necessary when road users need to make decisions about the choice of a route to take when navigating the road networks. We represented u_8 as the **time of the day** (e.g. morning – rush hour, afternoon, evening), u_9 is the **road condition to destination** (wet, slippery, bumpy), and u_{10} is the **road emergency/alert** (nature, location, severity). This profiling information is automatically captured by some certain sensors within the users' mobile devices and provided to other subsystems for further processing.

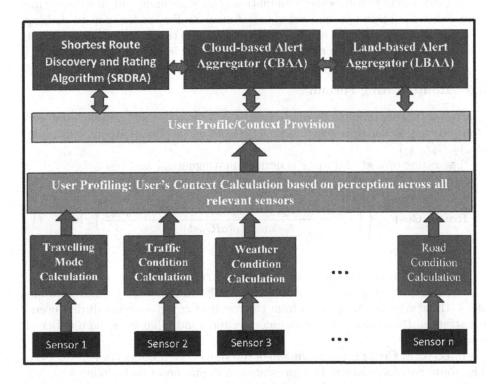

Fig. 2. User profiling (context-sensitive) subsystem

When routing information needs to be provided to a user, the user profile decuple, $(u_1, u_2, \ldots, u_{10})$ will be mapped with the travel model, quintuple, $(t_1, t_2, t_3, t_4, t_5)$ of a discovered route for rating purpose to determine how best the route correlates with the user profile. We established the parameters for the travel model by using t_1 to represent the **distance from user's current location to a POI** using the discovered route, t_2 represents the **traffic condition along the discovered route** (e.g. speed-limit, congestion), t_3 represents the **road condition along the discovered route** (dry, wet, bumpy, etc.), t_4 represents the **road incidents along the discovered route** (accident, road-block, abduction, etc.), while t_5 represents the **weather condition along the discovered route** (rainy, snowy, cloudy, etc.)

4.4   The Route Rating Subsystem

The authors in [22] stated that the choice of route taken by a road user is a mix between decision-making under certainty and uncertainty. In [23], the choice of route was categorized based on attributes including characteristics of travelers, characteristics of routes (road, traffic, environment), characteristics of the trip and characteristics of other circumstances. In this paper, we propose a Route Rating subsystem that uses the combination of user profiling and crowd sourcing approaches to obtain personalized views of users traffic modes so as to develop a robust and user sensitive weighted averages for the traffic parameters that are used in our proposed route rating formula presented in Eq. (1).

4.5   Route Rating Formula

The results of user profiling discussed in Sect. 4.3 serve as input into the proposed Route Rating formula presented in Eq. (1) based on the Travel Model, quintuple, $(t_1, t_2, t_3, t_4, t_5)$.

The rating or cost of a route is derived mathematical as:

$$\textbf{Route Cost} = \left\{ \left(\frac{(t_1 w_1) + (t_2 w_2) + (t_3 w_3) + (t_4 w_4) + (t_5 w_5)}{max(totalCost)} \right) x10 \right\} \quad (1)$$

where:

$t_1, t_2, t_3, t_4, and t_5$ are the traffic parameters representing the Traffic Model

$w_1, w_2, \ldots, w_5$ are the weighted averages assigned to individual traffic parameters (these averages are derived from the result of crowd-sourcing during users' registration, the values will become more refined and reliable as the number of users increases).

max(total Cost) is the maximum of the sum of the product $t_1 w_1 \ldots \ldots w_5 t_5$. The route cost formula can be represented in Sigma notation as follows:

$$\textbf{R(TM, UP)} = \left\{ \left(\frac{\displaystyle\sum_{i=1}^{5} f_i(P.W)}{max \displaystyle\sum_{i=1}^{5} f_i(P.W) \neq \emptyset} \right) x10 \right\} \quad (2)$$

Where:

R(TM, UP) is the route cost or rating derived from the mapping of the User Profile, UP and Travel Model, TM.

$f_i(PW)$ is a function representing the product of a traffic parameter, **P** and its corresponding weight parameter, **W**.

The weighted average assigned to each of the route cost parameters in Eq. (2) will differ depending on the travelling mode of the user. If the user is a pedestrian, for instance, the distance to destination and instances of road incidents might generate lower weighted averages compared to when the user is driving.

4.6   Rationale for the Route Rating Parameters

In a survey conducted in [24], the researchers discovered that the factors that are pertinent to the choice of route taken by bikers are the condition of the roads, volume of traffic, the speed of motor vehicles along the route, and the distance to destination. The results of the survey show that the speed of motor vehicles and volume of the traffic contributed largely to the overall decision made by bikers on the choice of route taken and were respectively rated 100% and 97%, with 100% rating indicating greatest contribution. Several researchers suggest that the choice of driving a car along a route is mostly affected by the travel time, road category, road safety, scenic quality, and the number of traffic lights and stop signs [25, 26]. The results of the work in [22] indicate that the probability of selecting a route decreases with a rise in the travel time, and drivers tend to select the routes with lower tolls. The authors in [27] also identified seven factors that pedestrians consider favourable when selecting a route to take to a POI. These factors include shorter distance, lower travel time, even sidewalks, connected links, less crossing and barriers, low congestion level, and safety.

As a summary, we discovered from the various literature that the factors that are common to road users (bikers, drivers and pedestrians) when choosing a route to get to a POI include distance to the POI, road condition, level of congestion, and instances of traffic incidents. We therefore used these factors as bases for formulating our proposed Road Rating formula. To the best of our knowledge, we noticed that none of the literature considers the road weather conditions as a factor that can influence the choice of route by road users. Due to varying geographic factors, the weather condition along a particular route might be significantly different from that of another route. Since weather conditions affect the ease of biking, driving or walking along a route, we therefore consider the use of weather conditions as one of the factors to be considered while rating a route using our Route Rating formula as shown in Eqs. (1) and (2). We also restate here that the weights to be assigned to these traffic parameters including the weather conditions will be the weighted average derived as a result of the crowd-sourced data from users' initial or periodic survey discussed in Sect. 4.1.

5   The Context-Sensitive Mobile Alert Subsystem

The Context-Sensitive Mobile Alert subsystem of our proposed architecture is illustrated in Fig. 3. Traffic related data are automatically sensed by the Alert Sensing Layer and transferred to the Alert Detection Layer periodically. Traffic data can be received from the cell phone sensors, Google Map API, and related systems to profile the user. At the Alert Detection Layer, the received traffic data and the user behavior are analyzed to derive a profile for the user. The result of the user profiling is further analyzed and compared with normal traffic data to detect abnormal traffic conditions. This abnormal traffic data is sent to the Alert Processing Layer in the cloud where the abnormal traffic data is aggregated (**Message Aggregation**) using the Cloud-Based Alert Aggregator (CBAA). Before processing, the received message is authenticated to validate the source of the message (Message Authentication). This is a crucial component of the CBAA as the mechanism prevents instances of malicious users or hijackers from using the system to create public panics or as a tool for terrorism. The authenticated message is then processed using a proposed hybrid Data Analytic Engine that compares the current data with historical data and then translate or adapt the message into an alert standardized format (**Message Adaptation/Translation**). The translated alert message is then sent by the CBAA to each affected subscriber (within a determined radius of the incident, depending on the type and the severity of the incident) in a format that matches their profiles (**Alert Dissemination**). For instance, if the travelling mode is driving/biking, an audio alert is sent to the user but if the traveling mode is walking/running a textual alert is sent to the user.

5.1   The Cloud-Based Alerts Aggregator and the Optimal Route Algorithm

The results of user profiling (generated by the User Profiling subsystem) and the rating of the route currently occupied by the user (generated by Route Rating subsystem) are sent by a user's mobile device periodically (proactive service) or on-demand (reactive service) to the CBAA. As an improvement over existing cloud-based ITS systems, we anticipated instances of cloud system faults and failures by designing two-layer alerts/traffic data aggregators by implementing a CBAA while still maintaining a redundant Land-Based Alert Aggregator (LBAA). The LBAA acts as a cache for offline access, especially for rural ITS users to traffic messages when the CBAA experiences faults or failures.

The CBAA uses the user profile received to discover all available alternate routes from the current position of the user to the POI using the Dijkstra's Shortest Path Algorithm (DSPA) [28]. For a particular alternate route discovered by DSPA, the CBAA checks its database to see if there are current Travel Model data available. If such data exist, the CBAA uses the Route Rating formula described in Sect. 4.5 to calculate the route cost and rate the route. If there is no current Travel Model data, The CBAA will first use the Google Map API data to determine the real-time Travel Model data for the route. If there is

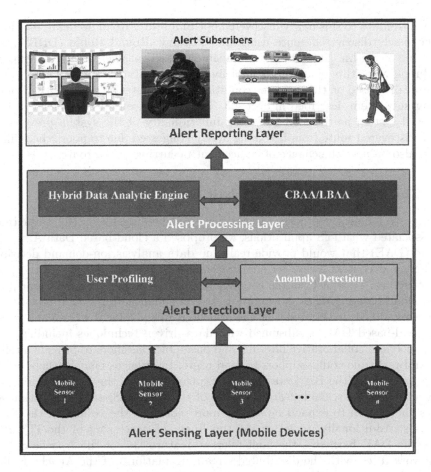

Fig. 3. Context-sensitive mobile alert subsystem

no current Travel Model data for the route, then the CBAA will generate the Travel Model data by triggering the hybrid Data Analytic Engine subsystem (see Fig. 4). The Data Analytic Engine subsystem, using our proposed hybrid Data Analytic algorithm, discussed in the next section, will analyze the massive historical traffic data stored in the cloud to generate the requested Travel Model data for the alternate route. The CBAA will perform the above process for all the discovered alternate routes and at the end will generate a list of available routes with their ratings in a descending order.

The CBAA then compares a user profile with the list of shortest routes generated to determine an optimal route for that user. The implication of this design is that two users traveling on a particular route might be rerouted to different routes depending on their individual profiles. The CBAA sends this optimal route information to a particular user in need of rerouting service via the user's mobile device. When the optimal route information gets to the user, the user will reroute to this newly discovered optimal route. Road users are rerouted to the newly discovered route using the Dynamic Round Robin (DRR) load balancing algorithm [29]. The DRR is a simple, resilient, weighted but dynamic scheduling algorithm that in our implementation, will allocate routes to users dynamically based on the real-time condition of the routes as rated by the Route Rating subsystem described in Sect. 4.3. This is an essential component of the proposed system as the load balancing functionality of the system prevents a newly discovered route from becoming overly congested due to poor scheduling, and it also reduces the chance of an accident occurring in the route.

5.2 The Cloud-Based Data Analytic Engine Subsystem

In order to efficiently process the complex and heterogeneous Big Data that are associated with ITS applications, we proposed a cloud-based Data Analytic Engine (DAE) that would provide real-time data analysis, on-demand decision support, and context-aware recommendations to the various users of the ITS infrastructure. To transform the heterogeneous and complex ITS data, our proposed cloud-based DAE as shown in Fig. 4 is an enhanced form of Apache Stark framework [30, 31] hybridized with the Apache Kafka [32] for Big Data analytics. The cloud-based DAE is subsumed with data-driven techniques including features selection, collaborative filtering, and ensemble classifiers to provide intelligent and real-time traffic support to road users. In order to manage the storage and processing of the Big Data that are captured within the ITS network, the DAE leverages the scalable feature [33–35] of the Apache Spark framework that allows the system to expand by adding more nodes as the volume of the data increases. Additionally, to foster the timeliness of processing of the ITS Big Data, the DAE harnesses the fault-tolerant feature [36] of the Apache Spark framework fused with the distributed streaming platform of the Apache Kafka to provide swift and efficient real-time streaming and data analytic within the ITS infrastructure.

Some additional features of Apache Spark that we implement in the DAE for ITS Big Data analytic includes the use of a dedicated resource dispenser and a result accumulator called the driver program. The driver program enables a smooth coordination of all the data processing operations within the ITS and reconfiguration of lost partitions effortlessly without depleting the information. The driver program also ensures that there is no loss of critical information between the data analytic engine and the alert subscribers. The DAE with the aid of the driver program stores intermediate results in memory instead of disk, and supports ample system workloads such as interactive processes, batch processing, iterative procedures, machine learning, and graph processing. These are essential functions necessary for the efficient processing of the ITS Big Data. We introduced a filter-based feature selection model to the implementation of the DAE so as to eliminate noise and data redundancy from the complex and heterogeneous data aggregated from the alert originators. This is crucial for the optimal performance of our proposed collaborative filtering model. Collaborative

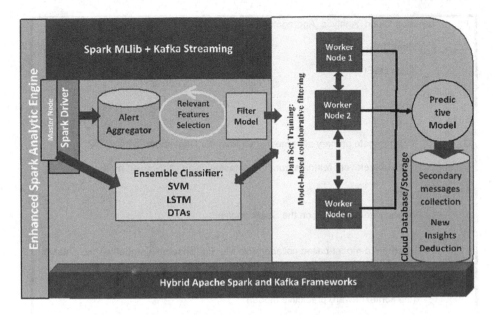

Fig. 4. Cloud-based data analytic engine subsystem

filtering [37] is a domain-independent prediction that explores historical and current data of the users to make intelligent recommendations for the users based on their current need.

In Fig. 5, we present our proposed Data Analytic algorithm that controls the DAE. The algorithm uses a filter-based features selection model to remove redundant and noisy data from the avalanche of dataset coming from the alert originators. We implement a model-based collaborative filtering technique so as to benefit from the advantages of ensemble machine learning classifiers [38]. This approach allows us to harness the strength of multiple machine learning techniques so as to perform predictive analytic and provide intelligent recommendations of the optimal route to users. Specifically, our proposed algorithm uses ensemble machine learning classifiers consisting of a hybrid of three machine learning methods including Support Vector Machine (SVM), Long Short-Term Memory (LSTM) and Decision Tree Algorithm (DTA). We are taking the advantage of the strength of SVM at being able to process heterogeneous and nonlinear data, and combining it with LSTM which is highly efficient in the analytics of historical data. Another advantage of this hybridization is the use of DTA which is capable of handling both regression and classification problems. Regression and classification considerations are desirable data analytic procedures for implementing robust ITS infrastructures.

```
1        function Cloud_Analytic_Aggregator ( ):

2            Start DAE( )

3            From DAE( )

4        Do

5            {

6                Aggregate primary alert messages from the Originators,

7                select relevant features from the datasets using filter-based model

8            }

9        For each worker node j on the Spark engine:

10   {
11           Perform a model-based collaborative filtering (Ensemble model) on the dataset
             coordinated through the   master node.

12           Aggregate the results of the training from the worker nodes on the master node
             (the context-aware predictive model)

13   }

14   Save the Predictive Model and relay it to the land-based servers

15   Collect   secondary messages from the mobile devices and store on the land-based
     servers

16   Use the Predictive Model to deduce new insights from the secondary data

17   Provide intelligent context-aware decision support to the road users

18   return
```

Fig. 5. ITS data analytic algorithm

6   Conclusion and Future Research Direction

In this paper, we presented a simple, inexpensive but fully functional Context-Sensitive Cloud-based Mobile Alert and Optimal Route Discovery and Rating for ITS infrastructures. Our goal is to provide a transportation system that will allow traffic data including alerts to be aggregated into a cloud environment where such data can be analyzed by our proposed hybrid Data Analytic algorithm. Our algorithm is derived by combining enhanced features of Apache Spark and Kafka frameworks for efficient real-time analysis and alert/traffic message dissemination to ITS users. Our proposed Data Analytic Engine performs two essential functions including analysis of received alert messages to detect traffic anomalies and the analysis of traffic data to generate required Traffic Model for a particular road user based on the user profile as received from the mobile devices. We anticipated instances of system faults and failures by designing two-layer alerts/traffic data aggregators by implementing a Cloud-Based Alert Aggregator (CBAA) while still maintaining a redundant Land-Based Alert Aggregator (LBAA). The LBAA acts as a cache for offline access to traffic messages when the CBAA experiences faults or failures.

In our future research, we plan to implement, investigate and analyze the performance of the proposed algorithms operating within the Cloud-Based ITS architecture as the algorithms support real-time and high quality communication between road users mobile devices and the CBAA. We will also investigate the validity of the traffic parameters used in this research along with their assigned weights, so as to establish their correctness. We anticipate that there will be some other design and implementation issues that will emanate as a result of the proposed architecture. Therefore, we will address these challenges and related issues in our future publications.

References

1. Toroyan, T.: Global status report on road safety. Inj. Prev. **15**(4), 286–289 (2009)
2. Zheng, K., Zheng, Q., Chatzimisios, P., Xiang, W., Zhou, Y.: Heterogeneous vehicular networking: a survey on architecture, challenges, and solutions. IEEE Commun. Surv. Tutor. **17**(4), 2377–2396 (2015)
3. U.S. Department of Transportation (2020) About ITS - Frequently Asked Questions. https://www.its.dot.gov/about/faqs.htm. Accessed 28 Apr 2020
4. U.S. Department of Transportation Effects on Intelligent Transportation Systems Planning and Deployment in a Connected Vehicle Environment (2018). https://ops.fhwa.dot.gov/publications/fhwahop18014/fhwahop18014.pdf. Accessed 24 Apr 2020
5. Ezell, S.: Explaining international IT application leadership: intelligent transportation systems. ITIF-The Information Technology & Innovation Foundation, Washington, DC (2010). https://itif.org/files/2010-1-27-ITS-Leadership.pdf. Accessed 3 May 2020
6. Vanajakshi, L., Ramadurai, G., Anand, A.: Intelligent Transportation Systems Synthesis Report on ITS Including Issues and Challenges in India, Centre of Excellence in Urban Transport (2010)
7. Young, K.: Overcoming Barriers to ITS Deployment in Korea, Presentation to the ITS World Congress (2008)
8. Li, R., Jiang, C., Zhu, F., Chen, X.: Traffic flow data forecasting based on interval type-2 fuzzy sets theory. IEEE/CAA J. Autom. Sinica **3**(2), 141–148 (2016)
9. Vorhies, B.: The Big Deal About Big Data: What's Inside-Structured, Unstructured, and Semi-Structured Data (2013). http://data-magnum.com/the-big-deal-about-big-data-whats-inside-structured-unstructured-and-semi-structureddata/. Accessed 24 Apr 2020
10. Brooks, R.R., Sander, S., Deng, J., Taiber, J.: Automobile security concerns. IEEE Veh. Technol. **4**(2), 52–64 (2009)
11. Zhu, L., Yu, F.R., Wang, Y., Ning, B., Tang, T.: Big data analytics in intelligent transportation systems: a survey. IEEE Trans. Intell. Transp. Syst. **20**(1), 383–398 (2019). https://doi.org/10.1109/TITS.2018.2815678

12. Hilbert, M., López, P.: The world's technological capacity to store, communicate, and compute information. Science **332**(6025), 60–65 (2011)
13. Wang, W., Krishnan, R., Diehl, A.: Advances and Challenges in Intelligent Transportation: The Evolution of ICT to Address Transport Challenges in Developing Countries (2015). https://openknowledge.worldbank.org/handle/10986/25006. Accessed 24 Apr 2020
14. Assunção, M.D., Calheiros, R.N., Bianchi, S., Netto, M.A.S., Buyya, R.: Big Data computing and clouds: trends and future directions. J. Parallel Distrib. Comput. **79**(80) 3–15 (2013)
15. Waze Apps (2020). https://www.waze.com/. Accessed 3 May 2020
16. Chowdhury, M., Apon, A., Dey, K.: Data Analytics for Intelligent Transportation Systems. Amsterdam, The Netherlands (2017)
17. Leetaru, K., Wang, S., Cao, G., Padmanabhan, A., Shook, E.: Mapping the global Twitter heartbeat: the geography of Twitter. **18**(5)(2013). https://firstmonday.org/article/view/4366/3654. Accessed 3 May 2020
18. Inrix Traffic Apps (2016). http://inrix.com/mobile-apps/. Accessed 3 May 2020
19. Moovit Apps (2018). http://moovitapp.com/. Accessed 3 May 2020
20. Gaode Apps2 (2019). http://gaode.com/. Accessed 3 May 2020
21. Balogun, V.F., Obe, O.O., Balogun, T.M.: Location-based mobile alert system for intelligent transportation system. Int. J. Adv. Res. Eng. Appl. Sci. (IJAREAS) **3**(1), 11–26 (2017)
22. Ringhand, M.: Factors influencing drivers' urban route choice. Ph.D. Dissertation (2019). https://www.researchgate.net/publication/335422150-Factors-influencing-drivers%27-urban-route-choice. Accessed 24 Apr 2020
23. Bovy, P.H.L., Stern, E.: Route Choice: Wayfinding in Transport Networks, vol. 9. Springer, Dordrecht (1990)
24. Segadilha, A.B.P., da Penha Sanches, S.: Identification of factors that influence cyclists' route choice. Procedia-Soc. Behav. Sci. **160**, 372–380 (2014)
25. Tawfik, A.M., Rakha, H.A.: Network route-choice evolution in a real-time experiment: a necessary shift from network to driver oriented modeling. In: 91st Annual Meeting of Transportation Research Board Paper Compendium DVD 12-1640 (2012)
26. Papinski, D., Scott, D.M., Doherty, S.T.: Exploring the route choice decision-making process: a comparison of planned and observed routes obtained using person-based GPS. Transp. Res. Part F: Traffic Psychol. Behav. **12**(4), 347–358 (2009). https://doi.org/10.1016/j.trf.2009.04.001
27. Chamali, H., Baman Bandara, W.S.: Analysis of factors affecting pedestrian route choice. J. Chem. Inf. Model. **53**(9), 1689–1699 (2013)
28. Dijkstra, E.W.: A note on two problems in connexion with graphs. Numerische mathematik **1**(1) 269–271(1959)
29. Farooq, M.U., Shakoor, A., Siddique, A.: An efficient dynamic round robin algorithm for CPU scheduling. In: IEEE International Conference on Communication, Computing and Digital Systems, pp. 244–248 (2017)
30. Seshasayee, A., Lakshmi, J.V.N.: An insight into tree based machine learning techniques for big data analytics using Apache Spark. In: International Conference on Intelligent Computing, Instrumentation and Control Technologies (ICICICT), pp. 1740–1743 (2018)
31. Sarumi, O.A., Leung, C.K., Adetunmbi, O.A.: Spark-based data analytics of sequence motifs in large omics data. Procedia Comput. Sci. **126**, 596–605 (2018)

32. Le Noac'h, P., Costan, A., Bougé, L.: A performance evaluation of Apache Kafka in support of big data streaming applications. In: IEEE International Conference on Big Data (Big Data), pp. 4803–4806 (2017)
33. Jiang, F., Leung, C.K., Sarumi, O.A., Zhang, C.Y.: Mining sequential patterns from uncertain big DNA in the Spark framework. In: IEEE BIBM, pp. 874–88 (2016)
34. Matei, Z., et al.: Apache Spark: a unified engine for big data processing. Commun. ACM **59**(11), 56–65 (2016)
35. Sarumi, O.A., Leung, C.K.: Scalable data science and machine learning algorithm for gene prediction. In: The 7th International Conference on Big Data Applications, pp. 118–126 (2019)
36. Cardoso, P.V., Barcelos, P.P.: Definition of an architecture for dynamic and automatic checkpoints on Apache Spark. In: IEEE 37th Symposium on Reliable Distributed Systems (SRDS), pp. 271–272 (2018)
37. Venil, P., Vinodhini, G., Suban, R.: Performance evaluation of ensemble based collaborative filtering recommender system. In: IEEE International Conference on System, Computation, Automation and Networking (ICSCAN), pp. 1–5 (2019)
38. Thepade, S.D., Kalbhor, M.M.: Ensemble of machine learning classifiers for improved image category prediction using fractional coefficients of Hartley and sine transforms. In: Fourth International Conference on Computing Communication Control and Automation (ICCUBEA), pp. 1–5 (2018)

Carpooling Systems Aggregation

Porfírio P. Filipe$^{(\boxtimes)}$ and Rodrigo D. Moura

Instituto Superior de Engenharia de Lisboa, Lisbon, Portugal
porfirio.filipe@isel.pt

Abstract. Intelligent transportation systems are advanced software applications that support innovative requirements related to several transportation devices. Those applications are vital to mitigate traffic congestion and consequent environmental issues, becoming the transport more efficient and sustainable. In this context, appears the carpooling system idea, which can be described as a facilitator for sharing available seats in a private vehicle that performs a journey.

The main goal of this paper is to argue about the design of a distributed aggregator, which is a new paradigm, to handle information from carpool clubs according to a previously negotiated agreement. The aggregator emerges as a coordinator of carpooling systems, with their own administrations that autonomously manage rewards, penalties and admissions maintaining the privacy and trust among its restricted group.

For this, it is proposed a pure P2P unstructured architecture to support the aggregation of the carpooling systems. The experimental evaluation of this architecture was carried out by developing and installing a demonstrator composed by three instances of carpooling systems, based on a proposed reference implementation, which unify and upgrade, the most common requirements in the market highlighting users' privacy and trust. In order to represent hypothetical carpool clubs each carpooling system instance was populated with its own fictional data.

Keywords: Carpooling · Ridesharing · Sustainable mobility · Carpooling system · Aggregation · P2P architecture

1 Introduction

1.1 Sustainable Mobility

According to International Energy Agency, 80% of primary energy demand is based in fossil fuels, and they are responsible for 90% of CO_2 emissions [1]. A significant part of those emissions is produced by huge traffic jams in big cities. Over the years, many studies focused this environment issue, but few had proposed a real and practical solution to the overuse of private transport. Those studies show an average of 1.45 passengers per vehicle, and the urgency of change those poor numbers [2].

Intelligent Transport Systems (ITS) are vital to increase safety and to solve traffic jams issues. They can make transportation more efficient and sustainable applying information and communication technologies to all modes of passenger and freight transport [3]. In this context, carpooling appears as an emergent transport mode, where

A. L. Martins et al. (Eds.): INTSYS 2020, LNICST 364, pp. 52–71, 2021.
https://doi.org/10.1007/978-3-030-71454-3_4

a carpooling system can be described as a facilitator for sharing available seats in a private vehicle that performs a journey.

The widespread availability of broadband Internet services allows the deployment of powerful tools for carpoolers to meet potential companions and reach an agreement to share a journey [4]. This opportunity created by the Internet became the best way to inspire innovative strategies to support carpool clubs [5].

1.2   Background

Intelligent transportation systems appeared in a spontaneous way based on technological advances considered revolutionary for the urban mobility area. In Portugal, the road transports are responsible for a significant part of energy consumption based in petroleum products. There are strategies to solve this issue, for instance, the use of public transports, bicycle or carpooling also known as ridesharing.

According to a study made by Cetelem (Observador Cetelem Automóvel) there are several reasons for the population, do not join to carpool clubs. Following the Fig. 1, 46% of the population with age of 55 or more older and 38% with ages between 18 and 34 prefer to drive alone. This type of choice is more common in countries such as United States of America (USA) and Germany. In Japan, for instance, most of the people prefer to trust their vehicle to another driver [6].

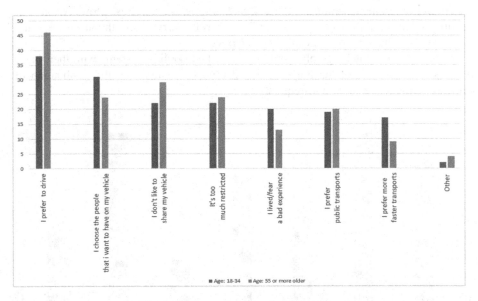

Fig. 1. Reasons for not using carpooling

At the city of Aspen in Colorado, it was carried out a survey asking the residents their opinion about incentives to use carpooling systems [7]. The most common answers were: (i) more preferential parking locations, (ii) additional benefits such as coupons or prizes, (iii) more convenient carpool pass retrieval, (iv) more convenient way to find those traveling similar routes (matching system), (v) emergency ride home to provide flexibility and (vi) financial reward for carpooling.

In Portugal, carpooling still do not have much impact. It is more common the use of carsharing, that consists in renting a specific vehicle, for a given journey. Considering that carsharing is less efficient in terms of resources, the carpooling has a lot of room to grow [8].

The most relevant advantages of carpooling are clearly the economic and the incentive for socialization between passengers. However, as is natural, there are disadvantages associated with travelling with strangers, for instance, lack of privacy and trust [9]. To mitigate these disadvantages, some of carpool clubs recommend that their users should register using social networks, such as Facebook, Twitter, or Instagram, to ensure the veracity of the user profile.

1.3 Related Work

One of the most valuable proposals of ITS to reduce traffic jam and help to save CO_2 emissions is carpooling, that has been recommended since long time ago.

Currently, there is a significant and growing set of carpooling systems. As part of the present work, in order to produce an overview focusing the most frequent characteristics of carpooling systems, it was carried out a study that includes ten carpooling systems that was judged relevant. In practice, it was not possible to have the specification and/or implementation of the selected carpooling systems. However, it was possible to carry out this study assuming the user role, carrying out the installation and registration of the analyzed systems and interfaces.

In Fig. 2 is depicted a graph about ten studied carpooling systems with their basic features. The analysis of the graph in Fig. 2 reveals the fact that the publication of demand announcements is not frequent.

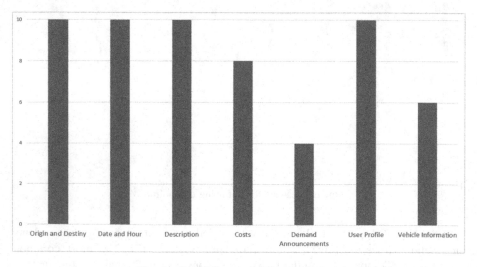

Fig. 2. Carpooling systems basic features

In Fig. 3 is depicted a graph about ten studied carpooling systems with their advanced features. The analysis of the graph in Fig. 3 reveals three features that are not frequent, namely, CO_2 calculator, waypoints and matching system.

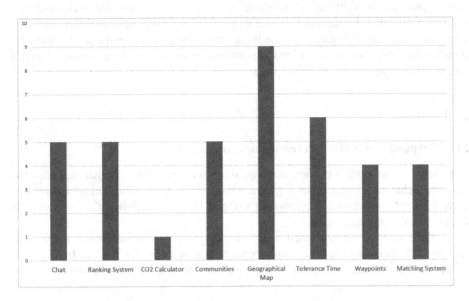

Fig. 3. Carpooling systems advanced features

About the authentication and authorization mechanisms, the studied carpooling systems use social networks or institutional email to ensure the veracity of the user's profile. However, in half of the studied systems, the administrators do not control users.

1.4   Contribution

Currently, this paradigm is becoming more well-known because of growing enhancements in information and communication technologies. In our opinion, the carpooling systems are threatened by a monopoly with a few international players that operate at a global level without a common legal framework compromising privacy and trust of the users. Major worldwide market players in information technology are involved in conflicts related to the reusing and selling of information that belongs to its users [10].

The main contribution of this work is the design of a distributed aggregator, which is a new paradigm, to handle information from carpool clubs according to a previously negotiated agreement. The aggregator emerges as a coordinator of carpooling systems, with their own administrations that autonomously manage rewards, penalties and admissions maintaining the privacy and trust among its restricted group. The aggregator allows the user of a carpooling system to manipulate, transparently, respecting the negotiated agreements, the published announcements by other carpool clubs [11].

1.5   Organization

This paper is organized in four sections. The first section, this one, includes an overview related to sustainable mobility, background, and related work. Additionally, this section, presents the contribution and these document organization. The second section presents a reference implementation for carpooling systems, the aggregator architecture, and the aggregation gateway. The third section refers the experimental evaluation devising demonstration scenarios and the obtained results. The fourth section, the final one, is about conclusion and future work.

2   Proposal

2.1   Carpooling System Reference Implementation

A reference implementation often accompanies a technical standard that describes the expected behavior of any other implementation of it. It is important to establish a reference implementation for carpooling systems in order to define the requirements and behavior of the aggregator.

In the scope of the presented study at Sect. 1.3, it was elaborated a use case diagram [12] that includes the most frequent and relevant use cases. In Fig. 4 is presented the use case diagram that refers two actors, namely: anonymous and registered.

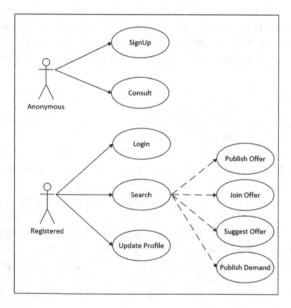

Fig. 4. Use case diagram of the reference implementation

Anonymous users can register (Sign up) or consult (Consult) announcements overviews with the basic information. The registration facility assigns to the user a Universally Unique Identifier (UUID) [13] allowing the users to create their profile indicating the following attributes: first and last name, email address, password, passport photo, birth date and mobile phone number.

Registered users can, after authenticating themselves (Login), search for detailed announcements (Search) or update their profile (Update Profile). Typically, authentication is performed by indicating the user's identifier and a password. As an alternative to the identifier, the email address or the mobile phone number can be typed. The Search case allows the users to access and carry out the actions associated to the announcements, namely: publish an offer announcement (Publish Offer) or demand (Publish Demand), joining an offer (Join Offer) or suggesting an offer announcement to satisfy a explicit demand announcement (Suggest Offer). Only users with a valid driving license and with at least one associated vehicle can publish offer announcements that can be suggested by him (Suggest Offer) to satisfy an explicit demand announcement.

In Fig. 5 is depicted the carpooling system reference architecture with three layers: service layer, logical layer, and data layer.

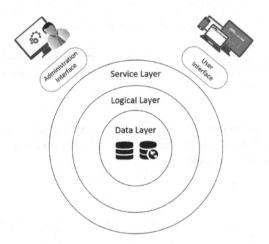

Fig. 5. Carpooling system reference architecture

In order to anticipate requirements associated with the user's privacy and trust, which are not common in the market, but considered to be urgent for the success of the carpooling systems, we suggest to implement the following requirements, such as: (i) confirmation of registration by the administrator; (ii) minimization of personal and historical data; (iii) only provide the necessary strictly information for each moment of interaction between the passenger and the carpooling system; (iv) adoption of pseudonyms to avoid the disclosure of user's real names; (v) additionally, should be considered the current legal framework on data protection.

Service Layer
The service layer is responsible for providing access to the components of the carpooling system. Essentially, this layer exposes a set of services that are intended to be consumed by the interfaces for users, administrators, and sponsors. On the other hand, this layer encapsulates the logic of the components controlling the transactions managed by the carpooling system. Thus, the service layer, that provides a Service API, does the decoupling between the components of the carpooling system and the current interfaces or the interfaces targeted for future development.

Logical Layer
The logical layer deals with the behavior of the carpooling system. In Fig. 6 shows the components that make up the logical layer, which are described below.

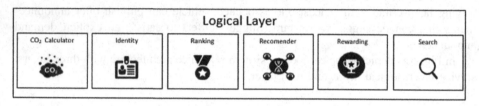

Fig. 6. Logical layer components

The logical layer supports the activities of the carpooling system, for instance, data processing, data search and report building, more generally, all the processing behind the human interface (BackOffice).

CO₂ Calculator
The CO_2 Calculator component calculates the production of CO_2 by a specific vehicle used in a journey (each vehicle model has its own CO_2 emission rate). In Fig. 7 is depicted an example of a journey.

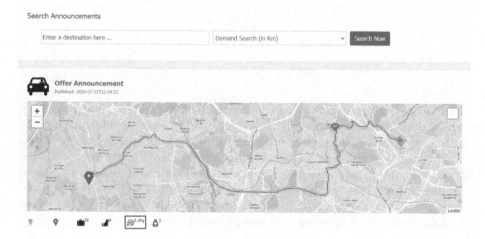

Fig. 7. Offer announcement with CO_2 calculation

The CO_2 rate associated to the vehicle model is 112 g/Km. The distance in this journey was 19.64 km. Consequently, the total of CO_2 released in this journey is 2.2 kg.

Identity

The identity component is in charge of the user's identity management. In Fig. 8 is depicted the domain model of the user. The administrator of the carpool club exclusively accesses the sensitive data, which are first and last name, email, nationality, birth date, identification document and driving license.

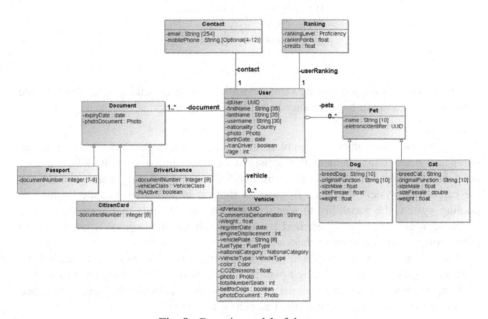

Fig. 8. Domain model of the user

The data that is exchanged between the users are, specifically: username (pseudonym), profile picture, raking data and partial information about the vehicle. For this, the username is generated randomly to not compromise the user's identification.

In addition to vehicle data, the user model also records data about pets, dogs, or cats, which can be indicated in announcements and included in journeys.

Ranking

The ranking component is responsible for managing the ranking value and level of the users.

The administrator of each carpool club defines the rules for awarding points. These points can represent rewards or penalties. The rewards can be, namely: (i) register at the carpool club, (ii) publish an announcement, (iii) subscription of an offer announcement, (iv) evaluation of users and (v) choose an economic vehicle. The penalties can be, namely: (i) unsubscribe an offer announcement or (ii) cancel an offer announcement. Additionally, the rewards points are converted into credits, which are managed by the reward system. In Table 1 shows an example of the rules processed to determine the ranking level.

Table 1. Ranking level assignment rules

Ranking	
Value	Level
0 to 50	Beginner
51 to 100	Amateur
101 to 500	Professional
501 to 2000	Veteran
2001 to 1000000	Master

On the other hand, the ranking value determines the user ranking level. For this, the administrator can define the ranking level assignment rules.

Recommender

The recommender component implements a matching algorithm that determines published offer announcement that satisfy a demand announcement. When a user publishes a demand announcement, there may exist corresponding announcements on the carpooling system database. Because of that, is important to include in the carpooling system the capability to identify offer announcements that correspond. The matching algorithm is parameterized by a geographical or temporal window to find similar origins, destinations or dates and times.

For instance, if the geographical window for origin is 2 km, this means that will be matched announcements with origin within a circle with 2 km radius. For instance, if the temporal window for departure date/time is 10-min, this means that will be matched announcements with departure centred at a 20-min interval.

Rewarding

The rewarding component manages the user's credits, allowing the user to convert them into desired rewards previously recorded by the sponsors of the carpool club. A reward is defined by a description, a quantity, and a validity interval. The rewards can be, for instance: free parking, fuel discounts, and cinema tickets. In Fig. 9 is presented an example of data included in the QRCode.

Barcode format	QR_CODE
Parsed Result Type	TEXT
Parsed Result	The idUser: 56e425f8-11ea-87d9-0a002700000f The User Name: jewell.ziemann58 The Sponsor: XPY

Fig. 9. Example of data included in the QRCode

The conversion of credits into rewards is carried out by generating a QRCode that includes the consumed credits, the name of the sponsor, user's identifier, and the username. In Fig. 10 is depicted the generated QRCode.

Fig. 10. Generated QRCode

The QRCodes can only be generated for rewards/donations previously configured by the sponsors of the carpool club.

Search

The search component allows finding announcements, which can be archived using a multi-attribute filter, for instance, (i) search through a destination within a circle; (ii) search for announcements subscribed by the user; (iii) search for announcements published by the user. In Fig. 11 is depicted the domain model of the announcement.

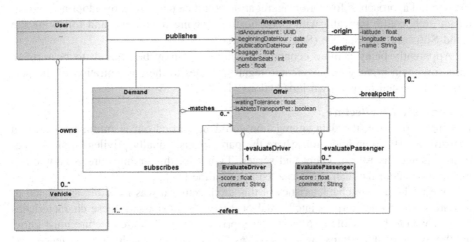

Fig. 11. Domain model of the announcement

The announcement can be classified as Offer or Demand. For an offer announcement, it is mandatory to have associated at least one vehicle, which may have zero or more subscriptions.

Data Layer

The data layer maintains data about the users and announcements. For this, a relational database and a geographic database are putted in place [14].

2.2   Aggregator

Regarding, the recent proliferation of carpooling systems, we propose a new paradigm to facilitate the coordination between carpooling systems respecting its autonomy. This paradigm is materialized by an aggregator, which combines, at runtime, data from multiple carpooling systems avoiding data replication and data centralization according to data protection issues.

The aggregator architecture should facilitate, for the members of a carpool club, the transparent manipulation of the announcements published by other clubs with established agreements. In our opinion, agreements are the desirable way for carpool clubs to negotiate, protecting the interests of their users and offering a more robust service [15].

Data Scraping

In a first approach, the data managed by the aggregator could be acquired directly from the websites of the existing carpooling systems. This process does not require data migration and may involve some improvements in the existing carpooling systems.

However, in addition to the feedback about publication and subscription of announcements and the requirement for the users to have registration, there are still legal problems with the use of this web data without prior agreement.

Multi-tenant Architecture

In a second approach, information aggregation could be performed by adopting a multi-tenant architecture typically with cloud hosting, paying for the use and following the cloud Software as a Service (SaaS) paradigm.

Apparently being a more economical solution, it may be difficult to bear rising costs, maintain privacy and overcome legal obstacles to the concentration of the personal data hosted in unknown jurisdictions [16].

Peer-to-Peer Architecture

In a third approach, the data aggregation could be carried out at runtime adopting a Peer-to-Peer (P2P) architecture, where the participants, equally privileged, simultaneously assume the role of client and server. Typically, this architecture is adopted to distribute content that can be consumed at real time [17].

Due to the unique characteristics of this architecture it was indelibly associated to activities that do not respect intellectual property. In other hand, these characteristics have proven to be suitable to protect user's privacy [18]. This architecture must know all the participant systems, which requires, in a first approach, the existence and maintenance of additional systems to support a discovery protocol. This kind of architecture, designated by hybrid P2P architecture, is considered partially centralized because of the data needed for the discovery protocol [19]. In Fig. 12 depicts the hybrid P2P architecture with a single server, which introduces a single point of failure and bottleneck.

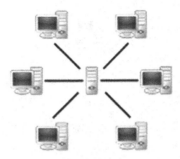

Fig. 12. Hybrid P2P architecture

The need of servers leads to dependent on third parties introducing costs that must be shared. In this scenario, it seems desirable to adopt the P2P architecture, completely decentralized, without servers and avoiding points of failure and bottlenecks.

In Fig. 13 is depicted a pure P2P unstructured architecture, which supports a dynamic interaction between the participants.

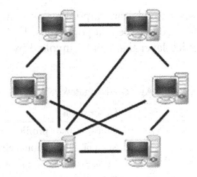

Fig. 13. Pure P2P unstructured architecture

Considering the presented arguments, it is proposed that the aggregator follows a pure P2P unstructured architecture.

2.3 Aggregation Gateway

In order to support carpooling systems aggregation, carpooling systems must be upgraded adopting an aggregation gateway, which will be the ambassador of a carpool club as part of a distributed aggregator.

From another point of view, the aggregator is dynamically composed, at runtime, by the online gateways. The local aggregation gateway accesses remote gateways and vice-versa. A carpooling system upgrade is illustrated in Fig. 14 that includes the proposed aggregation gateway.

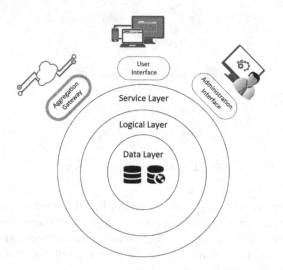

Fig. 14. Carpooling system upgrade

The aggregation gateway extends the carpooling system in order to support the interaction agreement established between carpool clubs. In Table 2 is enumerated the exposed services of the service layer that can be invoked by the aggregation gateway.

Table 2. Aggregation gateway services

Letter	Service	Description
A	GET/user/profile/	Consults user profile
B	GET/announcement/s/	Searches for announcements
C	GET/announcement/	Consults an announcement
D	PUT/announcement/subscription/	Subscribes an announcement
E	POST/announcement/evaluate/	Evaluates a user based on announcement
F	POST/announcement/suggest/	Suggests an offer to a demand announcement

The agreement is previously negotiated and configured by the local administrator. A unidirectional agreement is configured through a Uniform Resource Locator (URL) and a random serial key. A bidirectional agreement can be completed defining a reciprocal configuration.

In Fig. 15 and Fig. 16 is depicted the administrator interface that can be used to configure a set of agreements.

Fig. 15. Agreements management of "daBoleias" and "eventos.Boleias"

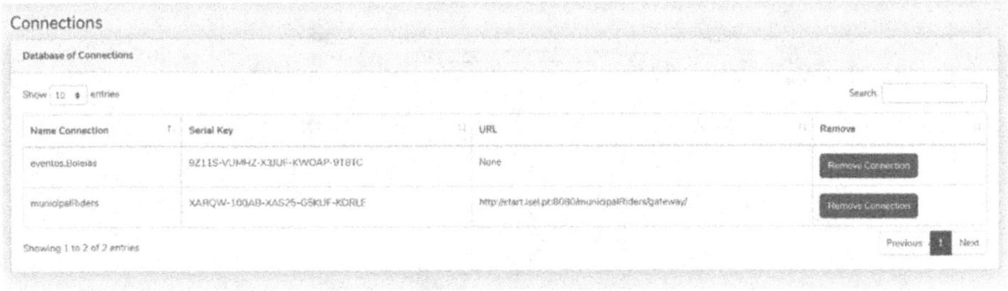

Fig. 16. Agreements management of "daBoleias" carpool club

In the interest of preserve the autonomy of carpool clubs, the aggregation gateway must implement a distributed announcement search and subscription process converting the user's ranking.

Ranking Conversion
The ranking conversion is implemented upgrading the A method (see Table 2) that adopts a rule based on an interchange fee established by the local administrator. However, the interchange fee can be dynamically determined, using the average of the two involved rankings.

Distributed Search
The distributed announcement search is implemented upgrading the B method (see Table 2) assuming a limited quantity of returned announcements. The quantity of return announcements is a configuration parameter managed by the local administrator considering efficiency issues.

Thus, in a first interaction, the local search launches remote searches to obtain a set of announcements for each online carpool club. The returned announcements are loaded in a persistent memory and sorted in order to acquire a previously limited set of announcements. The following announcements are those that remain in memory. When the memory is emptied, it is launched a new distributed search indicating the next iteration number.

3   Experimental Evaluation

The experimental evaluation of the proposed architecture was carried out by implementing a demonstrator composed by three instances of the reference implementation presented in Sect. 2.1. In order to represent hypothetical carpool clubs each instance was populated with its own fictional data.

In Fig. 17 is depicted the interaction diagram between carpool clubs, namely "boleias.Eventos", "daBoleias" and "municipalRiders". The systems names are inspired by Portuguese names.

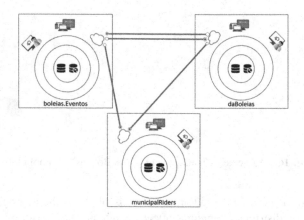

Fig. 17. Demonstrator P2P architecture

In Fig. 18 is depicted the announcements feed of "daBoleias" carpool club.

Fig. 18. Feed announcements screen

The announcements are sorted, by default, according to departure date and time. When the user wants to see more announcements, he or she must scroll down. The experimental evaluation covers four scenarios detailed below.

#1 Scenario: User Ranking

Carpooling clubs may have its own rules for adding user ranking points, which causes divergences between user's rankings. For instance, the user Annie Granger with the pseudonym "cindie-satterfield38" registered at "municipalRiders" has a user ranking value of 205 points. However, the same user at "daBoleias" has 41 for ranking value because the interchange fee, configured by the administrator, is 80% and at "eventos. Boleias" club the ranking value is 194.75 due to an interchange fee of 5%.

#2 Scenario: Search for a Journey

Registered users can search for journeys using a multi-attribute filter. For instance, when Arieta Benson, with the pseudonym "maryjane-smith28" registered at "daBoleias" carpool club wants to search for a journey to "Belém Cultural Center" she indicates that destination and the desired radius. The result set may include announcements published locally, by users from "daBoleias", or remotely, by others users from "municipalRiders" or from "eventos.Boleias". In Fig. 19 is depicted an example of the search.

Fig. 19. Offer announcement search screen

In Fig. 20 is depicted the subscription screen used to indicate the pickup point and the weight of luggage. The user can select and subscribe one of the displayed announcements or, if he or she does not select any, he or she can publish a correspondent demand announcement based on existing search filter values.

Fig. 20. Subscribe announcement screen

When the user subscribes an announcement, he or she must indicate the pickup point and optionally the weight of the luggage.

#3 Scenario: Consent Subscription

The users that publish offer announcements are notified when a subscription occurs. For instance, the user Marco Robertson, with the pseudonym "chong.collier03" of "municipalRiders" carpool club, receives a notification stating that someone wants to join the journey he announced. After the user "chong.collier03" consents the subscription, "maryjane-smith28" of "daBoleias" carpool club can check more detailed information, such as the users who subscribed the announcement and details about the vehicle.

In order to solve the notification, the user "chong.collier03" must access the consent screen, in Fig. 21, to accept or decline the subscription.

Fig. 21. Consent subscription screen

In Fig. 22 is depicted the screen, available after consent, with additional details about the subscribed announcement.

Fig. 22. Screen after subscription consent

After the journey, the users must fill the evaluation form. Each traveler must rate between 1 and 5 stars. This rating allows the calculation, by the ranking component, of the ranking points and credits that will be assigned to each user.

In Fig. 23 is depicted the journey evaluation form of the user chong.collider03 from "municipalRiders" carpool club that evaluates the user "maryjane-smith28" of "daBoleias" carpool club in the context of a journey.

Fig. 23. Evaluation of a user from "daBoleias" carpool club

The user "maryjane-smith28" from "daBoleias" carpool club receives a similar screen with the same goal.

4 Conclusion and Future Work

The presented work is a recent development fitted in the initiatives around sustainable mobility promoted in our laboratory. Regarding, the recent proliferation of carpooling systems, is argue the relevance of the coordination between carpooling systems implementing a pure P2P architecture to support the aggregator dynamically composed at runtime. For this, is devised a carpooling system reference implementation based on our own presented study in order to establish the requirements for the aggregation gateway that extends and integrates the carpooling systems within a distributed aggregator. This approach allows the registered users in a carpool club, to manipulate announcements published by other carpool clubs.

The experimental evaluation is based on our own distributed aggregator that coordinates three instances of the carpooling system reference implementation currently deployed in our laboratory, which can be freely accessed by URL start.isel.pt.

Additionally, is available by URL www.start.isel.pt/daBoleiasVM, also for free use as is, a virtual machine in.ova [20] format (see Fig. 24), which was prepared for "daBoleias" carpool club demonstration that can be considered as a beta version of an autonomous carpooling system.

Fig. 24. Download screen for virtual machine

As future work, we intend to follow and adapt to our approach the progresses in Intelligent Carpooling System (ICS) [21], mainly the use of Global Positioning System (GPS) at real time to increase the flexibility of the negotiation for announcements subscriptions [22]. Explore available cloud environments, in order to develop a reference carpooling system as a native cloud application. Finally, we intend to take advantage of emergent improvements related to trust in semantic P2P architectures [23].

References

1. IEA Data Database. https://www.iea.org/energyaccess/database/. Accessed 21 July 2020
2. Occupancy rates of passenger vehicles. https://www.eea.europa.eu/data-and-maps/indicat ors/occupancy-rates-of-passenger-vehicles/occupancy-rates-of-passenger-vehicles. Accessed 21 July 2020
3. Anderson, J., Sutcliffe, S.: Intelligent transport systems (ITS) – an overview. IFAC Technol. Transfer Dev. Countries 99–106 (2000)

4. Mallus, M., Colistra, G., Atzori, L., Murroni, M., Pilloni, V.: Dynamic carpooling in urban areas: design and experimentation with a multi-objective route matching algorithm. Sustainability 9(2), 254 (2017). https://doi.org/10.3390/su9020254
5. Ferreira, J., Filipe, P., Martins, P.: Cooperative transportation infrastructure. In: International Conference on IT and Intelligent Systems (2013)
6. O Observador Cetelem, Auto A Fratura Automóvel, p. 92 (2020)
7. Aspen. Carpool Survey (2017). https://www.surveymonkey.com/r/XNJ8D72. Accessed 21 July 2020
8. Carpooling: Muito Mais do que Andar à Boleia com Estranhos. https://www.e-konomista.pt/carpooling/. Accessed 21 July 2020
9. Correia, G., Viegas, J.: Carpooling and carpool clubs: clarifying concepts and assessing value enhancement possibilities through a stated preference web survey in Lisbon, Portugal. Transp. Res. Part A: Policy Pract. 45(2), 81–90 (2011). https://doi.org/10.1016/j.tra.2010.11.001
10. Olsson, L., Maier, R., Friman, M.: Why do they ride with others? Meta-analysis of factors influencing travelers to carpool. Sustainability 11(8), 2414 (2019). https://doi.org/10.3390/su11082414
11. Tahmasseby, S., Kattan, L., Barbour, B.: Propensity to participate in a peer to peer social network based carpooling system. J. Adv. Transp. 50, 240–254 (2015)
12. UML Use Case Diagrams. https://www.uml-diagrams.org/use-case-diagrams.html. Accessed 21 July 2020
13. Universally Unique Identifier (UUID) URN Namespace. https://tools.ietf.org/html/rfc4122. Accessed 21 July 2020
14. Luaces, M., Brisaboa, N., Paramá, J., Viqueira, J.: A Generic Architecture for Geographic Information Systems, January 2004
15. Chaulagain, R., Pandley, S., Basnet, S., Shakya, S.: Cloud based web scraping for big data applications. In: Conference: 2017 IEEE International Conference on Smart Cloud (SmartCloud), November 2017
16. Gomes, C.: Estudo do Paradigma Computação em Nuvem, Master Dissertation by Instituto Superior de Engenharia de Lisboa, December 2012
17. Huang, F., Ravindran, B., Jensen, E.D.: RT-P2P: a scalable real-time peer-to-peer system with probabilistic timing assurances. In: Conference: 2008 IEEE/IPIP International Conference on Embedded and Ubiquitous Computing (EUC 2008), Shanghai, China, 17–20 December, vol. I (2008)
18. Vimal, S., Srivatsa, S.K.: A Survey on Various File Sharing Methods in P2P Networks
19. Baccaglini, E., Grangetto, M., Quacchio, E., Zezza, S.: A study of an hybrid CDN–P2P system over the PlanetLab network. Signal Process.: Image Commun. 27, 430–437 (2012)
20. Ova. https://www.reviversoft.com/pt/file-extensions/ova. Accessed 21 July 2020
21. López-García, D.A., Torreglosa, J.P., Vera, D.: A decentralized P2P control scheme for trading accurate energy fragments in the power grid. Int. J. Electr. Power Energy Syst. 110, 271–282 (2019)
22. Friginal, J., Gambs, S., Guiochet, J., Killijian, M.-O.: Towards privacy-driven design of a dynamic carpooling system. Pervasive Mob. Comput. 14, 71–82 (2014). https://doi.org/10.1016/j.pmcj.2014.05.009
23. Mawlood-Yunis, A.-R., Weiss, M.: From P2P to reliable semantic P2P systems. Peer-to-Peer Netw. Appl. 3(4), 363–381 (2010).

An Individual-Based Simulation Approach to Demand Responsive Transport

Sergei Dytckov[✉], Fabian Lorig, Johan Holmgren, Paul Davidsson,
and Jan A. Persson

Department of Computer Science and Media Technology,
Internet of Things and People Research Center,
K2 – The Swedish Knowledge Centre for Public Transport, Malmö University,
205 06 Malmö, Sweden
{sergei.dytckov,fabian.lorig,johan.holmgren,
paul.davidsson,jan.a.persson}@mau.se

Abstract. This article demonstrates an approach to the simulation of Demand Responsive Transport (DRT) – a flexible transport mode that typically operates as a combination of taxi and bus modes. Travellers request individual trips and DRT is capable of adjusting its routes or schedule to the needs of travellers. It has been seen as a part of the public transport network, which has the potential to reduce operational costs of public transport services, to provide better service quality for population groups with limited mobility and to improve transport fairness. However, a DRT service needs to be thoroughly planned to target the intended user groups, attract a sufficient demand level and maintain reasonable operational costs. As the demand for DRT is dynamic and heterogeneous, it is difficult to simulate it with a macro approach. To address this problem, we develop and evaluate an individual-based simulation comprising models of traveller behaviour for both supply and demand sides. Travellers choose a trip alternative with a mode choice model and DRT vehicle routing utilises a model of travellers' mode choice behaviour to optimise routes. This allows capturing supply-side operational costs and demand-side service quality for every individual, what allows for designing a personalised service that can prioritise needy groups of travellers improving transport fairness. By simulating different setups of DRT services, the simulator can be used as a decision support tool.

Keywords: Demand Responsive Transport · Simulation

1 Introduction

Demand Responsive Transport (DRT) describes a range of transport services where the vehicles' routes are dynamically planned based on trip requests by

© ICST Institute for Computer Sciences, Social Informatics and Telecommunications Engineering 2021
Published by Springer Nature Switzerland AG 2021. All Rights Reserved
A. L. Martins et al. (Eds.): INTSYS 2020, LNICST 364, pp. 72–89, 2021.
https://doi.org/10.1007/978-3-030-71454-3_5

travellers. Most commonly, DRT is realised as a minibus taxi-like service, where a fleet of vehicles is serving travel requests in a door-to-door manner within a specified area. In contrast to conventional taxis, ride-sharing among multiple travellers is one of the features that allows reducing operational costs of DRT. However, DRT may take more restricted forms closer to regular Public Transport (PT) bus service. For example, it can be a corridor service with defined start and final stops but flexible intermediate stops between them [36]. Most commonly, DRT is applied in two forms: as a special transport service for population groups with mobility limitations or as replacement of regular bus service in rural low-density areas [49].

In this work, the main characteristics of DRT are: 1) Service is open for everyone – it is not a special transport service but DRT may adapt to requirements of a specific population group or purpose. 2) A traveller has to inform the system about pick-up and drop-off points – this differs the service for traditional PT. 3) The service responds to changes in demand by either altering its route and/or its schedule. 4) The fare is charged on a per passenger and not a per vehicle basis. Thus taxi is not DRT, yet, DRT trips can be executed by taxi vehicles.

There is growing interest to use DRT for the general public and with the real-time serving of requests. However, many trial cases of new DRT systems were discontinued due to a variety of reasons including insufficient financial results, poor marketing, low integration to the regular public transport network or lacks in the service design [10]. Pettersson [40] concludes that new technologies do not seem to improve the success of DRT services by itself and we argue that the service needs to better adapt to conditions of a specific geographical area and population to be successful.

The potential of DRT services has been extensively studied through simulations [5, 25, 30, 34, 38, 42–44, 47, 52]. Still, each case is unique and the DRT service needs to be designed in accordance with the conditions of the specific case. In case of the DRT service Kutsuplus in Helsinki, Finland, a simulation was built prior to the implementation of the physical service showing that DRT is more efficient than PT at high demand levels [21]. After the service was discontinued, the final report shows that the demand prediction was inaccurate [16]. A realistic simulation could help decision-makers (politicians, authorities and PT actors) to assess the effectiveness of a DRT service and the whole PT network before doing expensive trials.

DRT in its nature is similar to other on-demand transport modes, like shared autonomous vehicles, and simulation of them can be done very similarly. We focus on DRT to highlight non-private use of service vehicles, ride-sharing and social goals of the service that DRT is usually associated with. With the simulation, we want to find a balance between social benefits and operational costs. According to a study in UK [23], actors see social objectives as the main reason to introduce DRT. We want to help decision-makers to understand what design of a DRT service is most beneficial to the target demand groups and how to achieve synergies between different target groups to enable better DRT performance.

In this article, we suggest and demonstrate an approach to the simulation of DRT and analyse benefits and disadvantages of such an approach. When developing the simulation, there were the following two goals: 1) To develop a simulation capable of providing decision support for decision-makers; 2) To study how DRT, if seen as a part of PT network, may affect the mobility opportunities and what population groups may benefit the most. We are developing an agent-based simulation approach where the traveller behaviour is in the centre of simulation and DRT is directly connected to PT. Our approach allows for simulating a DRT system where social objectives are optimised when routing vehicles, what allows tuning of the service towards the needs of the travellers.

2   Related Work

Traditionally, DRT is used as paratransit service, or as a replacement for low-demand bus lines in rural areas [49]. But there is a trend that travellers change their travel behaviour towards less predictable travels and expect more personalised service, what opens up a potential for flexible transport services such as DRT [39]. In a series of interviews, Davison et al. identify existing market niches that DRT occupies and opportunities for future market penetration [7]. They also note that unsuccessful DRT cases are often caused by the realisation of inappropriate DRT scheme for the target purpose. To overcome this issue, the suitability of a DRT design should be evaluated in advance to their implementation. In this regard, this section presents different approaches for the simulation, analysis and design of on-demand transport services and relates them to the approach we present in this paper.

2.1   Simulation of On-demand Transport Modes

Traditionally, transport is studied using macro-models that simulate traffic flow based on different characteristics such as flow or density to estimate the utilisation or congestion of larger street segments [15]. They approximate the dynamics of interactions between actors. Ramezani and Nourinejad show how macroscopic fundamental diagrams can be used to optimise the dispatching of taxis taking into account traffic conditions [41]. Macroscopic fundamental diagrams relate vehicle density and flow rates in a traffic network and need to be generated using real traffic data or other individual-based simulation approaches. Yang, Wong and Wong used an analytical modelling approach to find an equilibrium state of the taxi market for different scenarios of managing taxi [56]. While this approach allows for maximising social objectives (amount of trips, waiting time and costs), it is difficult to use it for the evaluation of service quality for heterogeneous travellers or for optimising the service for specific groups of travellers. This is because macroscopic approaches do not explicitly model interactions between actors.

Micro-simulations, in contrast, focus on modelling the behaviour of individual autonomous units such as travellers and DRT vehicles. Numerous of micro-simulation studies have been presented on on-demand modes of transport such as autonomous shared vehicles, which operate similar to DRT. In both cases, the used simulation methodology is very similar. One major difference is that ride-sharing is not considered in the majority of studies on autonomous shared vehicles. Instead, vehicles are only shared between users [3,18,26,29,50]. Ride-sharing is an important feature of DRT, hence, in the remainder of this section, we present only studies on DRT and on-demand mobility with ride-sharing.

2.2   Analysis and Design of On-demand Transport Modes

In attempts to analyse theoretical advantages of on-demand transport modes, most simulation studies explore modelled service on unrealistic road networks [34] with randomly generated demand [33,38], by serving all the recorded trips by DRT [1,30] or by defining an arbitrary number of trips [1,5,11]. The goal of these studies is to estimate the required amount of vehicles and costs for DRT. Only a limited amount of studies considers realistic environments and demand [8,25,46,48]. As we aim to provide a decision for DRT introduction to a specific area, we need to consider both realistic road network and demand model.

We consider DRT as a service that complements PT rather than replacing or competing with it. In our vision, DRT is integrated into the PT network. In most of studies of DRT (e.g., [25,38,43,44,46,52]) and other on-demand transport modes (e.g., [3,11,18,30,31]) PT is considered a separate standalone service, sometimes in direct competition to other existing transportation services. On-demand transport, such as autonomous vehicles, are often seen as a leading mode in future transportation but it has potential to increase demand due to reduction of travel costs, new user groups and recontextualisation of trip time [53]. Improving roads does not solve road congestion, although the degree of effect is in discussion [4,19]. PT is more efficient in moving high volumes of travellers [28]. The generalised costs of public transport for society is half the cost of private transport when considering external costs such as air pollution, climate change and road accidents [20]. Thus, we see the ride-sharing aspect of DRT and connection of DRT to PT (that could also help to promote PT), as a potential way forward for improving transport equity and sustainable future and focus our efforts on building a simulation that helps to estimate the effects of a scenario with DRT integrated with PT.

An important aspect of our study is the integration of DRT into PT network. In literature, DRT is often opposed to PT. For instance, Leich and Bischoff show that replacing PT with DRT results in marginal benefits [25]. However, the combination of PT and DRT may be more efficient than solely PT when the demand level is low. With higher demand, in contrast, PT becomes more efficient [27]. To achieve a higher level of social welfare, the same vehicle fleet may be used as demand-responsive or as regular timetabled transport depending on demand level [45]. A combination of DRT and PT may be more efficient if DRT vehicles are allowed to drive travellers to any of the available PT transfer stations [24]. Shen, Zhang, and Zhao presented a simulation approach to study the integration of autonomous vehicles into the public transport network [48].

These studies show that DRT integrated into PT network may be more efficient than PT or than PT and DRT as competing services.

3   Simulation of Demand Responsive Transport

The overarching goal of our work is to develop a simulation tool that can provide decision support to decision-makers in the process of designing a DRT system for a specific area. The simulation helps to evaluate different service options: level of route flexibility, target population groups or geographical coverage. We see DRT as a service that may actively optimise its behaviour at the vehicle routing phase towards social objectives. In line with this, we see DRT as a part of public transport (PT) and strive to find a way to optimise the connection between the services, as PT plays an important role in sustainable transportation (where social aspects are as important as economical) [28]. We see a need to develop a simulation approach capable of simulating DRT together with PT and capturing not only economical characteristics but also social value that a DRT service could bring.

Traditional paratransit DRT services require booking of a trip at least one day in advance. To make DRT attractive for other population groups, we consider a flow of requests to the DRT service with real-time requirements (meaning that trip is requested to be executed as soon as possible) or with small booking time (a trip is executed at the same day as request). This assumption makes the demand dynamic what is a challenge for the simulation process. The dynamic nature of DRT makes it more difficult to simulate it with conventional macro-simulation approaches. Macro-simulations have to approximate travel times and do not allow to capture the details of service quality, making it harder to estimate the social value of a DRT service. Thus, we apply agent-based micro-simulation that allows for modelling individual behaviour.

3.1   Simulation Approach

The overall simulation process is shown in Fig. 1. When a traveller, which is modelled as an autonomous agent, is planning a trip, he or she requests the service (through a trip planner) to find available travel options. The service generates trips that include DRT as well as the combination of DRT and PT and other conventional travel options. Then traveller chooses one of the options and books it if it involves DRT. If DRT is booked, the service updates its vehicles' routes and vehicles execute them. Travel requests come into the system dynamically during the day and vehicles' routes can be modified even when a vehicle is already executing journeys.

With the simulation approach that integrates a model of travel behaviour, we may evaluate a DRT service with a complex behaviour of the service that balances between economical and social goals providing suitable mobility options for everyone. DRT service routes the vehicles according to its optimisation goals which can be formulated multi-objective optimisation problem. The economical

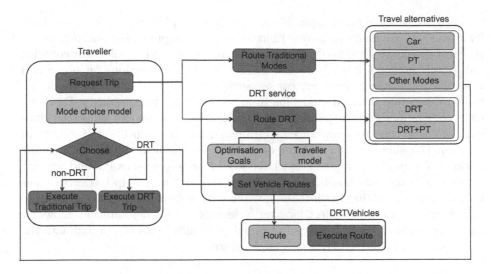

Fig. 1. Overview of the simulation approach.

objective of DRT is to minimise its operational costs, the major part of which are the number of vehicles running and distance driven. The value of a travel can be represented by its utility (or disutility) and the social objective is to maximise the utility for travellers (or minimise the disutility). Such a numeric representation allows for integrating social objective into the optimisation function for vehicle routing, allowing, in turn, to balance between economical and social objectives when routing DRT vehicles.

In a micro-simulation, we have an opportunity to model the utility a trip provides to a traveller and even model traveller choice (a probability that accepts the proposed DRT trip). Accounting for that, the service may provide sub-optimal trip alternatives (from the point of view of a traveller), which still will be likely accepted by travellers, to improve the overall performance. Additionally, this allows implementing a heterogeneous service scheme, meaning that different population groups or purposes of travel may be routed differently according to the needs of people and priority of service. For example, trips to work or hospital require specific arrival times that must be kept, while shopping trips may be more flexible. Persons with movement limitations may be of higher priority for the service and minimising walking distance is of higher priority than total travel time for them. A DRT service can be designed with hard restrictions to target the needs of specific population groups (e.g. by setting predefined stop points, restricting who can use the service). If such restrictions are applied on the stage of routing trips, there is an opportunity to use "soft" restriction putting priority to the trips the service is intended to serve, but still allowing other trip types, what could help with the service overall efficiency.

Travel behaviour (the actions of actual travellers) includes both the demand model, trip planning and mode choice. This behaviour is different and individual for each of the agents and depends on socio-demographic factors (e.g. age, family status, employment, or income) but also on geographical factors such as the place of residence as described in [9]. Demand and mode choice are complex multilevel problems in real life and include long-term decisions on home and workplace locations. Moreover, car ownership dictates everyday mode choice. Still, we separate demand modelling from mode choice for simplicity. By doing that, we can focus on the parameters of the system that we can simulate (influence of travel time to acceptance ratio) but ignore the connection of long-term decision (housing location and car ownership) to the availability of transport options. We implicitly assume that DRT would be perceived as PT and will not change the long-term housing and work decision but may help to decrease car use. We may argue that in short-term, while DRT is being adopted, it is unlikely that it will significantly affect long term decisions. This delimitation allows us to use travel surveys or otherwise recorded real-world data to approximate the behaviour of travellers if DRT was implemented.

3.2 Evaluation of the Approach

The benefit of such a request-oriented simulation approach is that the system might take into account personal and contextual information from travellers and generate trip alternatives according to both the needs of the travellers and system optimality, allowing the maximisation of social objectives. Alternatively, when travellers' behaviour is modelled realistically, one may use this approach to optimise service parameters such as travel cost, amount of vehicles or expected profits [30,34].

The drawback of this approach is that it relies heavily on the mode choice modelling while there is a very limited amount of data to build such models. Still, this opens up opportunities to study what type of behaviour shift is needed an efficient DRT operation. A benefit of our approach is that it allows explicit mode choice in each situation and that travellers are not required to use a service with insufficient quality, reducing the service load, thus, converging towards a transport equilibrium state. That is also a drawback of our approach – it represents a single day. If a traveller received service with sufficient quality in one day it does not guarantee that on a different day service would be able to provide the exact same quality.

Multiple similar simulations in the area of conventional and on-demand transportation have been done with MATSim [17,18,31]. The philosophy of MATSim lies in the co-evolution of supply and demand. Travellers in MATSim plan the trip mode at the beginning of a simulation cycle, evaluate their results after each day and replan their journeys for the next day. The problem with DRT simulation in MATSim is that a person requires to select DRT not knowing trip characteristics as waiting and travel time. And while in the evolutionary cycle the demand will adjust to the supply, a significant amount of simulation cycles are required to find the equilibrium.

In a way, travellers in MATSim learn average service quality and make an informed choice based on the average utility of DRT service. However, separating mode choice from building routes could result in a large amount of sub-optimal and unrealistic trips being accepted travellers, especially when a connection of DRT and PT is utilised. This brings down the potential of DRT and slows down the process of converging to the equilibrium state.

Our approach could benefit from MATSim philosophy: in multi-day simulations, travellers could accumulate the knowledge on service quality and utilise it in the decision process. Yet, simulation of DRT is a computationally expensive process: building routes and solving vehicle routing problems is NP-hard and should rely on heuristics for large-scale simulations. In our simulation experiments, the computational bottleneck was in constructing time-distance matrices between travellers and vehicles to build a vehicle routing problem. To relax this problem, a workaround has been made by [46]. The authors use MATSim to find a near-equilibrium state based on approximate time provided by DRT and then simulate this state in a custom simulator with advanced fleet management and routing.

A benefit of our implementation is that we designed the system based on DRT connected to PT. There are several extensions in MATSim: public transport, on-demand transport, multi-modal trips and carsharing. They allow adding this functionality to MATSim. For instance, one could expand the DRT route planning algorithm to plan the connection between DRT and PT. But so far, to our knowledge, existing studies in MATSim include DRT-like ride-share [35,38,52] and they do not utilise the MATSim philosophy of co-evolution. We also have not found examples where on-demand transport is connected with regular PT in the same network.

3.3   Simulation Prototype

This section describes the prototype of our simulator, focusing on how trip routing flow is implemented. We are developing an open-source simulator[1] based on other open-source projects. As we do not have a requirement to create a precise traffic micro-simulation so vehicle movement is implemented as event-driven simulation. Vehicles teleport between picking up and delivering travellers according to travel times estimated by the trip planner. If a vehicle needs to be rerouted when it is moving, its current position can be extracted from the planned route.

The trip generation flow is depicted in Fig. 2. Processing of trip requests starts from OpenTripPlaner[2] (OTP) and it is a central tool for generating trip alternatives for requests. It uses Open Street Maps[3] and PT timetables in the format of General Transit Feed Specification (GTFS) to find multi-modal trip alternatives that can combine car, walking, public transport, bicycle. Routing a direct trip by DRT is straightforward: we build a vehicle routing problem, calculating time and distance matrix between all the trip start and trip end positions with the help of Open Street Routing Machine[4] (OSRM) which works

---

[1] https://github.com/serdyt/DRTsim.
[2] https://www.opentripplanner.org.
[3] https://www.openstreetmap.org/.
[4] http://project-osrm.org.

significantly faster than OTP and solve the resulting vehicle routing problem with jsprit[5]. Finding a DRT+PT trip involves two steps: first, with the use of OTP, we find a trip with the "kiss and ride" mode, when a traveller is assumed to be driven from a starting position to a bus stop as a passenger in a car; then, we replace the car leg with DRT building a vehicle routing problem and solving it with jsprit in the same way as with the direct DRT trip.

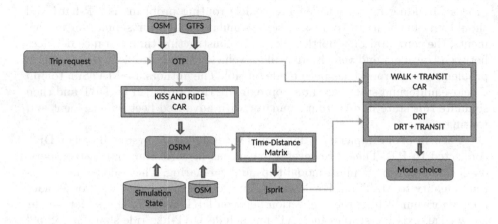

Fig. 2. The process diagram of routing trip alternatives.

Building a naïve optimisation problem including all of the currently active requests resulted in a computational bottleneck limiting the scalability. A time-distance matrix between all the geographical points involved is required to solve the optimisation problem. The size of such a matrix is quadratic to the number of requests R: $O(R^2)$, as each new request adds new origin and destination to the matrix. In our first experiments (described in more details in the Sect. 3.4), planned vehicle routes involved on average 19 travellers per vehicle, what means OSRM needs to find all to all shortest paths between 600 points (for 30 vehicles), which took around 15 s to compute, what limits the simulation possibilities. A smarter algorithm for data preparation for vehicle routing problem is required, like in [1], filtering out the vehicles that cannot be utilised in serving of a new request.

3.4 Experiments

The prototype was evaluated with a simulation experiment on the municipality of Sjöbo in southern Sweden. Travel demand for commuters (travellers going to the workplace and back with either home or work activities located in the target area) was modelled based on a regional Swedish survey of travel habits [14] with modified four-step modelling approach [9]. Trip attraction and production

---

[5] https://github.com/graphhopper/jsprit.

were modelled with a linear regression model. Trips were distributed into the origin-destination matrix with tri-proportional fitting. The trip matrix was disaggregated into individual trips by sampling locations of houses and workplaces. Additionally, the desired time of the trip was assigned based on the recorded distribution of work trips. A sample of about 15% of the total amount of commuters was simulated, what corresponds to the current public transport ridership in the target area. The demand was served by 30 DRT vehicles executing door-to-door trips withing the borders of target municipality and door-to-PT transfer if the trip crossed the borders of the municipality. Travellers request a trip two hours in advance to the approximated trip start time. When routing vehicles, service used the desired time of arrival for trips to work and the desired time of departure for trips from work as a hard constraint. Both service and travellers were using the same model of traveller behaviour: a DRT trip is accepted if

$$t_{DRT} < t_{CAR} \times 1.5 + 15\,\text{min}. \tag{1}$$

In other words, travellers accept a DRT trip if service was able to generate a DRT trip within this time window, where either arrival or departure times are fixed. The service is allowed to modify confirmed trips even at runtime as long as the trip duration would fit in the specified time windows of each traveller.

For the experiments, the simulation received data on 1900 real-world trips as input. Approximately 1450 of these trips were executed with DRT on a simulated day by a fleet of 30 vehicles. As shown in Fig. 3, most of the time (39%) there was no ride-sharing and only one passenger was on board of the DRT vehicle. Only in 19% of vehicles' travel time, two or more travellers were present. At the same time, when using 30 vehicles, the rejection ratio was around 24% (rejection happened when the DRT service could not provide a trip within the time window, according to Eq. 1). This low performance may be explained by the non-uniform distribution of demand, as shown in Fig. 4. Vehicles were ready to operate during the whole 24-h period but travellers show two distinct peaks in the demand. The

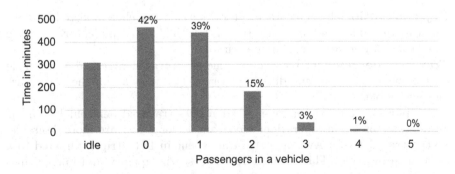

Fig. 3. Amount of time a certain number of people (0 to 5) was in the DRT vehicles. "Idle" represents the time vehicles spent in a depot. Values above the bars show the percentage of total travel time the vehicles were running with the corresponding amount of passengers ignoring idle time.

demand during peak hours is 3.4 times higher than average daily demand so there is little possibility for ride-sharing outside peak hours and many vehicles are idling. At the same time, the high rejection ratio around 24% indicates that 30 vehicles cannot handle the peak level of the demand.

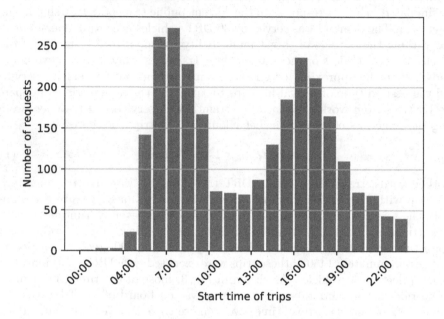

Fig. 4. Distribution of requested trip times.

We have conducted a sensitivity analysis serving the same demand with different amount of vehicles as shown in Table 1. We extracted the key performance indicators to compare the scenarios. They are:

- **Rejection ratio:** The percentage of the trips that travellers rejected (or trips violating the time windows restriction, Eq. 1). This is an indicator of service quality and lower values are more desirable.
- **Travellers per vehicle:** The average amount of travellers served by a vehicle during one day. This is an indicator of service efficiency and higher values are more desirable.
- **VKT per vehicle:** The number of kilometres travelled per vehicle. This is an indicator of service operational costs and lower values are more desirable.
- **Extra travel time:** Average extra time spent in DRT trip, compared to a direct trip by a car. This is an indicator of service quality and lower values are more desirable.
- **Direct vehicle kilometre per DRT vehicle kilometre:** The ratio of the length of the direct trips (trip by a direct path from origin to destination) to the actual length of DRT trips.

- **Direct travel minutes** (not explicitly shown in Table 1): The total time of direct trips, if they are executed by a car. Excludes detour time from travel time. This is an indicator of service efficiency and lower values are more desirable.
- **Direct minutes per hour:** The amount of direct travel minutes executed by an average DRT vehicle in an hour. This is an indicator of service efficiency and higher values are more desirable. For example, this value is always equal to 1 for private cars, as car always executes a direct path; the value is equal to 2 if two travellers (family members) are going to the same place in the same car; the value is equal to 0.5 if a taxi needs to ride 30 min to pick up a traveller and ride 30 min to the destination.

In Table 1, we see that the system behaves according to expectations: when more vehicles are utilised, it is possible to serve more travellers and the rejection ration decreases. At the same time, the average number of travellers and number of vehicle kilometres per vehicle decreases together with the number of direct minutes per hour, indicating that the cost efficiency of service is decreasing. Extra travel time, however, stays approximately the same as it is restricted by the mode choice model. We should note that extra travel time in DRT slightly increases together with the number of vehicles in the scenarios with 20, 30 and 40 vehicles, but drops in the scenario with 50 vehicles. When the amount of vehicles is low and service is overloaded, the service selects the trips that can be executed most efficiently. When the amount of vehicles is increasing to the level when the service has an opportunity to serve most inconvenient trips, there is less room for ride-sharing and more trips are executed in a taxi manner.

Table 1. Sensitivity analysis

Number of vehicles	20	30	40	50
Rejection ratio, %	42	24	12	4
Travellers per vehicle	55	48	42	36
VKT per vehicle	772	671	585	516
Extra travel time, %	33.1	33.3	34.5	33.7
Direct VKT per DRT VKT	0.85	0.85	0.84	0.85
Direct minutes per hour	44	38	33	28

4 Discussion and Future Work

Multiple optimisation issues need to be solved during the simulation. The trip planner needs to find trip alternatives, rank them to provide most promising alternatives to a traveller, find and rank possible DRT to PT transfers (which again involves a loop of searching for PT alternatives) and solve a vehicle routing problem. According to our goal, to balance social objectives, the model of traveller behaviour is included in all of the aforementioned operations. This results in the distribution of the behaviour model making it less transparent and harder to comprehend and potentially inhibits knowledge transit to decision-makers. To prevent this, the same model of traveller behaviour should be used on different steps of finding trip alternatives and better analysis and visualisation tools need to be developed to understand the impact of DRT design decisions on social objectives.

OTP uses heuristics and trip ranking to limit the amount of generated trip suggestions. When filtering out trip alternatives, OTP uses parameters like walk and transfer reluctance, that define how walking is perceived comparing to in-vehicle time or waiting time. These parameters are hidden from a final user (decision maker) but it also opens up an opportunity for contextualised and personalised travel planning that takes into account these parameters. A benefit of OpenTripPlaner is that it would be straightforward to integrate context-aware travel planing into the simulation.

The second optimisation engine is jsprit that optimises vehicle routes according to a cost function. In the first experiments, we used the default cost function that minimises operational costs.

$$C = C_{const} + \sum_{v \in Vehicles} C_{distance} + C_{time} \qquad (2)$$

Reduction of transportation cost with sharing a ride is only a part of the DRT objective. This optimisation function does not allow for direct optimisation of social objectives such as quality of service. Especially for investigating the viability of a DRT service, a trade-off between the service costs and the quality of service needs to be made by the decision-maker. Thus, extending the simulation with this respect would be desirable.

To account for social objectives, we need to model traveller behaviour on this level to predict traveller satisfaction from a trip. Behaviour in transport modelling (most often in form of mode choice) is dominated by econometric utility-based models [2,22]. To build such a model, we need to have real-world statistics on usage of the service. As we don't have access to such data, we are limited to either stated preference surveys (similar to [30,51]), or approximate value of time (similar to [18] or [12,54]).

As a temporary measure, we implemented rule-based behaviour. A person interested in DRT accepts a proposed journey if travel time is within an interval of $m \times t_{direct\ travel} + c$, where the constant c accounts for time that would be spent for parking a car and multiplier m represents tolerance to detours. There are two alternatives to how to apply this formula: to the whole trip or the DRT leg only. If we consider car users then it is meaningful to compare direct car time to the whole trip, yet the people already using PT could prefer to other transportation modes to access PT stops like being a passenger in a car, using a car to drive to PT stop or scooters or bikes. While such a time window puts a restriction to trip length, it does not penalise the increase in travel time and does not account for other trip characteristics like waiting time, transfer convenience, on-route rescheduling. Improvements to optimisation function open up more elaborate multi-objective optimisation.

We use routes built by OTP to teleport vehicles between pick-up and drop-off locations, according to the approximated travel time of vehicle path. We use OTP output for navigators to track vehicle positions during the route, but in a rural area, where long straight roads do exist, it is preferable to turn a vehicle in between navigation points. It should be possible to connect a high precision micro-simulator like SUMO with Traffic Control Interface [55] that simulates exact positions of vehicles at each moment in time.

PT in general and DRT in our view serves social purposes among others. To measure how mobility levels are affected by DRT we need to have metrics measuring that. Accessibility is one of the typical metrics. [37] identify high-level metrics like route length or amount of activity centres linked by PT network, but it is not directly applicable to DRT. At the best case, a person may receive a taxi level of service. But in a heavily loaded system, possibilities for each request would be limited by previous requests and a dynamic state of the service (position of vehicles and their routes).

Another interesting approach for optimisation of DRT is the dynamic allocation of stop points. If DRT is working in a non-door-to-door manner, fixed stop points are typically assigned and travellers are forced to walk to the closest stop point. There is an opportunity to utilise the flexibility of DRT to optimise the position of pick-up points if they are dynamically allocated [6,13,32]. Similarly, when DRT has a connection to PT, DRT to PT transfer points can be optimised what increases overall efficiency [24].

5 Conclusions

In this article, we present an agent-based simulation approach to DRT that introduces a traveller behaviour model into DRT service planning process allowing the service to adapt to the needs of the target population groups or utilise contextual information for trip planning. Such an approach requires an appropriate travellers' behaviour model (mode choice) so that travellers realistically choose DRT only when it is convenient for them. Our simulation focuses on the scenarios when DRT service is open to the general public, but it may prioritise some population groups and adapt to their needs. It allows optimising between social goals (providing mobility means for target population groups) and economical goals (minimising operational costs).

We evaluate this simulation approach and compare it to the alternatives. The weak point of macro-simulations and analytical approaches is in the approximation of detour time for DRT. A simulation approach implemented in MATSim may better capture service quality that users learn in time but may struggle to implement a feedback loop for adjusting route optimisation algorithms. The approach we present allows using contextual data to provide personalised trips according to the needs of travellers. It allows evaluating DRT service with soft priorities without hard restrictions, thus contributing to transport fairness and allows dynamically adjusting supply-side parameters and optimisation of service parameters. A combination of two approaches may be beneficial, but would result in a very high computational load. Here, further studies are required. The integration of DRT and PT into one service is the second highlight of this article – it allows more realistic and more practical DRT service designs. Most works consider DRT as a separate service, we argue that to capture the transfers between services, allows optimising both service performances.

We developed a prototype of simulation based on open-source tools OpenTripPlanner, jsprit and Open Source Routing Machine and identified opportunities for future work and possible extensions. Finally, we conducted a simulation study of commuter trips to demonstrate the approach. This simulation study indicates that it is challenging to achieve high efficiency of a service just by increasing the number of DRT vehicles to serve the demand. Additionally, we identify the direct trade-off between cost-effectiveness and service quality.

Acknowledgements. This work has been partially funded by the Interreg ÖKS fund within the Intelligent Mobility of the Future in Greater Copenhagen project.

References

1. Alonso-Mora, J., Samaranayake, S., Wallar, A., Frazzoli, E., Rus, D.: On-demand high-capacity ride-sharing via dynamic trip-vehicle assignment. Proc. Natl. Acad. Sci. **114**(3), 462–467 (2017)
2. Ben-Akiva, M., Bierlaire, M.: Discrete choice methods and their applications to short term travel decisions. In: Hall, R.W. (ed.) Handbook of Transportation Science. International Series in Operations Research & Management Science, pp. 5–33. Springer, Boston (1999). https://doi.org/10.1007/978-1-4615-5203-1_2
3. Boesch, P.M., Ciari, F., Axhausen, K.W.: Autonomous vehicle fleet sizes required to serve different levels of demand. Transp. Res. Rec. **2542**(1), 111–119 (2016)
4. Cervero, R.: Road expansion, urban growth, and induced travel: a path analysis. In: Dialogues in Urban and Regional Planning, pp. 310–343. Routledge (2006)
5. Charisis, A., Iliopoulou, C., Kepaptsoglou, K.: DRT route design for the first/last mile problem: model and application to Athens, Greece. Public Transp. **10**(3), 499–527 (2018)
6. Czioska, P., Kutadinata, R., Trifunović, A., Winter, S., Sester, M., Friedrich, B.: Real-world meeting points for shared demand-responsive transportation systems. Public Transp. **11**(2), 341–377 (2019)
7. Davison, L., Enoch, M., Ryley, T., Quddus, M., Wang, C.: Identifying potential market niches for Demand Responsive Transport. Res. Transp. Bus. Manag. **3**, 50–61 (2012)
8. Deflorio, F.P., Dalla Chiara, B., Murro, A.: Simulation and performance of DRTS in a realistic environment. In: Proceedings of the 13th Mini-Euro Conference on Handling Uncertainty in the Analysis of Traffic and Transportation Systems and the 9th Meeting of the Euro Working Group on Transportation Intermodality, Sustainability and Intelligent Transport Systems, pp. 622–628 (2002)

9. Dytckov, S., Lorig, F., Davidsson, P., Holmgren, J., Persson, J.: Modelling commuting activities for the simulation of demand responsive transport in rural areas. In: Proceedings of the 6th International Conference on Vehicle Technology and Intelligent Transport Systems, VEHITS, vol. 1, pp. 89–97 (2020)

10. Enoch, M., Potter, S., Parkhurst, G., Smith, M.: Why do demand responsive transport systems fail? In: Transportation Research Board 85th Annual Meeting (2006)

11. Fagnant, D.J., Kockelman, K.M.: Dynamic ride-sharing and fleet sizing for a system of shared autonomous vehicles in Austin, Texas. Transportation 45(1), 143–158 (2018)

12. Fosgerau, M., Hjorth, K., Lyk-Jensen, S.V.: The Danish value of time study. Technical report (2007)

13. Gökay, S., Heuvels, A., Krempels, K.H.: On-demand ride-sharing services with meeting points. In: Proceedings of the 4th International Conference on Vehicle Technology and Intelligent Transport Systems, pp. 117–125 (2019)

14. Hedlund, J.: This is how we travel in Skåne - travel survey 2018. Report: https://utveckling.skane.se/publikationer/rapporter-analyser-och-prognoser/resvaneundersokning-i-skane/. (in Swedish)

15. Helbing, D., Hennecke, A., Shvetsov, V., Treiber, M.: Micro- and macro-simulation of freeway traffic. Math. Comput. Model. 35(5–6), 517–547 (2002)

16. Helsinki Regional Transport: Kutsuplus-final report (2016). https://www.hsl.fi/en/news/2016/final-report-kutsuplus-trial-work-develop-ride-pooling-worth-continuing-8568

17. Hörl, S.: Agent-based simulation of autonomous taxi services with dynamic demand responses. Procedia Comput. Sci. 109, 899–904 (2017)

18. Hörl, S., Balac, M., Axhausen, K.W.: Dynamic demand estimation for an AMoD system in Paris. In: 2019 IEEE Intelligent Vehicles Symposium (IV), pp. 260–266. IEEE (2019)

19. Hymel, K.M., Small, K.A., Van Dender, K.: Induced demand and rebound effects in road transport. Transp. Res. Part B Methodol. 44(10), 1220–1241 (2010)

20. Jakob, A., Craig, J.L., Fisher, G.: Transport cost analysis: a case study of the total costs of private and public transport in Auckland. Environ. Sci. Policy 9(1), 55–66 (2006)

21. Jokinen, J.P., Sihvola, T., Hyytiä, E., Sulonen, R.: Why urban mass demand responsive transport? In: 2011 IEEE Forum on Integrated and Sustainable Transportation Systems, pp. 317–322. IEEE (2011)

22. Koppelman, F.S., Bhat, C.: A self instructing course in mode choice modeling: multinomial and nested logit models. Transportation Research Board (2006)

23. Laws, R., Enoch, M.P., Ison, S.G., Potter, S.: Demand-responsive transport schemes in England and Wales and considerations for their future. In: Transportation Research Board 87th Annual Meeting (2008)

24. Lee, A., Savelsbergh, M.: An extended demand responsive connector. EURO J. Transp. Logist. 6(1), 25–50 (2017)

25. Leich, G., Bischoff, J.: Should autonomous shared taxis replace buses? A simulation study. Transp. Res. Procedia 41, 450–460 (2019)

26. Levin, M.W., Kockelman, K.M., Boyles, S.D., Li, T.: A general framework for modeling shared autonomous vehicles with dynamic network-loading and dynamic ride-sharing application. Comput. Environ. Urban Syst. 64, 373–383 (2017)

27. Li, X., Quadrifoglio, L.: Feeder transit services: choosing between fixed and demand responsive policy. Transp. Res. Part C Emerg. Technol. 18(5), 770–780 (2010)

28. Litman, T.: Evaluating Public Transit Benefits and Costs. Victoria Transport Policy Institute, Victoria (2015)

29. Liu, J., Kockelman, K.M., Boesch, P.M., Ciari, F.: Tracking a system of shared autonomous vehicles across the Austin, Texas network using agent-based simulation. Transportation **44**(6), 1261–1278 (2017)
30. Liu, Y., Bansal, P., Daziano, R., Samaranayake, S.: A framework to integrate mode choice in the design of mobility-on-demand systems. Transp. Res. Part C Emerg. Technol. **105**, 648–665 (2019)
31. Loeb, B., Kockelman, K.M., Liu, J.: Shared autonomous electric vehicle (SAEV) operations across the Austin, Texas network with charging infrastructure decisions. Transp. Res. Part C Emerg. Technol. **89**, 222–233 (2018)
32. Lyu, Y., Lee, V.C., Ng, J.K.Y., Lim, B.Y., Liu, K., Chen, C.: Flexi-sharing: a flexible and personalized taxi-sharing system. IEEE Trans. Veh. Technol. **68**(10), 9399–9413 (2019)
33. Ma, T.Y.: On-demand dynamic Bi-/multi-modal ride-sharing using optimal passenger-vehicle assignments. In: 2017 IEEE International Conference on Environment and Electrical Engineering and 2017 IEEE Industrial and Commercial Power Systems Europe (EEEIC/I&CPS Europe), pp. 1–5. IEEE (2017)
34. Ma, T.Y., Klein, S.: Integrated microtransit services with chance-constrained dynamic pricing and demand learning. arXiv preprint arXiv:2001.09151 (2020)
35. Maciejewski, M., Nagel, K.: Simulation and dynamic optimization of taxi services in MATSim. VSP Working Paper 13-0 (2013)
36. Mageean, J., Nelson, J.D.: The evaluation of demand responsive transport services in Europe. J. Transp. Geogr. **11**(4), 255–270 (2003)
37. Miller, P., de Barros, A.G., Kattan, L., Wirasinghe, S.: Analyzing the sustainability performance of public transit. Transp. Res. Part D Transp. Environ. **44**, 177–198 (2016)
38. Navidi, Z., Ronald, N., Winter, S.: Comparison between ad-hoc demand responsive and conventional transit: a simulation study. Public Transp. **10**(1), 147–167 (2018)
39. Nelson, J.D., Wright, S., Masson, B., Ambrosino, G., Naniopoulos, A.: Recent developments in flexible transport services. Res. Transp. Econ. **29**(1), 243–248 (2010)
40. Pettersson, F.: An international review of experiences from on-demand public transport services. Working Paper (2019)
41. Ramezani, M., Nourinejad, M.: Dynamic modeling and control of taxi services in large-scale urban networks: a macroscopic approach. Transp. Res. Procedia **23**, 41–60 (2017)
42. Ronald, N., Thompson, R., Haasz, J., Winter, S.: Determining the viability of a demand-responsive transport system under varying demand scenarios. In: Proceedings of 6th ACM SIGSPATIAL International Workshop on Computational Transportation Science, pp. 7–12 (2013)
43. Ronald, N., Thompson, R.G., Winter, S.: Comparison of constrained and ad hoc demand-responsive transportation systems. Transp. Res. Rec. **2563**(1), 44–51 (2015)
44. Ruch, C., Lu, C., Sieber, L., Frazzoli, E.: Quantifying the benefits of ride sharing. Working Paper (2019). https://www.research-collection.ethz.ch/handle/20.500.11850/367142
45. Sayarshad, H.R., Gao, H.O.: Optimizing dynamic switching between fixed and flexible transit services with an idle-vehicle relocation strategy and reductions in emissions. Transp. Res. Part A Policy Pract. **135**, 198–214 (2020)
46. Segui-Gasco, P., Ballis, H., Parisi, V., Kelsall, D.G., North, R.J., Busquets, D.: Simulating a rich ride-share mobility service using agent-based models. Transportation **46**(6), 2041–2062 (2019)

47. Shen, C.W., Quadrifoglio, L.: Evaluation of zoning design with transfers for paratransit services. Transp. Res. Rec. **2277**(1), 82–89 (2012)
48. Shen, Y., Zhang, H., Zhao, J.: Integrating shared autonomous vehicle in public transportation system: a supply-side simulation of the first-mile service in Singapore. Transp. Res. Part A Policy Pract. **113**, 125–136 (2018)
49. Spielberg, F., Pratt, R.H.: Traveler Response to Transportation System Changes Handbook, 3rd edn, chap. 6. Demand-Responsive/ADA. No. Project B-12A FY'99, The National Academies Press (2004)
50. Spieser, K., Treleaven, K., Zhang, R., Frazzoli, E., Morton, D., Pavone, M.: Toward a systematic approach to the design and evaluation of automated mobility-on-demand systems: a case study in Singapore. In: Meyer, G., Beiker, S. (eds.) Road Vehicle Automation. LNM, pp. 229–245. Springer, Cham (2014). https://doi.org/10.1007/978-3-319-05990-7_20
51. Te Morsche, W., Puello, L.L.P., Geurs, K.T.: Potential uptake of adaptive transport services: an exploration of service attributes and attitudes. Transp. Policy **84**, 1–11 (2019)
52. Viergutz, K., Schmidt, C.: Demand responsive - vs. conventional public transportation: a MATSim study about the rural town of Colditz, Germany. Procedia Comput. Sci. **151**, 69–76 (2019)
53. Wadud, Z., MacKenzie, D., Leiby, P.: Help or hindrance? The travel, energy and carbon impacts of highly automated vehicles. Transp. Res. Part A Policy Pract. **86**, 1–18 (2016)
54. Wardman, M.: Public transport values of time. Transp. Policy **11**(4), 363–377 (2004)
55. Wegener, A., Piórkowski, M., Raya, M., Hellbrück, H., Fischer, S., Hubaux, J.P.: TraCI: an interface for coupling road traffic and network simulators. In: Proceedings of the 11th Communications and Networking Simulation Symposium, pp. 155–163 (2008)
56. Yang, H., Wong, S.C., Wong, K.I.: Demand-supply equilibrium of taxi services in a network under competition and regulation. Transp. Res. Part B Methodol. **36**(9), 799–819 (2002)

Dependable and Efficient Cloud-Based Safety-Critical Applications by Example of Automated Valet Parking

Christian Drabek[1]([✉]), Dhavalkumar Shekhada[1], Gereon Weiss[1], Mario Trapp[1], Tasuku Ishigooka[2], Satoshi Otsuka[2], and Mariko Mizuochi[3]

[1] Fraunhofer IKS, Munich, Germany
{christian.drabek,dhavalkumar.shekhada,gereon.weiss,
mario.trapp}@iks.fraunhofer.de
[2] Research and Development Group, Hitachi Ltd., Ibaraki, Japan
{tasuku.ishigoka.kc,satoshi.otsuka.hk}@hitachi.com
[3] Hitachi Europe GmbH, Schwaig, Germany
mariko.mizuochi@hitachi-eu.com

Abstract. Future embedded systems and services will be seamlessly connected and will interact on all levels with the infrastructure and cloud. For safety-critical applications this means that it is not sufficient to ensure dependability in a single embedded system, but it is necessary to cover the complete service chain including all involved embedded systems as well as involved services running in the edge or the cloud. However, for the development of such Cyber-Physical Systems-of-Systems (CPSoS) engineers must consider all kinds of dependability requirements. For example, it is not an option to ensure safety by impeding reliability or availability requirements. In fact, it is the engineers' task to optimize the CPSoS' performance without violating any safety goals.

In this paper, we identify the main challenges of developing CPSoS based on several industrial use cases and present our novel approach for designing cloud-based safety-critical applications with optimized performance by the example of an automated valet parking system. The evaluation shows that our monitoring and recovery solution ensures a superior performance in comparison to current methods, while meeting the system's safety demands in case of connectivity-related faults.

Keywords: Cyber-Physical Systems of Systems · Automated recovery · Monitoring · Fail-operational · Graceful degradation · Self-awareness

1 Introduction

Nowadays, Cyber-Physical Systems (CPS) become more and more flexibly interconnected with other services as well as with local and remote infrastructure.

A. L. Martins et al. (Eds.): INTSYS 2020, LNICST 364, pp. 90–109, 2021.
https://doi.org/10.1007/978-3-030-71454-3_6

For instance, off-loading software services of embedded systems into cloud computing environments bears the potential to offer more features and to bypass resource restrictions of local CPS. This will further become essential, as upcoming autonomous machines with artificial intelligence capabilities have an insatiable need for computational power [25]. Moreover, cloud infrastructure facilitates better maintainability and scalability, e.g., easier service upgrades and data aggregation of multiple machines. Such interconnected CPS can be seen as a *Cyber-Physical System-of-Systems (CPSoS)* [6]. Examples range from intelligent networked vehicles over industrial control systems to collaborating robots. However, in many application scenarios these machines also perform safety-critical functions. In consequence, this means that it is not sufficient anymore to ensure the safety of single systems. Instead, it is necessary to ensure the safety of the complete CPSoS including all systems and services. As an additional challenge, a CPSoS is not static, but integrates and removes systems and services from different vendors dynamically at runtime. Moreover, it is unavoidable to use non-safe components such as the communication infrastructure or cloud servers. This requires the CPSoS to be resilient. In case a service temporarily fails or is not available at all, the CPSoS should still work safely. To this end, the CPS might continue in a degraded mode and resume with full capacity, when the cloud service becomes available again.

In this paper, we examine the challenges of developing safe CPSoS considering various different practical application scenarios. Focusing on optimizing efficiency without violating safety, we introduce our design approach that holistically covers safety and other dependability requirements. We illustrate the application of our approach using an industrial case study realizing an *Automated Valet Parking (AVP)* service. Eventually, we evaluate our approach using a simulation-based prototype of the AVP. In this evaluation, we focus on service availability due to communication problems and show the advantages of the resulting dynamic management using dedicated monitoring and recovery solutions over the current approaches only considering the local assurance or optimization of single systems. We compare the performance of the approaches by measuring the average speed of the vehicles in the parking area. Summarizing, the main contribution of the paper is the introduction and the practical evaluation of a holistic design approach for safety-critical CPSoS.

The remainder of the paper is outlined as follows. Section 2 introduces several industrial use cases of CPSoS and their high-level requirements, which we use to derive the general challenges posed by such systems. Section 3 discusses related work on optimizing and analyzing CPSoS. In Sect. 4, we present our approach for the design of safe and efficient CPSoS by example of an AVP system. The evaluation described in Sect. 5 compares the performance of the designed CPSoS with a pure local variant, before we conclude the paper in Sect. 6.

2   Challenges and Use Cases of CPSoS

CPSoS comprise several subsystems and components. These in turn may also include safety-critical applications. In comparison to traditional CPS which act on their own (e.g., control units in a car or industrial control systems), CPSoS combine them into highly interconnected large systems. Therewith, the independence of these autonomous units is abolished and their correct function is considered on system level. For instance, machine learning-based systems can leverage cloud infrastructure to compute complex scenarios or remote operation of a vehicle requires the whole control chain to function correctly. For identifying the main challenges of upcoming CPSoS, exemplary industrial use cases have been selected and are presented in the following.

2.1   Industrial Use Cases of CPSoS

The following use cases introduce applications of CPSoS and provide examples for industrial scenarios. For brevity, only selected challenges are listed for each use case.

Vehicle Remote Operation (VRO) (cf. Fig. 1, left) is a use case that considers remotely driving a vehicle to a safe place with the situation-wise adequate speed, e.g., in case of a failure or unavailability of a driver. This requires *real-time execution and sensor data upload* with low latency and jitter for control stability, and local fallback in the vehicle to guarantee minimum safety, e.g., if the link to the remote service is lost suddenly.

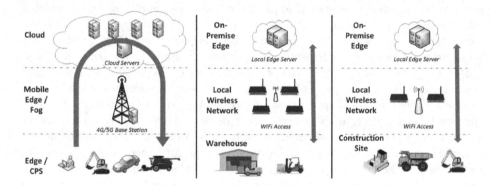

Fig. 1. Use cases: Vehicle Remote Operation (left), Warehouse Management (middle) and Construction Site Management (right).

The use case *Warehouse Management* (WM) (cf. Fig. 1, middle) describes moving shipments within an automated warehouse. Tasks are sent to automated forklifts which operate at low vehicle speeds in the warehouse. Scalability needs to address sharing of sensor information between vehicles and infrastructure. Moreover, efficiency of the system, e.g., the ability to quickly move goods when needed, is important and stand-still should be avoided.

With the use case *Construction Site Management* (CSM) (cf. Fig. 1, right) individual construction machine operation at a restricted construction site is considered. The operation of local machinery, e.g., excavators or bulldozers, is automated based on the fusion of each machine's sensor data. As such, challenges arise from data uploads for continuous training and logging, as well as maintenance to update local maps, tasks and software in general.

As an example of a CPSoS in which domain boundaries are vanishing, the use case of *Cross-Domain Unknown Services* (CDUS) (cf. Fig. 2, left) considers cross-domain service orchestration. The specific use case addresses the usage of services of other domains after successful authentication. We refer to them as unknown services, as they are developed independently without considering each other and information must be translated between domains. For example, an automated valet parking system cannot directly process information from construction sites in the parking area, but will benefit from knowing which part of the area is not available. As unknown services need to interact, establishing interoperability between the involved systems without compromising security or safety is a prominent challenge.

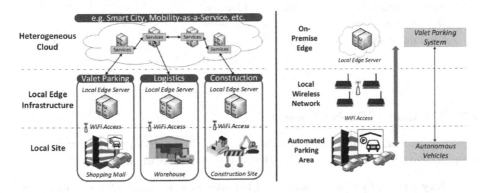

Fig. 2. Use cases: Cross-Domain Unknown Services (left) and Automated Valet Parking (right).

The *Automated Valet Parking (AVP)* use case (cf. Fig. 2, right) includes a management of automated vehicles in a restricted parking area. Mainly, the *Parking Area Management* assigns the best free parking space to arriving vehicles and allows a safe remote navigation by sending trajectories to the vehicles moving at low speeds. This is carried out by monitoring and controlling blocks of the parking area and granting driving permissions to vehicles. As for all CPSoS, the comprising subsystems are usually developed independently, but need to interface with each other. Unless the parking area is limited to a specific group of vehicle manufacturers, AVP needs to be an open system. Therefore, standards are required to ensure interoperability. Moreover, to cover cases where no or only limited communication is possible, a safe fallback is needed. This use case is studied and evaluated within this work and therefore presented in more detail in Sect. 4.

While only selected challenges have been introduced when presenting the above application use cases to provide examples, many challenges apply to several of the use cases. To summarize the challenges, Table 1 presents an overview of the identified challenges for each of the above application use cases.

Table 1. Challenges of industrial use cases of CPSoS

Challenge	VRO	WM	CSM	CDUS	AVP
Safety to ensure no collision with obstacles	✓	✓	✓	✓	✓
Efficiency to avoid stand-still		✓	✓		✓
Real-time execution with low latency	✓	✓	✓	✓	✓
Real-time sensor data upload	✓				
Scalability of sharing real-time sensor information		✓	✓		✓
Interoperability between different manufacturers	✓	✓	✓	✓	✓
Connectivity for control data	✓	✓	✓	✓	✓
Security against hijacking	✓	✓	✓	✓	✓
Data uploading for continuous training and logging		✓	✓		
Maintenance w.r.t. map, task and software updates		✓	✓		
Self-awareness to monitor and recover remote control	✓	✓	✓	✓	✓

2.2   Common CPSoS Challenges

Based on our analysis of the examined use cases, we derived the following common challenges of upcoming CPSoS in such safety-critical environments:

- **Safety and efficiency:** Faults and threats must be identified and managed dynamically, i.e., by providing suitable countermeasures.
- **Real-time:** Planning of flexible and reliable end-to-end architectures, including dynamic allocation of distributed resources.
- **Connectivity & interoperability:** Interfaces definitions & standardization for cross-domain inter-operation is needed.
- **Security:** Identification and mitigation of additional threats created by widening the system boundaries.
- **Data-uploads & maintenance:** Collect training data and distribute updates of the various subsystems without interfering with normal operation.

These challenges share the need to provide an in-time and complete overview of the present CPSoS state. For this, run-time monitoring mechanisms at different levels of a CPSoS are indispensable. By this, a so-called *self-awareness* at run-time can be achieved, which constitutes the basis for taking measures to keep the system in a safe and performant state. The goal of managing such a CPSoS is to increase availability and meet reliability, particularly considering defective resources and the integration of unknown services. In order to achieve resilient behavior of a CPSoS, in general diverse changes of different nature, prospect, and timing [13] must be considered. By embedding self-adaptation as fault-tolerance mechanisms into CPSoS it is capable to optimize the performance, while meeting dependability requirements. We have selected the AVP use case for detailed study and evaluation, because of the availability of detailed specifications and its requirements for safety and optimized performance.

3   Related Work

When designing CPSoS [26], ensuring safety and optimizing performance are two of the main challenges. Previous approaches related to our work are briefly introduced in the following.

For optimizing performance of CPSoS, diverse approaches and tools are already available [4]. Optimization tools like FogNetSim++ [17], iFogSim [7], EdgeCloudSim [24] focus on the simulation of edge-, fog-, cloud-systems and support identifying optimal parameters or deployments for specific scenarios. In addition, network simulations like ns-3 [19] and OMNET++ [27] can provide estimates on the performance of specific network infrastructures for a CPSoS. However, these tools do not consider the safety of the system.

Approaches targeting to provide reliability develop patterns to identify host or network failures, or in general, violations of safety properties [23] and apply specific recovery strategies to provide fault tolerance in distributed systems [14,15]. Others aim to establish resilience for stateful IoT applications [16] by enabling the recovery of their states. In case a safety-critical function cannot be easily stopped or replaced, graceful degradation [9], which reduces functionality in order to retain safety properties even under the presence of certain faults, has proven useful. If faults and desired reconfigurations are known beforehand, the availability in fail-operational automotive systems can be planned and verified already at design time [20]. While general safety requirements and distribution of functions for automated valet parking have been analyzed [22], we focus on the presence of an unreliable connection between cloud and vehicle. As already discussed by other authors [12], we pursue a state-based monitoring approach for this challenge in safety-critical CPSoS.

In comparison, safety-related approaches often focus to ensure the systems' safety properties, not its performance or availability. An alternative example considering performance optimization is a safety envelope used within autonomous systems [11], which allows a system to optimize its performance within this operating envelope by monitoring violations. Therefore, a tighter integration of methods for safety analysis into other software-engineering disciplines could benefit both sides [3,5]. Our approach leverages such an integration in an iterative process of identifying safety and performance faults and, thereby, allows a novel improvement of a design for both mitigation and optimization.

4   Design of Safe and Efficient CPSoS

As previously motivated, designing safety-critical CPSoS that are safe and yet efficient is a challenging task. The design of such systems is a multivariate optimization problem in order to always provide the best possible performance, while fulfilling safety requirements at any time. While a holistic approach is required to ensure no safety requirements are missed, CPSoS quickly become large and complex. Therefore, this complexity needs to be broken down during design. In the following, we describe our design approach for such systems (cf. Fig. 3).

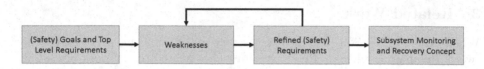

Fig. 3. Overview of our design approach for efficient safety-critical CPSoS.

An initial requirements analysis in the first step defines the top-level requirements of the CPSoS and utilizes safety analysis methods to identify the main safety goals in terms of additional requirements. Moreover, it manifests an architecture draft that enables the analysis of critical interactions between subsystems. In the next step, weaknesses of the system and its subsystems are iteratively identified and mitigated by refining the requirements as well as documenting assumptions and verification methods. Finally, self-awareness of subsystems is established by deriving monitors from the requirements that identify important changes in the current context and thereby trigger the planned recovery methods.

We use the example of an AVP system with a centralized, cloud-based *Valet Parking System (VPS)* that guides *autonomous vehicles (AV)* to demonstrate our approach. In the automotive domain, safe design against hardware failures is performed according to the functional safety standard ISO 26262 [1] and safety design against performance limitations is performed according to ISO/PAS 21448 [2].

4.1 Top-Level Requirements

The top-level requirements are utilized to sketch the desired features of the CPSoS. For brevity, we only present the headline of each requirement, which provides a short summary of its description. Nevertheless, this level of detail should be sufficient to follow the general idea of the design approach. The definition of top-level requirements can be quite coarse. They will be refined, broken down and assigned to subsystems in the next phase. The main purpose of the top-level requirements is to describe the important functional and non-functional goals of the system.

For the AVP use case, we consider the following functional requirements:

FR-1   Management of parking space (occupied or empty).
FR-2   Connection between AV and VPS when AV enters the service area.
FR-3   Find suitable, empty parking space.
FR-4   Calculate trajectory (based on vehicle properties) and send to AV.

| FR-5 | Move AV to parking space by referring to trajectory of FR-4. |
| FR-6 | Terminate VPS for AV when it arrives at the target space. |

With a preliminary hazard and risk analysis (HARA), the following dependability requirements have been identified. The first two requirements are related to the system's safety, while the remaining improve reliability and availability.

DR-1	Local emergency stop.
DR-2	Remote emergency stop.
DR-3	Detect unreachable parking place and request another.
DR-4	Communication diversity in physical architecture.
DR-5	Collision prevention by free space detection and block control.
DR-6	Wrong waypoint and parking place detection.

Based on these top-level requirements, a possible architecture design of the AVP system has been developed, as shown in Fig. 4. VPS and AV do not know each other's internal architecture, as they will be developed by different vendors. However, the systems need to interface with each other. The identification and description of necessary interfaces are facilitated, if exemplary architectures are assumed. After receiving a parking request, the parking area management identifies a suitable destination and planning generates a trajectory. *Traffic Monitor (TM)* passes trajectories and permissions to AVs. Trajectories describe waypoints to the destination, e.g., a parking place, and permissions allow the AV to proceed to a certain waypoint. *Trajectory Following Control (TFC)* in the AV is then responsible for following this trajectory as permitted. The AV's sensors are utilized to trigger *Passed Notifications (PN)* sent to TM. In turn, TM updates its database of permissions and locations. PN will also trigger a new parking request if the destination is not reachable.

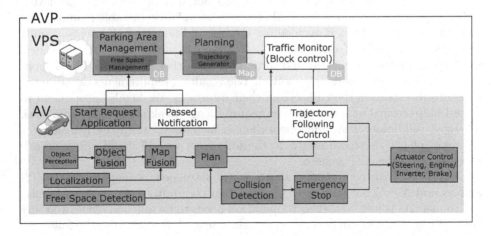

Fig. 4. Exemplary architecture design for an AVP based on requirements.

4.2 Iterative Weakness-Driven Design Refinement

In the next phase of our approach, we use an iterative weakness-driven design refinement to uncover the system's weaknesses and to integrate countermeasures along the refinement. In order to denote not only safety-related issues, i.e., faults, we define the term *weakness* as *any deviation from the system's intended function*. This could be with respect to a potential safety hazard or failure [1], a security threat or vulnerability [21], or a breach of performance thresholds. The general intent is to identify potential weaknesses of the CPSoS and determine what conditions are necessary to handle them on subsystem level.

The inputs to this phase, top-level requirements and a draft of the system architecture, have been presented in the previous subsection. Potential weaknesses are systematically identified using a HAZOP-oriented process [8], i.e., by applying a set of guide-words to the requirement descriptions. Examples for guide words are *not, more, less, early* and *late*. To scrutinize the consistency of the requirements, the following questions are used in addition to common HAZOP guide-words:

- Internal: How can the subject itself fail to fulfill the requirement?
- External: What external influences can cause the subject to fail (the intend of) the requirement?
- Integrity: Are there any terms, definitions or values used by the requirement that can impact its intend, if chosen incorrectly?

Each of the identified weaknesses needs to be resolved by verification, assumptions, or other requirements. A *verification* describes a method to verify why a weakness will not occur or is mitigated sufficiently. An *assumption* is a statement describing a property that is assumed to be valid. Therefore, assumptions are formulated to document parts of the system that are expected to work or resolved by the detailed design of an individual subsystem. For example, we assume a correct implementation of requirements but will not specify how this is achieved. Other requirements that resolve weaknesses either refine vulnerable requirements to detail how the failure is avoided, or impose additional requirements to mitigate cause or effect of certain faults. New requirements may introduce new weaknesses that are identified and mitigated in further iterations. This is continued until all weaknesses are resolved. The resulting requirements describe the roles of subsystems in the CPSoS and their interfaces. We highly recommend to record bidirectional relations between requirements, weaknesses and resolutions. Thereby, validation of an implementation is facilitated, when the reason for a requirement can be traced easily. In the following, we will detail our approach by example of the AVP system.

AVP is a CPSoS comprising independently developed, resilient systems: VPS and several AVs. They each may provide their own mitigation strategy in case the connection is lost. Yet, their cooperation needs to be safe and efficient at any time. Without the loss of generality, we select *loss of connection* in the following as exemplary fault to outline our approach and its related weaknesses, as they cannot be handled by a single system of the CPSoS individually. As this is a high-level analysis targeting cloud-based autonomous CPS, functional safety aspects of single systems are less of concern, which is documented using assumptions. The critical parts, where the two CPS types interface with each other, can be identified already in the architecture draft. An extract of the analysis with their main requirements and the identified weaknesses related to the loss of connection from the first iteration are given in Table 2. The weaknesses are also assigned to categories for indicating the kind of deviation, e.g., reliability for safety-related faults or performance in case they merely impact the efficiency.

Table 2. Extract of requirements and identified weaknesses of TM, TFC and PN before the first refinement.

System	ID	Cat.	Top-Level Req.	Short summary
TM	R4	Gen.	FR-5, DR-2, DR-5, DR-6	TM shall monitor and control access to blocks based on trajectories calculated by Planning
	V4a	Rel.	DR-2, DR-5, DR-6	TM can fail to monitor cars
	V4b	Rel.	DR-2, DR-5, DR-6	TM can fail to control manually driven cars
	V4c	Rel.	DR-2, DR-5, DR-6	TM can fail to control not connected cars
	V4d	Perf.	FR-5	TM can be slow to provide access to blocks
	V4k	Perf.	FR-5	TM can receive passed notifications late or never
TFC	R8	Gen.	FR-5, DR-2, DR-5, DR-6	TFC shall calculate actuator controls based on the trajectory and permission provided by VPS and the information from perception chain
	V8c	Rel	FR-5, DR-2, DR-5, DR-6	TFC can fail to receive or process permissions from VPS
PN	R18	Gen.	FR-5, FR-6, DR-6	PN shall signal right after a block was cleared by the vehicle
	V18c	Perf.	FR-5, FR-6	PN can send the notification too late

The first iteration addresses the fault of TFC not receiving permissions. Therefore, a new requirement requires TFC to stop the vehicle if no permission is provided in time. In addition, this prohibits rogue movement of AVs in the parking area. Care must be taken that an AV is always able to stop in time and will not move without permission, i.e., by slowing down at the end of the permitted trajectory. We assume that there are no manual operated vehicles in the parking area and thus, TM is in sole control of all movement. This addition makes the system safe, and we will refer to this as *Mitigation Variant 1 (MV1)* in the evaluation section. However, additional performance weaknesses remain.

AVs can get stuck, if they have neither permission nor connection. Hence, after a specified timeout, its own TFC shall permit a trajectory based on the AV's sensors. However, from the perspective of TM, this is a rogue AV. Moreover, insufficient monitoring of parking area by the TM is now a safety issue, as it may provide a conflicting permission to another AV, if it does not sufficiently locate the rogue AV. Further, if VPS never receives a pass notification, it is forced to reserve the permitted space infinitely. Therefore, a requirement for VPS to track vehicles using infrastructure sensors is added and the architecture is updated as in Fig. 5. We assume sensors to work as expected. While VPS can now notice rogue AVs, TM also needs to validate and possibly adjust already provided permissions. To mitigate the weakness of AVs relying on outdated information, permissions sent from TM have a limited lifetime. Therefore, an AV must be capable to stop in time before a permission becomes invalid. Depending on the selection of timeouts, it may directly switch to permissions based on its own sensors. Moreover, to facilitate predictability of an AV's movement, VPS should send a complete trajectory to AVs initially, which is followed even by a disconnected AV. We define this as *Mitigation Variant 2 (MV2)*. More weaknesses could be identified, e.g., that a trajectory may get blocked by an obstacle, but are beyond the scope of this example.

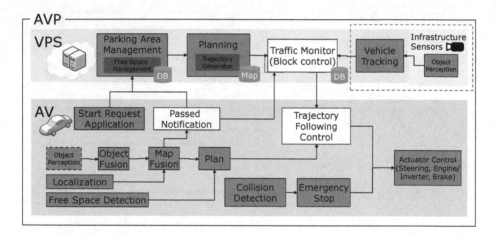

Fig. 5. Exemplary architecture design extended with infrastructure sensors.

4.3   Monitoring and Recovery Concept

With the next step of our approach, we map the identified requirements to a monitoring and recovery concept for each subsystem. At this stage, the requirements already capture the critical interaction patterns between the individual systems, so that the remainder of each system can be developed independently. However, to make it more explicit what a subsystem must monitor and what reactions are required for coordinated interactions, this is formulated as monitoring and recovery concepts. Transforming the requirements of the critical interactions into a monitoring and recovery concept has the additional benefit that this enables an abstract simulation of these interactions without full implementations of each subsystem. This helps to validate the concept early. In summary, the monitor identifies current context states and the recovery will adjust the operation to remain in a safe and efficient overall system state. The monitor aggregates all information that must be observed in order to establish a *self-awareness* of critical changes in the environment or within the system itself. The recovery will change operation parameters or start and stop services as needed to reach the state inferred by the weakness analysis. The behavior needs to be managed dynamically based on current context. However, this can still be planned at design time, if the involved capabilities are known. Thereby, existing concepts for graceful degradation in the automotive domain [9] can be used to facilitate the integration of recovery in alignment with ISO 26262 and ISO/PAS 21448. In the following, we explain how the monitoring and recovery concepts for the AVP example were derived.

In MV1, an AV stops and waits if there is no permission update, e.g., because of a lost connection. As the scope of this paper is limited to such faults, an AV will never act outside the expectations of VPS and there is no specific need for a monitor or recovery on VPS side from a safety perspective. In contrast, AVs must ensure they are always able to stop in time. While a monitor could be designed to directly observe the state of the connection, just a loss-of-connection is no direct safety hazard to AVP. A hazardous situation would arise only if the AV overshoots its permitted trajectory. In this case, it is much more effective for the monitor to observe AV's ability to stop before this occurs. Therefore, the monitor must keep track of the remaining distance to the end of its permitted trajectory (D_p), get an estimate of the current brake distance (D_b) and compare the two. If the difference is less than a given minimum distance (D_m), recovery needs to force the AV to decelerate. This is illustrated in Fig. 6. The minimum distance must be larger than the distance traveled by the AV between two checks and can be calculated based on the rate at which this check is performed and the (maximum) speed of the vehicle in the parking area. The monitor will thereby signal the AV if it approaches the boundary of its permission and the recovery will force the AV to decelerate. If the permission is extended again, the AV may proceed normally again. Actually, the resulting monitor is independent of a lost connection and also triggers if VPS updates were received but the AV needs to yield right of way at an intersection.

Fig. 6. Monitoring and recovery concept for AV in mitigation variant 1.

In MV2, an AV also mitigates the weakness that it may get stuck at some place with no connection. In this case, other AVs may be moving without permission from the cloud. An AV must be able to receive updates of permissions issued by VPS. Otherwise, they might be outdated and not reliable anymore. The critical property for this is the time since the last update (T_u), which is accompanied by two thresholds. The first specifies when the remote permissions should be considered outdated (T_o). The other indicates the time when local permissions may be issued (T_l). The chosen thresholds may allow for an overlap of remote and local permission $(T_o \geq T_l)$, or an AV will have to stop before it can switch to local sensors $(T_o < T_l)$. While the monitor for MV1 only checks the distance, for MV2 an AV's monitor also has to consider the time needed to slow down. Therefore, T_b specifies the time needed to slow down to stop or to the speed currently permitted by local sensors. The overall monitoring and recovery concept for MV2 is shown in Fig. 7. This consists of three separate monitors, where recovery will react to their combined state. T_m is the margin, i.e., the amount of time reserved for cycle times and processing.

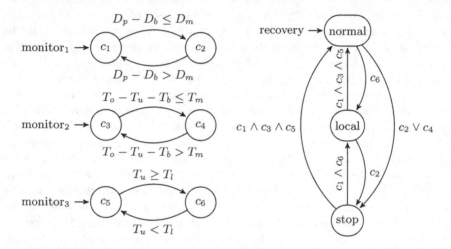

Fig. 7. Monitoring and recovery concept for AV in mitigation variant 2.

If AVs are moving on their own permissions, VPS is required to monitor for this and needs to recover conflicting permissions. The VPS' responsibility is to provide such updates to connected AVs. Therefore, VPS must track the AVs in the parking area. Locations provided by AVs can and will likely be affected by similar connection losses as provided permissions. Therefore, secondary means are required, e.g., using infrastructure sensors to monitor AVs. Moreover, the VPS must check if the rogue AV interferes with existing permissions and must update those accordingly. This works like a remote emergency brake, but allows for a more graceful deceleration if updates can be provided early.

As MV2 utilizes two sources for permissions, the concept must ensure that they cooperate well. This is achieved by putting strict requirements on when an AV may provide its own permission, so that the VPS will always have sufficient time to adapt permissions for other AVs or that the permission of other (temporarily) disconnected AVs will expire. A critical situation could arise, if an AV moves without permission of VPS into space that is reserved for another car. Thus, an AV may only move into space it has no permission for, if it ensures (using its own sensors) that no other car will reach the space in time $T_i + T_o + T_m$, where T_i is the additional time needed by infrastructure sensors to identify the rogue AV's intent and by VPS to update permissions.

A longer permission lifetime (T_o) improves performance, as this allows bridging longer gaps in permission updates. However, any not connected AV must be able to predict its clearance for at least this duration. A shorter permission lifetime will lessen this need, but also limits the maximum speed of AVs, as they must be able to safely switch to local permissions or stop by the end. Tuning of these parameters is beyond the scope of this paper and would require including details about capabilities of the AVs' sensors.

5   Evaluation

We evaluate the effectiveness of the proposed concept in simulations of the AVP use case. While we also verify the concept's safety by checking no collisions occur, the primary goal is evaluating the potential benefits in efficiency by using an optimized and safe cloud-based control despite unreliable connections between VPS and AVs. Therefore, we compare the presented cloud-based mitigation variants with scenarios where AVs use only their own sensors to calculate permissions. We neglected further optimizations of the control algorithms, e.g., we are using randomly assigned parking places and the shortest route instead of carefully selected waypoints that would allow cars to avoid each other. We believe scenarios utilizing the cloud are likely to benefit more from them, as decisions can be based on more information.

5.1   Evaluation Setup

An overview of the evaluation setup is shown in Fig. 8. The evaluation uses an abstract representation of the AVP system to simulate scenarios. The Robot Operating System (ROS) [18] is used in its second version, ROS2, as middleware to connect cloud node and car nodes. The parking area is divided into blocks that are controlled by the VPS cloud node. Every 300 ms, the VPS will broadcast updated permissions to all registered AVs, i.e., up to which block they are allowed to proceed. In turn, AVs send their updated location to VPS with a rate of 200 ms after moving based on the permission and used mitigation variant. ROS2's simulation time was used with 100 ms steps and messages could only be processed by the receiver in the next step.

There is a new car node created for each AV that enters the parking area. It starts at one of the designated entry points, registers with the VPS and requests to park. The VPS selects a parking place and calculates waypoints using A* algorithm and the AV receives this as a list of blocks. The movements, actions and permissions of AVs can be visualized using RViz [10] for further inspection (cf. Fig. 9).

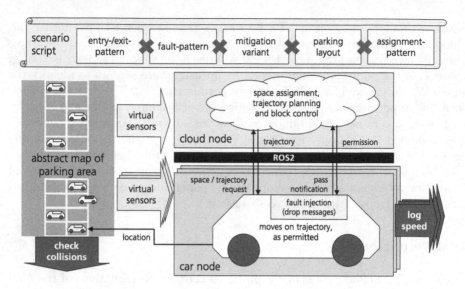

Fig. 8. Overview of the simulation setup used for evaluation.

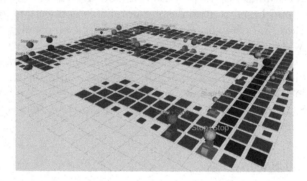

Fig. 9. Screenshot of simulation visualization. VPS permissions are represented by blocks tainted in an AV's color. The size of orbs above AVs correlates to the duration since the last update from VPS, red color indicates expired VPS permissions. The AV's current action is shown as text. (Color figure online)

Each scenario has a duration of 200 s and comprises modular scripts for which all sensible combinations were run. Pattern modules define random distributions that would allow for unlimited variants based on their parameters. To get comparable results and reduce noise, sets with entry-/exit-patterns and fault-patterns were generated beforehand and then used in respective combinations. AVs enter during the first 135 s with an average inter-arrival delay of 2, 4, or 20 s. They start to exit between 30 to 60 s later. This is used to model a busy parking area, while also imitating realistic parking behavior. Failures of connections have been injected based on either a permanently jammed location and radius, e.g., to simulate a failed access point, or time-based patterns per AV. These were mitigated by MV1 and MV2.

When MV2 is in its *local* operating state (cf. Fig. 7), it uses local sensors to generate its permissions. To focus the simulation on evaluating the effects of loss of connectivity and eliminate the choices of sensor types and perception algorithms, it was assumed that local sensors will safely grant permissions up to and including the next block the AV has not yet entered. In the simulation, local permission is granted if no other vehicle can enter the block within T_o, i.e., the time until permissions are outdated. In the evaluation, T_o and T_l were fixed to 3 s. A block that can be reached from more than one other block, i.e., intersections, may only be permitted if the AV has completely entered the adjacent block. Similarly, two offline design variants are included in the evaluation for comparison: *Local Sensors (LS)* is MV2 with the time since the last update (T_u) set to infinity and, therefore, will never use the *normal* operating state. As a result, AVs using LS still receive waypoints from the VPS but ignore received permissions. To see the possible effects of improved local sensors, an additional block may be permitted in *Local Sensors 2 (LS2)*.

Scenarios can take an amorphous layout that is based on a real parking area, or square grid parking layouts with a side-length of 11 or 21 blocks. They can be seen in Fig. 10. Finally, the random seed for the parking place assignment completes the scenario.

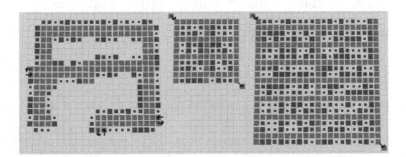

Fig. 10. The parking area layouts used by scenarios. Blue blocks are parking places and sized according to the suitable vehicle size. Arrows indicate entry and exit points. (Color figure online)

As metric for the efficiency of the system in each scenario, the *average speed* of AVs is calculated based on the duration from receiving waypoints to reaching the destination and length of this path. To verify the safety of the proposed concept, a check for (near) collisions of AVs has been implemented that reports if two AVs occupy the same block.

5.2   Evaluation Results

Figure 11 presents an overview of the average speed in meters per second, observed in the presence of various faults, more details can be derived by Table 3. The column headings name the mitigation variant and fault pattern. In **jam**, a third of the parking area around an intersection is permanently without connection. A repeated pattern of a functioning connection for around X seconds followed by a disruption for Y seconds is designated with **cXdY**. No faults occurred in **none**. LS and LS2 do not consider permissions issued by VPS and are thus unaffected by connection faults. Subset cross-validation among 44 random seeds for space assignments showed no significant influence on the average speed with all other factors equal. Therefore, we present results averaged across all random seeds.

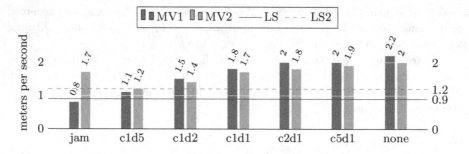

Fig. 11. Average speed of the variants for different fault patterns.

Table 3. Average speed of AVs in meters per second for selected scenarios.

Layout	Entry	LS *	LS2 *	MV1 jam	c1d5	c1d2	c1d1	c2d1	c5d1	none	MV2 jam	c1d5	c1d2	c1d1	c2d1	c5d1	none
Grid11	2s	0.8	1.1	0.4	0.4	0.6	0.9	1.2	1.2	1.5	1	0.6	0.6	0.8	1	1	1.2
	4s	1	1.3	0.6	1.2	1.8	1.9	2	2.1	2.1	1.9	1.4	1.5	1.9	2	2.1	2.1
	20s	1.3	1.6	1.1	1.8	2.2	2.2	2.2	2.3	2.3	2.2	1.9	2.1	2.2	2.2	2.3	2.3
Grid21	2s	0.9	1.2	0.7	0.6	0.8	1.3	1.7	1.8	2	1.4	0.8	0.7	1.1	1.5	1.5	1.7
	4s	1.1	1.4	1.1	1.6	2.4	2.6	2.6	2.7	2.8	2.4	1.7	1.9	2.5	2.5	2.6	2.8
	20s	1.4	1.7	1.7	2.5	2.9	2.9	2.9	3	3	2.8	2.2	2.7	2.9	2.9	3	3
real	2s	0.7	1	0.9	0.9	1.6	1.9	2	2.1	2.2	1.6	1.1	1.3	1.6	1.8	1.8	2.1
	4s	1	1.3	1	1.7	2.2	2.3	2.3	2.4	2.5	2.1	1.8	2.1	2.3	2.3	2.4	2.5
	20s	1.2	1.5	1.7	2.1	2.4	2.5	2.5	2.6	2.6	2.3	2	2.3	2.5	2.5	2.6	2.6
*		0.9	1.2	0.8	1.1	1.5	1.8	2	2	2.2	1.7	1.2	1.4	1.7	1.8	1.9	2

It can be seen that doubling the distance of local permissions, i.e., the change from LS to LS2, yields only a small improvement in speed. The 2 s entry interval easily leads to congestion, especially in small parking areas and if VPS cannot provide frequent updates to AVs. This is visible by the overall low speed in Table 3 for layout Grid11 with 2 s entry time. In all other cases, both MVs about double the speed compared to LS and are only slightly affected by the worse connection. MV1 performs minimally better than MV2 with good connection, as it does not need to account for AVs moving without permission.

However, with longer connection losses, MV1 performs worse and even blocks the parking area. The fault *jam* will bring MV1 to a halt and need manual recovery, as AVs cannot get new permissions. For offline AVs, the VPS is not able to revoke permissions as they never expire. When using MV2, this is no issue and speed is only mildly affected even by permanent jams. AVs that do not manage to pass through the jam completely based on VPS permissions, can use their local sensors to escape it. A VPS that can detect and react to such possible rogue movement using infrastructure sensors, allows safety to remain ensured, when combined with permission lifetimes and rules that define if a vehicle may permit movement to itself.

In this simulation, the cloud based approaches could double the speed compared to using only local sensors, which will provide shorter wait times for users of such systems and help to avoid bottlenecks during rush hours by proving a higher throughput. Such a safe optimization could only be achieved by integrating the safety-analysis into the design process of the system.

The example analysis and the abstract simulation used for evaluation are focused on faults caused by connection problems. Real systems need to prepare for all kinds of faults and threats, e.g., uncertain sensors, failing actuators or malicious users. Nevertheless, they can be included in further iterations of the presented process and appropriate mitigation strategies can be developed. In overall, the results show that our approach improves efficiency in terms of average speed without compromising the CPSoS safety.

6   Conclusion

The advent of CPSoS brings along major advantages with respect to potential service-based applications but also bears great challenges with respect to meeting dependability requirements of safety-critical functions. By the examples of various industrial CPSoS use cases we could identify several common challenges. With the selected case study of an automated valet parking system, we show the performance optimization of a CPSoS while meeting the respective safety demands. Our monitoring and recovery solution further highlights the potential of such a performance optimization with respect to managing car parking under varying connection conditions. Thus, we showcase the potential for performance optimization of safety-critical applications in CPSoS.

In future work, we plan to target more extensive safety-critical applications of CPSoS like Mobility-as-a-Service solutions and additional methods to improve their performance, while meeting dependability requirements.

Acknowledgments. The research leading to these results has partially received funding from the Bavarian Ministry of Economic Affairs, Regional Development and Energy as Fraunhofer High Performance Center Secure Intelligent Systems.

References

1. Road Vehicles - Functional Safety. Technical Report ISO 26262:2018 (2018)
2. Road vehicles - Safety of the Intended Functionality. Technical Report ISO/PAS 21448 (2019)
3. Biggs, G., Juknevicius, T., Armonas, A., Post, K.: Integrating safety and reliability analysis into MBSE: overview of the new proposed OMG standard. INCOSE Int. Symp. **28**(1), 1322–1336 (2018). https://doi.org/10.1002/j.2334-5837.2018.00551.x
4. Brogi, A., Forti, S., Guerrero, C., Lera, I.: How to place your apps in the fog: state of the art and open challenges. Softw.: Pract. Exp. (2019). https://doi.org/10.1002/spe.2766
5. Clegg, K., Li, M., Stamp, D., Grigg, A., McDermid, J.: A SysML profile for fault trees—linking safety models to system design. In: SAFECOMP, pp. 85–93 (2019). https://doi.org/10.1007/978-3-030-26601-1_6
6. Engell, S., Paulen, R., Reniers, M.A., Sonntag, C., Thompson, H.: Core research and innovation areas in cyber-physical systems of systems. In: Berger, C., Mousavi, M.R. (eds.) CyPhy 2015. LNCS, vol. 9361, pp. 40–55. Springer, Cham (2015). https://doi.org/10.1007/978-3-319-25141-7_4
7. Gupta, H., Vahid Dastjerdi, A., Ghosh, S.K., Buyya, R.: iFogSim: a toolkit for modeling and simulation of resource management techniques in the Internet of Things, Edge and Fog computing environments. Softw. Pract. Exp. **47**(9), 1275–1296 (2017). https://doi.org/10.1002/spe.2509
8. International Electrotechnical Commission: Hazard and Operability studies (HAZOP studies) - Application guide. Technical Report IEC 61882:2016
9. Ishigooka, T., Otsuka, S., Serizawa, K., Tsuchiya, R., Narisawa, F.: Graceful degradation design process for autonomous driving system. In: Romanovsky, A., Troubitsyna, E., Bitsch, F. (eds.) SAFECOMP 2019. LNCS, vol. 11698, pp. 19–34. Springer, Cham (2019). https://doi.org/10.1007/978-3-030-26601-1_2
10. Kam, H.R., Lee, S.-H., Park, T., Kim, C.-H.: RViz: a toolkit for real domain data visualization. Telecommun. Syst. **60**(2), 337–345 (2015). https://doi.org/10.1007/s11235-015-0034-5
11. Koopman, P., Wagner, M.: Challenges in autonomous vehicle testing and validation. SAE Int. J. Trans. Saf. **4**, 15–24 (2016). https://doi.org/10.4271/2016-01-0128
12. Kopetz, H., Bondavalli, A., Brancati, F., Frömel, B., Höftberger, O., Iacob, S.: Emergence in cyber-physical systems-of-systems (CPSoSs). In: Bondavalli, A., Bouchenak, S., Kopetz, H. (eds.) Cyber-Physical Systems of Systems. LNCS, vol. 10099, pp. 73–96. Springer, Cham (2016). https://doi.org/10.1007/978-3-319-47590-5_3
13. Laprie, J.C.: From Dependability to Resilience. DSN (2008)
14. Lauer, M., Amy, M., Fabre, J.C., Roy, M., Excoffon, W., Stoicescu, M.: Resilient computing on ROS using adaptive fault tolerance. J. Softw.: Evol. Process **30**(3), e1917 (2018). https://doi.org/10.1002/smr.1917
15. Ledmi, A., Bendjenna, H., Hemam, S.M.: Fault tolerance in distributed systems: a survey. In: 2018 3rd International Conference on Pattern Analysis and Intelligent Systems (PAIS), pp. 1–5, October 2018. https://doi.org/10.1109/PAIS.2018.8598484

16. Ozeer, U., Etchevers, X., Letondeur, L., Ottogalli, F.G., Salaün, G., Vincent, J.M.: Resilience of stateful IoT applications in a dynamic fog environment. In: Proceedings of the 15th EAI International Conference on Mobile and Ubiquitous Systems: Computing, Networking and Services - MobiQuitous 2018, pp. 332–341. ACM Press, New York (2018). https://doi.org/10.1145/3286978.3287007
17. Qayyum, T., Malik, A.W., Khan Khattak, M.A., Khalid, O., Khan, S.U.: FogNet-Sim++: a toolkit for modeling and simulation of distributed fog environment. IEEE Access **6**, 63570–63583 (2018). https://doi.org/10.1109/ACCESS.2018.2877696
18. Quigley, M., et al.: ROS: an open-source robot operating system. In: Proceedings of the IEEE International Conference on Robotics and Automation Workshop on Open Source Software, vol. 3, p. 6 (2009)
19. Riley, G.F., Henderson, T.R.: The ns-3 network simulator. In: Wehrle, K., Güneş, M., Gross, J. (eds) Modeling and Tools for Network Simulation, pp. 15–34. Springer, Heidelberg (2010). https://doi.org/10.1007/978-3-642-12331-3_2
20. Schleiss, P., Drabek, C., Weiss, G., Bauer, B.: Generic management of availability in fail-operational automotive systems. In: Tonetta, S., Schoitsch, E., Bitsch, F. (eds.) SAFECOMP 2017. LNCS, vol. 10488, pp. 179–194. Springer, Cham (2017). https://doi.org/10.1007/978-3-319-66266-4_12
21. Schmittner, C., Griessnig, G., Ma, Z.: Status of the development of ISO/SAE 21434. In: Larrucea, X., Santamaria, I., O'Connor, R.V., Messnarz, R. (eds.) EuroSPI 2018. CCIS, vol. 896, pp. 504–513. Springer, Cham (2018). https://doi.org/10.1007/978-3-319-97925-0_43
22. Schönemann, V.: Safety requirements and distribution of functions for automated valet parking. Dissertation, Technische Universität Darmstadt (2019)
23. Sen, K., Vardhan, A., Agha, G., Rosu, G.: Efficient decentralized monitoring of safety in distributed systems. In: Proceedings of the 26th International Conference on Software Engineering, pp. 418–427. IEEE Computer Society, Edinburgh (2004). https://doi.org/10.1109/ICSE.2004.1317464
24. Sonmez, C., Ozgovde, A., Ersoy, C.: EdgeCloudSim: an environment for performance evaluation of edge computing systems. Trans. Emerg. Telecommun. Technol. **29**(11), e3493 (2018). https://doi.org/10.1002/ett.3493
25. Thompson, N.C., Greenewald, K., Lee, K., Manso, G.F.: The Computational Limits of Deep Learning. arXiv:2007.05558 [cs, stat], July 2020
26. Törngren, M., Sellgren, U.: Complexity challenges in development of cyber-physical systems. In: Lohstroh, M., Derler, P., Sirjani, M. (eds.) Principles of Modeling. LNCS, vol. 10760, pp. 478–503. Springer, Cham (2018). https://doi.org/10.1007/978-3-319-95246-8_27
27. Varga, A., Hornig, R.: An overview of the OMNeT++ simulation environment. In: Proceedings of the 1st International Conference on Simulation Tools and Techniques for Communications, Networks and Systems & Workshops, pp. 1–10. ICST, Marseille (2008)

Effective Non-invasive Runway Monitoring System Development Using Dual Sensor Devices

Rahul Sharma[1](✉), Fernando Moreira[1], Gabriel Saragoça[1], and João Ferreira[2]

[1] Tecmic - Tecnologias de Microelectrónica, Lisbon, Portugal
rahul.sharma@tecmic.pt
[2] ISCTE-University Institute of Lisbon, Lisbon, Portugal
joao.carlos.ferreira@iscte-iul.pt
https://www.tecmic.com/, http://www.iscte-iul.pt

Abstract. At airports, the runways are always troubled by the presence of ice, water, cracks, foreign objects, etc. To avoid such problems the runway is supposed to be monitored regularly. To monitor the runways a large number of techniques are available such as runway inspection mobile vans. These techniques are largely human dependent and need interruptions in the runway's operations for inspection. In this position paper, we suggest an alternative way to monitor the runway. This method is non-invasive in nature with the involvement of Light Detection and Ranging (LIDAR) sensors. In the methodology, we describe the schemes of labelling the data obtained from LIDAR using MARWIS sensors fitted in a mobile van. We describe the entire system and the underlying technology involved in developing the system. The proposed system has the potential of developing an efficient runway monitoring system because the LIDAR technology has proved its efficiency in several terrestrial mapping and monitoring systems.

Keywords: Runway monitoring · LIDAR · Machine learning

1 Introduction

Runways, taxiways, and aprons are some essential entities on all airports, and they need to be maintained well for the safety of the carriers and the passengers. On all airports, foreign objects, ice or water films, and structural defects (e.g., cracks) are the factors that impose a potential threat to the carriers. Due to such types of threats, the runways, taxiways, and the aprons are to be monitored regularly. Generally, the foreign objects found over taxiways and runways [24] can lead to accidents like that of Air France Flight 4590 on 25th July 2000, where due to the foreign object debris (FOD) an airplane crashed into a hotel killing 113 persons [3]. Amongst the foreign objects found at Airports 60% are metallic and 18% are of rubber materials, respectively [9]. Besides this, the aviation industry

A. L. Martins et al. (Eds.): INTSYS 2020, LNICST 364, pp. 110–121, 2021.
https://doi.org/10.1007/978-3-030-71454-3_7

has lost around 3.5 B€ just because of the problem caused by foreign objects [6]. Some radar-based systems can be used to detect foreign objects on the runways using millimeter-wave imaging [5,13,23]. These methods are non-invasive but interfere with current installations of the airport and therefore require special permission. Besides interference, the system is expensive and requires special training for installation and maintenance, and may not be suitable for mid-sized or small airports. Another non-invasive foreign object detection system uses the technology from the visual domain, where the videos and images were taken at different time intervals for foreign object detection [2,17]. Another method used Convolutional Neural Networks to build an automated system for region-based object detection using data obtained from the cameras mounted on a runway scanning vehicle [1].

Structural integrity is the other issue at airports that also leads to problems, including accidents because any flaw on the taxiway or runway impacts the aircraft's taxiing and landing (or take-off) [14]. An interesting work used robot mounted Ground Penetrating Radar and camera to detect cracks on the runway [7]. For non-invasive structural flaw detection on runways, a large number of methods were developed to identify cracks on the track using computer vision [15,19]. Ice and thin film of water are other problems that lead to the critical situation at airports especially during landing and take-off of the aircraft. Several sensor-based techniques exist that can be used to detect ice formation on the runways using microwaves [4] and capacitance [21] measurement of the surface.

The existing runway monitoring for the aforementioned problems is mostly invasive, therefore requires a lot of time to scan the tracks and eventually interrupts the operations at the airport. Ice formation, waterlogging and structural deformations are persistent problems and one scan a day is sufficient. However, the foreign objects require regular monitoring of the runway, and invasive methods cannot be used for this purpose. In this paper, we are suggesting a system that can monitor the entire runway in a non-invasive manner. The proposed system exploits the LIDAR technology to perform the real-time scanning of the runway. We describe several technologies that will be used to develop the proposed system. While describing these technologies we also justify: how the system can detect all the three types of anomalies found at the airports; how monitoring is possible in real-time; and how anomalies can be geo-referenced to determine their locations. The article is organized as follows. Section 2 describes some existing systems that are used to monitor the runways. Section 3 details the technologies necessary to build the proposed system. In Sect. 4 we describe the entire system for non-invasive runway monitoring along with the development information. We end this article in Sect. 5 with conclusions and directions to system development.

2   Related Runway Monitoring Systems

In this section, we provide information about some existing systems that are suitable for structural deformations on the runway, or identification of foreign objects, or water thickness on the tracks.

2.1 Monitoring Systems for Structural Deformations

The structural deformations are found everywhere at airports, but they become a security risk when encountered by airplanes, especially, on runways.

1 **RIS Hi-PAV**:

It is a road and runway assessment system that uses ground penetrating radar (GPR) to perform the survey of several road conditions (such as detecting cavities, and cracks) [8]. RIS Hi-PAV can scan the entire runways at a high speed (e.g. 260 Km/hr) using a single antenna. This system can be used to verify and test new roads. This system comes with a semi-automatic road sub-surface detection software (GRED 3D) that makes it easy to use and take little survey and processing time. This system is non-invasive but needs to use a mobile van to scan the entire runway and therefore interrupts the operations at the airports.

2 **Roadscanners**

The Roadscanner is a non-invasive system that comes with an entire package of runway monitoring, mapping, diagnostic, and inspection [18]. The Road-scanner runway system has three components: first, the Road Doctor Survey Van mounted with technologies (e.g., GPR and LIDAR) to scan the path on the airport wherever the Van goes; second, the Road Doctor Software that processes the data obtained from the Van; third, the team of expert consultants that interprets the processed data. This system is suitable for surface monitoring, sub-surface monitoring, quality control, maintenance optimization, and underground mapping. Though the system is very advanced, it does not perform the real-time monitoring of the entire runway and needs human supervision to carry out anomaly detection such as structural deformations.

2.2 Monitoring System for Foreign Objects

As described in the introduction, the foreign objects are very critical, especially when they are found on the runways of airports. In this section, we describe systems that are well-reputed in detecting FODs on runways.

1 **iFerret**^{TM}

iFerret^{TM} is an intelligent vision-based runway foreign object detection system. It is capable of real-time, automated foreign object detection, identification, and pin-point foreign object's location; recording, and post-event analysis; full visual assessment from ATC/Ground Ops Control [10]. With the software and Electro-Optic Sensors, iFerret automatically detects, locates, classifies, and records foreign objects at commercial airports and military airbases. The system uses color (i.e., green, yellow, and red) coding to classify the type of foreign object and its associated threat (i.e., no, medium, and high threat, respectively). The system is very effective, but it's difficult to train this system to identify the same object as foreign objects at a different light intensity. The system also has problems identifying small foreign objects having the same color as the floor.

2 Tarsier

The Tarsier system is an automatic runway FOD detection system, which uses millimeter-wave (MMW) radars to scan the runway surfaces continuously [20]. The radar performance is not affected by dust or heatwaves and pinpoints debris location in a precise range and bearing. Being non-invasive, this system provides foreign object detection also in low light conditions like shadow, darkness, rain, and fog. The system is capable of detecting foreign objects such as metal, plastic, rubber, glass, and organic matter. The status information is relayed to airport operators through a graphical display. Live video feeds from powerful MIL-SPEC day and night camera systems are automatically cued to allow object verification before someone is sent to remove debris. A high-resolution night camera combined with a near infra-red illumination tuned to the lens system far exceeds any competing night vision system. An event log records the data for historical analysis.

3 Background

3.1 LIDAR Technology for Terrestrial Scanning

The Light Detection and Ranging (LIDAR)is a methodology where a distance (range) of an object is calculated by projecting a laser beam on the object and sensing its reflection on a sensor. The variation in the time of reflected beam and changes in its wavelengths are used to build a 3-D image of the target object. Mostly, the range is determined using two techniques; first, using the phase of the beam; second, using the pulse of the beam. In this article, we focus on the ground-based terrestrial sensors and describe them with respect to the proposal. The importance of LIDAR for this proposal is based upon its non-invasive nature of scanning terrestrial surfaces. There are LIDAR systems that can achieve an accuracy of 5mm and cover a range of 800 m [11], therefore it is extremely suitable for detecting cracks, ice, water, and foreign objects on the airport runways.

The data produced by LIDAR is a set of data points in 3-D space, commonly known as Point Clouds. Figure 1 shows an example of a torus represented by a point cloud. Point clouds have been used for many purposes, such as 3-D CAD model for manufactured parts, and their quality inspection, etc. In our proposal, the point cloud is produced by scanning the airport's runway using the terrestrial LIDAR sensor. The RIEGL VZ-400i [11] (see Fig. 2) is one of the possible candidate LIDAR sensor that can be used in our proposed system. This device is used for: Forensic and Crash Scene Investigations, architecture surveying and facade measurements, surveying and monitoring, etc. RIEGL VZ-400i can scan a view of 100° × 360° in a range up to 800 m with an accuracy of 5 mm. The data acquisition speed is 500,000 measurements/sec with real-time geo-referencing simultaneously.

Fig. 1. Example point cloud representation of a Torus [16]

Geo-referencing is one of the important characteristics of the proposed system. Through geo-referencing, we intend to locate the anomaly on the runway. Preventive or curative actions are to be taken at the location of the anomaly, based upon the severity of the anomaly. The integrated GNSS receiver and high accuracy and precision of ranging of RIEGL VZ-400i enable near accurate geo-localization of the anomaly. The RIEGL VZ-400i provides real-time data flow through dual processing platforms; the first processing system performs system operations and waveform processing, and simultaneous acquisition of scan and image data; the second system provides onboard registration, geo-referencing, and analysis. The RIEGL VZ-400i also comes with a 3G/4G LTE modem, Wi-Fi, and Ethernet ports, therefore, enables its remote operations.

Fig. 2. LIDAR RIEGL VZ-400i [11]

3.2 MARWIS for Terrestrial Scanning via Vehicle

Mobile Advanced Road Weather Information Sensor (MARWIS) is a non-invasive anomaly detection system for road and runways [12]. MARWIS is a kind of mobile weather station that performs real-time detection of several road's and runway's critical parameters such as temperature, friction, etc. At runways, the

Fig. 3. MARWIS sensor assembly [12]

problems caused by waterlogging and ice formation can lead to disastrous situations. Besides this, the road conditions such as temperature, relative humidity, friction, etc., also add to the problem with runways. MARWIS is a solution to address the aforestated problematic road conditions at runways. MARWIS aids in classifying road conditions like dry, moist, wet, icy, snow, slush, chemically wet. It also calculates the road surface temperature, ambient temperature, water film height (up to 6 mm), dew point temperature, ice percentage, and friction. The data collected from MARWIS will be helpful in developing the proposed system as we can use these classification produced by MARWIS to label LIDAR data (Fig. 3).

3.3   XTraN^{TM} for Vehicle Monitoring

XTraN is a solution for efficiently managing fleets and teams. The system provides several functionalities such as fleet scheduling, achieving energy efficiency in vehicle-usage, etc. XTraN has an on-board processing unit [22] designed to record event in a vehicle. XTraN also provides various interfaces to a vehicle's sensors and enables sensor data collection for vehicle monitoring and fleet management related optimizations. XTraN's on-board processing unit can be easily installed on the majority of vehicles. XTraN on-board unit has a GNSS module that has an accuracy of 25 cm, an integrated UHF radio link (license-free band), and several communication ports (including RS-232, RS-485, 1-wire, USB, and CAN). XTraN on-board unit communicates with the main system by interfacing GPRS to one of its communication ports (Fig. 4).

The XTraN on-board unit also has digital I/Os and analog inputs that can be used to interface with some additional sensors, if required to complement the main source of data. Another advantage of this solution is that it accepts a wide voltage range (between 10-36V), with a typical consumption of 120mA, which makes it directly pluggable to the car battery without additional components. We intend to utilize the XTraN on-board unit and interface it with MARWIS to collect data related to the runway, and further utilize this data for labeling the LIDAR data.

Fig. 4. XTraN's on-board processing unit for monitoring vehicle [22]

4 Proposed System

In this section, we describe the proposed system and its functions. First, we detail the components of the system. Secondly, we discuss the possible field arrangement of the sensors at the runway and scenarios to collect the data.

4.1 Component of Runway Monitoring System

There are four major components of the proposed system; Sensors; Data Storage; Artificial Intelligence (AI) and Machine Learning (ML) Stack; User interface. Figure 5 shows the complete architecture of the proposed system.

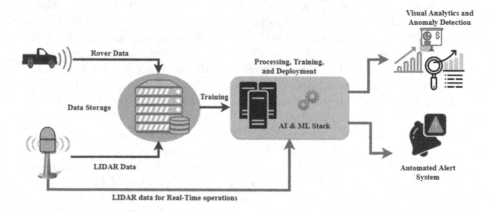

Fig. 5. Architecture of the runway monitoring system

1 **Sensors:** In the proposed system, we suggest using two types of sensors. LIDAR is the prime sensor of the system because it can 3-D scan the entire runway in a non-invasive manner (see Sect. 3.1 for LIDAR's description). The data sensed from LIDAR is utilized in two ways; saved in storage developing

ML models; and relayed to AI and ML stack for real-time operations (classification, visualization, etc.). MARWIS sensor is the second sensing device we propose to use in this system. MARWIS can be attached to the XTraN's on-board processing unit of the Rover to scan the runway for anomalies such as water film, ice, etc. (see Sects. 3.1 and 3.3 for the description of XTraN and MARWIS). Data from the Rover is also saved into the data storage that can be used to label the LIDAR data.

2 **Data Storage:** Data Storage (Lake) is created, to save the data obtained from the two sensor devices. The data from LIDAR sensors is converted in standard LAS format and stored as .las file in the data storage. The data obtained from the Rover can be stored in a database and saving various parameters captured (or calculated) by it. For every capture event, the time and GPS location of the rover is saved. This GPS location and time will help label the LIDAR data.

3 **AI and ML Stack:** There are three main purposes of this stack; data processing; modeling; and model deployment. In data processing, a stack of python scripting language along with libraries like Scikit-Learn, pandas Open3d, etc., can be used to process the data obtained from the rover and LIDAR, and label the LIDAR data. In modeling, a stack of python along with TensorFlow and Keras can be used to perform the classification operation by using the Convolutional Neural Network (CNNs). In modeling, we also perform tasks like clustering for unsupervised machine learning operations and use visualization libraries like the matplotlib, and seaborn for displaying the results. In model deployment, we pickle the learned model and deploy it to provide the classification in real-time. Besides python, the AI and ML stack also consist of the opensource tool CloudCompare to perform the data analysis and ML operations. We also intend to crop small images from the point cloud near to the georeference provided by the Rover data and use it to label the object in the point cloud.

4 **User Interface:** The system will have two types of interfaces; an automated alert system; and visual analytics and anomaly detection. The automated alert system is a dashboard that provides the output of the runway scan in real-time along with the anomalies identified by the system and their location. This system can help generate an automated alert based upon the severity of anomaly identified by the system. The second interface is also a dashboard but with a visual aid for example displaying the point cloud with several clusters in the cloud. This interface is also helpful to identify the unknown anomalies (via human interpretations) which are not identified during the training process.

As displayed in Fig. 5 we first store the data from the two runway scanning sources. The point cloud data from LIDAR is labeled using the geolocations of anomalies determined by the MARWIS sensor of the Rover. After processing and labeling the data, we train a CNN for the labeled point cloud data. Once the training completes and the model is validated, it is deployed to the real-time alert system. The visual analytics can also be performed by plotting the identified clusters.

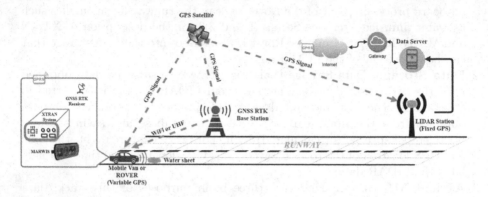

Fig. 6. Field view of the runway monitoring system

Figure 6 shows a field view of sensor deployment and data collection strategy on the runway. The Rover is mounted with the MARWIS and GNSS sensors. The LIDAR sensor is mounted over a pole with an integrated GNSS receiver. Both LIDAR and Rover send the sensed data to the data store via Ethernet and GPRS respectively. In the whole system, the data collection is the most crucial part because we need to send the Rover on the runway which interrupts the aviation service. Following are two data collection schemes that can be efficient:

1 **Data Collection Scheme 1**
   In this scheme, the LIDAR data is collected first. This collected point cloud data can be used as a reference and can be used to compare (using Cloud-Compare software) with other point clouds collected at different times. The geolocation of the anomalies identified by point cloud comparisons can be used by Rover to scan those locations and further label the anomaly. This scheme has the advantage that anomalies are identified in advance and Rovers can be sent to the runway to the specific locations on the runway. This also can save time needed to interrupt the runway for scanning.
2 **Data Collection Scheme 2**
   The labeling process takes place at the end of the data collection process. In this scheme, the LIDAR and Rover perform the runway scan simultaneously. This scheme has the advantage of identifying a large number of anomalies because the Rover scans the whole runway before coming back to the base.

4.2 Discussion

Due to the involvement of the laser-based scanning method, the proposed system can monitor the airport's runway in a non-invasive manner. The technologies we mentioned in this proposal are well proven for their domain and we intend to integrate them into a runway monitoring system. There are some issues we anticipate to encounter while developing the proposed system:

1 **Point Cloud Data Processing**
In this system, the laser signals will be processed into the point cloud by the in-built software to the LIDAR (i.e., REIGL VZ-400i device). However, the real challenge lies in the processing of the generated point cloud because the point cloud obtained from the terrestrial scan of the runway will be huge.

2 **Labeling Foreign Objects**
The list of foreign objects, whether living or non-living, is endless. It is practically impossible to label all foreign objects that are found on the runway because they vary from location to location.

3 **Size and Severity of Foreign Objects**
The LIDAR device suggested in this system can scan objects as small as 5 mm and we can also determine and label several small objects using the Rover. However, there are a lot of foreign objects (e.g. metal ball bearings, etc.) that are not recognized by MARWIS and they can be equally dangerous for the aircraft and the bigger objects. Labeling such kind of objects will also be a challenging task.

5   Conclusion

Air travel is considered the safest mode of transport. This achievement of the aviation industry is a result of highly efficient airport management. This management also includes the constant monitoring of the airport's assets, where the vigilance at runways, taxiways, and aprons are of high priority. Any problems occurring on these assets lead to delays in flights, increase costs, and in the worst-case results in accidents. In this article, we focused on three problems at the airports which are related to structural integrity, foreign objects, and water or ice. We surveyed several methods that solve either of the aforementioned problems, individually. Besides the methodologies, we also describe four runway monitoring technologies that are state of the art in the detection of foreign objects and structural deformation at the runways and taxiways.

Among the methods and technology reviewed for this work, some take a lot of time to scan the runways, therefore, interrupt the functioning of the airport. Some methods perform real-time monitoring operations but are dependent on human interventions to identify the objects and their exact location. In this article, we provide guidelines to develop a system that can monitor the airport's assets in real-time and in a non-invasive manner. The proposed system consists of LIDAR for non-invasive scanning of the airport's assets. The System also has MARWIS sensors mounted connected to the XTraN on-board processor of a mobile rover. We describe all components of the proposed system and its underlying technologies. We also explain two data collection schemes to label the LIDAR data based upon the location and category of anomaly sensed by the rover. The use of mature technologies of the proposed system has the potential to efficiently monitor the airport's assets in real-time and in a non-invasive manner. We also discuss some issues that are to be addressed before developing the system.

Acknowledgement. The work presented in this paper was carried out in the scope of the project Persistent Runway Monitoring (MPP-Monitorização Persistente de Pista SI IDT code of project is 039876), and we thank CENTRO 2020, Portugal 2020— Operational Program for Competitiveness and Internationalization (POCI), and European Union's ERDF (European Regional Development Fund) for funding the research work. We also thank our poject partners, Tecmic-Tecnologias de Microelectronica SA, INOV, and ANA Aeroportos de Portugal for their support.

References

1. Cao, X., et al.: Region based CNN for foreign object debris detection on airfield pavement. Sensors **18**(3), 737 (2018)
2. Chen, W., Xu, Q., Ning, H., Wang, T., Li, J.: Foreign object debris surveillance network for runway security. Aircr. Eng. Aerosp. Technol. **83**, 229–234 (2011)
3. Air France 4590. https://en.wikipedia.org/wiki/Air_France_Flight_4590. Accessed August 2020
4. Ezraty, R.: New-ice detection using microwave sensors. In: IGARSS 2003. 2003 IEEE International Geoscience and Remote Sensing Symposium. Proceedings (IEEE Cat. No. 03CH37477), vol. 1, pp. 270–272. IEEE (2003)
5. Feil, P., Menzel, W., Nguyen, T., Pichot, C., Migliaccio, C.: Foreign objects debris detection (FOD) on airport runways using a broadband 78 GHZ sensor. In: 2008 38th European Microwave Conference, pp. 1608–1611. IEEE (2008)
6. Foreign Object Debris and Damage Prevention. https://www.boeing.com/commercial/aeromagazine/aero_01/textonly/s01txt.html. Accessed August 2020
7. Gui, Z., Li, H.: Automated defect detection and visualization for the robotic airport runway inspection. IEEE Access **8**, 76100–76107 (2020)
8. RIS Hi-Pave for Road and Runway monitoring. https://www.stanlay.in/ground-penetrating-radars-equipment/hi-pave-gpr-for-pavement-engineering/ris-hi-pave/. Accessed August 2020
9. Hussin, R., Ismail, N., Mustapa, S.: A study of foreign object damage (FOD) and prevention method at the airport and aircraft maintenance area. In: IOP Conference Series: Materials Science and Engineering, vol. 152, p. 012038. IOP Publishing (2016)
10. IFERRET FOREIGN OBJECT & DEBRIS DETECTION. https://www.westernadvance.com/Aviation. Accessed August 2020
11. LIDAR Terrestrial Sensor RIEGL VZ-400i. http://www.riegl.com/nc/products/terrestrial-scanning/produktdetail/product/scanner/48/. Accessed July 2020
12. MARWIS - Mobile Advanced Road Weather Information Sensor. https://www.lufft.com/products/road-runway-sensors-292/marwis-umb-mobile-advanced-road-weather-information-sensor-2308/. Accessed July 2020
13. Nsengiyumva, F., Pichot, C., Aliferis, I., Lanteri, J., Migliaccio, C.: Millimeter-wave imaging of foreign object debris (FOD) based on two-dimensional approach. In: 2015 IEEE Conference on Antenna Measurements & Applications (CAMA), pp. 1–4. IEEE (2015)

14. Pasindu, H., Fwa, T.: Incorporating risk of failure into maintenance management of cracks in runway pavements. Transp. Res. Rec. **2177**(1), 114–123 (2010)
15. Peng, L., Chao, W., Shuangmiao, L., Baocai, F.: Research on crack detection method of airport runway based on twice-threshold segmentation. In: 2015 Fifth International Conference on Instrumentation and Measurement, Computer, Communication and Control (IMCCC), pp. 1716–1720. IEEE (2015)
16. Point cloud – Wikipedia, the free encyclopedia. https://en.wikipedia.org/wiki/Point_cloud. Accessed July 2020
17. Qunyu, X., Huansheng, N., Weishi, C.: Video-based foreign object debris detection. In: 2009 IEEE International Workshop on Imaging Systems and Techniques, pp. 119–122. IEEE (2009)
18. Roadscanners. https://www.roadscanners.com/services/airport-surveys/. Accessed August 2020
19. Sinha, S.K., Fieguth, P.W.: Automated detection of cracks in buried concrete pipe images. Autom. Constr. **15**(1), 58–72 (2006)
20. Tarsier Automatic Runway FOD Detection System. https://www.westernadvance.com/Aviation. Accessed August 2020
21. Troiano, A., Pasero, E., Mesin, L.: An innovative water and ice detection system for monitoring road and runway surfaces. In: 6th Conference on Ph. D. Research in Microelectronics & Electronics, pp. 1–4. IEEE (2010)
22. XTraN-Fleet Management. https://www.tecmic.com/portfolio/xtran/. Accessed July 2020
23. Yigit, E., Demirci, S., Unal, A., Ozdemir, C., Vertiy, A.: Millimeter-wave ground-based synthetic aperture radar imaging for foreign object debris detection: experimental studies at short ranges. J. Infrared Milli. Terahz Waves **33**(12), 1227–1238 (2012). https://doi.org/10.1007/s10762-012-9938-2
24. Zhongda, Y., Mingguang, L., Xiuquan, C.: Research and implementation of FOD detector for airport runway. In: IOP Conference Series: Earth and Environmental Science, vol. 304, p. 032050. IOP Publishing (2019)

Applications

Adopting Blockchain in Supply Chain – An Approach for a Pilot

Ulpan Tokkozhina[1,2], Ana Lucia Martins[1,2(✉)],
and Joao C. Ferreira[3]

[1] ISCTE - Instituto Universitário de Lisboa, Lisbon, Portugal
{ulpan_tokkozhina, almartins}@iscte-iul.pt
[2] Business Research Unit (BRU-IUL), 1649-026 Lisbon, Portugal
[3] Instituto Universitário de Lisboa (ISCTE-IUL),
ISTAR, 1649-026 Lisbon, Portugal
jcafa@iscte-iul.pt

Abstract. The world nowadays and business processes, in particular, are changing towards digitalization and reduction of time-consuming processes. Provenance and safety of products are becoming key factors for customers' trust, so traceability solutions are arising. One of the most up-and-coming disruptive technologies today is a Blockchain (BC). The aim of this article is to provide tentative framework of how to assess the level of success of BC technology in supply chain (SC) and the methods that should be used in such assessment. The fish SC will be used to illustrate the discussion and the traceability and trust issues will be enhanced. The pilot shows that BC can promote strategic alignment, provides convenience and could be used as market leverage issue by promoting traceability and consequently trust in the product available. Methods to be used or such endeavor are suggested. A future understanding of the importance for BC technology use, as a traceability provider from the perspective of a final customer, is detected as a path for further research.

Keywords: Blockchain technology · Methodological approach · Supply chain management · Traceability

1 Introduction

The interest in disruptive technology solutions for business processes is growing rapidly. Taking into consideration unforeseen emergency events of 2020, the digitalization and efficiency of operations is emergent as never before. In regard with emergency events [1] highlight the main criteria of supply chains: they need to be trustworthy, transparent, and share accurate real-time information, to assure the safety of global populations. The global supply chain is an industry, that is running two-thirds of the global economy [2], bringing to consumers everything that we eat, wear and use in everyday life. One of the most promising and disruptive technologies that has the potential to transform and improve supply chain activities is Blockchain [3].

Blockchain (BC) is an emerging technology, with potential applications to everyday life, from digital identity and voting to healthcare and legal contracts [4, 5]. It can

A. L. Martins et al. (Eds.): INTSYS 2020, LNICST 364, pp. 125–141, 2021.
https://doi.org/10.1007/978-3-030-71454-3_8

be characterized as an immutable digital ledger, that is building and keeping information in such a way that each player of a SC can track the real-time progress information [6]. The distributed nature of this technology, persistence and immutability of its records, and the ability to execute decentralized logic through smart contracts make BC-based products and services significantly different from those previously developed and based on the Internet – especially for sectors related to Industry 4.0 and supply chain [7]. BC is expected to become a "next holy grail for the enterprise", as it holds enormous potential for supply chain (SC) transformation, among other areas, in the ways of production, orders performing, transportation, delivery and consumption [8]. However, with a few exceptions, SCs are not considered to be a priority on the agenda of most countries with BC initiatives, even though interest is very high [9], empirical research is very limited due to the lack of knowledge among professionals about the potential of this technology [10].

In the adoption of BC in Supply chain management (SCM) [11] argues that all must start with the answer to two questions: "What to adopt" and "Where to start". Under the umbrella of the first question, [12] discusses and argues in favor of adopting a use case (which would be further developed into a pilot), nonetheless the second question still requests more detailed analysis. [13] suggest a framework for the mindful adoption of BC, which was extended by [12]. Further [12] proposed a guide for the "mindfulness of technology adoption" under the context of blockchain. Nonetheless, a more detailed methodological framework of how to assess the outcome of those pilots and their impact through the SC is still lacking.

While discussing the main advantages, constraints and resistances of BC technology use in SCM, the purpose of this article is to develop a tentative framework of how to assess the level of impact of BC technology in SC and the methods that should be used in that assessment.

The food industry has experienced many quality drawbacks in recent years. Public distrust in the provenance of seafood and some conservation operations is growing [14] and BC technology might be helpful to overcome such distrust. As so, following on [12] and [13] suggestion of starting the adoption of BC in SC with use cases and pilots, this article will focus on the specific SC for one product - fish. Such product, with fragile quality and high value as fish, shows to be a good example for a pilot. Consequently, the more detailed goal of this article is to assess the impact of the adoption of BC technology in SC trust in the fish industry. This paper will focus attention on the traceability feature of BC technology, as well as the recognition of this attribute in the B2B relations through the SC, together with the trust of the final customer in the product available. The need to conduct such research has already been stressed by [15] but to the best of our knowledge it is yet to be accomplished.

This paper will contribute to academia in terms of opening new paths to future researches and providing a detailed step-by-step explanation of how SC traceability can be reached using BC technology. At the same time, it contributes to practitioners and shows a potential benefit of BC technology implementation overview on the example of fish sector SC. To the best of our knowledge this is the first study of Portuguese use-case for BC technology implementation in such a specific sector. The novelty of the application of BC technology in SC justifies that a case approach is adopted [16]. The pilot of a Portuguese fish sector SC will be explored to develop the proposal to assess the impact of the adoption of BC technology in SC trust.

To fulfil the proposed goal, this research is based on existing literature on the topic as well as on interviews with key elements in the case SC. For confidentiality issues, the identity of the focal company in the pilot SC will not be disclosed and will hereafter be identified as Company X.

This paper is built as follows: Sect. 2 will present some of the acute literature on the topic, mainly highlighting BC characteristics, application and the adoption models, potential and main challenges to SCM, with the focus on traceability feature of BC for food SCs. Section 3 will give a brief understanding of BC initiatives in Portugal and Sect. 4 indicates a methodology that was used for this article construction. Section 5 introduces a pilot of Company X for the fish sector in Portugal, describing also the key management, building blocks and traceability processes, also discussing the assessment of the BC impact use in the pilot SC. Section 6 provides conclusions and paths for future research.

2 Literature Review

2.1 Blockchain Technology and Its Features

Blockchain technology, also defined as an encrypted digital ledger [17] is based on a decentralized peer-to-peer system [18], that is able to create a continuous, visible and sharable record of products transactions and movements around SC in a distributed manner [19]. BC is a set of chain block, that altogether represent a permanent and inviolable sequence of records and transactions that can be verified in the future. Keys and encryption secure the process, and each stakeholder is identified by their key [20]. This network is build based on the consensus achieved by different voting mechanisms and the chain is extended with a new block when the majority of participants agree with it [21].

Operations within BC are fully decentralized, and do not rely on an intermediary because all the transactions are being verified with smart contracts [22]. Unique features of smart contracts, such as automated process and tamper-proof system [23] together with the distributed nature of BC, improves upon automatization of ownership value and overall synchronization of business operations [24]. Smart contracts assumed to play a crucial role in partnership efficiency - since information is immutable, it leads to transparency and improvement of SC collaboration [25].

Due to self-executing codes, that are preventive to tampering or corrupting the execution of a given contract, every party is an equal custodian of the contract terms; which saves both costs and time in terms of contract revision, registration and verification [23]. However, building a high-quality smart contract is even more challenging than creating a traditional one, since experience in this field is not so widespread yet [2] and as a result, poor coding of smart contracts leads to problems [26].

2.2   Blockchain Technology for Supply Chain Management

By its nature, BC is increasing transparency throughout the SC, in this way providing reliance and confidence of products' provenance [10]. These encrypted ledgers provide a unified variation of truth through consensus protocols [27], thus enhancing the performance of SC that does not need to establish trust relationship among actors since every participant is a keeper of all information flow existing around SC [23]. Transparency of information regarding products and processes empowers suppliers to get engaged with further activities and decisions, such as strategies for development and innovation support [28].

At the era of the digital economy, SCs are still cyber-vulnerable: they are subjected to attacks due to their insecurity and are challenged with issues of trust both among suppliers as well as between supplier and consumer [29]. It is claimed that BC has an enormous potential to decentralize traditional SC and generate new networks of value combining it together with additive manufacturing, artificial intelligence and Internet of Things (IoT) [2].

BC IoT framework is expected to be a key driver that will boost SCM to the next level of analytics, enabling data democracy, and thus improving performance and productivity [8]. So, the next step of the digitalization will be the transformation of industrial companies, enabling the exchange of data and services between them, and implementation of smart contracts as a unified tool for the value transfer. BC implementation is potentially applicable to any sector from construction engineering [23] and parking spaces collaborative gamification [30] to diamond authentication [31] and the music recording industry [32]. BC applications are commonly implied to be used together with IoT solutions, as for instance using BC as a decentralized platform for IoT-based low-cost smart meters for energy consumption [33] or for handling charging processes of electric vehicles through mobile application [34]. BC use is "only limited by our imagination" [2]. One of the best-known logistics blockchain effectuations is the collaboration between IBM and Maersk – the use-case for container shipping [18]. Walmart is testing BC for food SC [2], some studies focus on conceptual models' applications, the case for electronic components is explored at [35] and agri-food at [36]. Safety is also an issue explored in the food business with [37]. General applications discussion is performed at [38]. Also, vegetables traceability is studied at [39] and for wine at [40].

2.3   Adopting Blockchain in Supply Chains

In the context of BC technology adoption to SCM and logistics, [13] completed four mindful dimensions of technology adoption by [41, 42] and introduce the fifth one. Those dimensions are as follows:

(1) *Engagement with the technology* – Are the technological features named clearly?
(2) *Technological novelty seeking* – Is there reasoning for the necessity of blockchain technology or can the business problem be solved with existing technology?
(3) *Awareness of local context* – How specifically will the use case fit into the supply chain context?
(4) *Cognizance of alternative technologies* – Are alternatives considered?
(5) *Anticipation of technology alteration* – Are use cases adaptable?

The listed dimensions were considered under the lens of key high-level SC objectives presented earlier by [6] which include cost reduction, speed, dependability, risk reduction, flexibility and sustainability. Since [13] were concerned with a threat of "a solution looking for a problem", [12] expanded those five principles and added one more dimension, which is a "contribution to high-level supply chain objectives". This dimension contributes to eliminate the risk of the unsuitability of BC technology in a potential use-case [12]. By virtue of this substantial dimension, in future, it will save resources and time for SC that will search for latter-day technology to implement.

2.4   Constraints of Blockchain Technology for Supply Chain Management Use

Undoubtedly, BC technology looks very attractive to scholars and practitioners, however, there is still a vast number of challenges for its integration into SC context. Numerous institutional, infrastructural, technical and regulatory challenges need to be embraced before BC-based solutions can reach their maturity stage [43]. Among others, challenges such as organizational readiness, scalability, technical expertise, [44] high cost of the technology and further regulation issues [45] may arise when implementing BC in the SC. Security issues of open access BC [46] and management procedures for BC used by multi-actor SCs [47] need to be addressed in future studies. A lot of BC initiatives have difficulties in emerging from the pioneering phase [48] and in the majority of cases, organizational changes are needed to be undertaken before this technology can be successfully adopted [49]. In general, all these constraints of a BC implementation imply a high risk of emergent technology adoption from scratch that also involves big costs [43]. Moreover, the literature on BC technology for SCM needs "theoretical substance and a theoretical foundation" [50] that could refine the understanding of such a novel phenomenon [26]. BC is claimed to be useful for traceability of goods within SC, boosting thus the overall transparency, however, organization and preparation of SCs themselves is essential before BC can be implemented [49].

2.5   Traceability for Blockchain-Based Supply Chains

BC is assumed to shed light into industry sectors' (e.g. food) complexity in terms of full traceability of SC networks [28]. Most of traceability standards are concentrated on the ability to follow the main characteristics of a product from origin to the final process destination throughout the SC [49]. The Typical food SC consists of many members, suppliers, producers, manufacturers, distributors, retailers, consumers and certifiers, among others; when connected together on a unified BC platform, every one of them will be able to update, add and check the real-time information about products [51]. Since every transaction is visible in the BC ecosystem, it should be easy to trace backward of the supply of each product or service with authenticity from a compliance or quality assurance perspective [23]. Traceability feature of BC brings the knowledge of the authenticity and origin of a product, as well as footprints of products' locomotion throughout the SC, bringing both commercial benefits in terms of brand reputation and serious safety measures [52]. Business requirements for BC-enabled traceability systems from the SC's focal companies view were addressed in [15] claiming that specific business requirements and technological evaluation of the business case development should be accurately analyzed.

Some of the main challenges in SCM is product traceability and supplier dependability, satisfaction and trust; it will impact on the performance of the entire SC [53]. Issues, such as traceability of products supplier dependability and end-to-end time and quality of service are all crucial for the success of SCs.

It is clear in the literature, that traceability is a relevant issue to several parties in the SC. However, traceability may not be recognized for having similar relevance for every element of the SC. The extend of this relevance is yet to be discussed, as well as the impacts or utility of traceability.

2.6 Traceability for Food Supply Chains

Food quality is a big concern to society, moreover, assuring quality throughout global and complex supply chains is very challenging for food and beverage industries. At the same time, issues like legal regulations, food standards and corporate social responsibility criteria, including also environmental sustainability concerns, should be highly considered [54]. Thus, product traceability from origin producer to the final consumer is an essential problem to solve. BC disruptive technology can give solutions to this problem by managing the identity of process stakeholders and associate immutable transaction block of product transactions, allowing food retailers to keep a track and react rapidly for recalls, assuring, thus, safety issues and reducing the chance of illnesses caused by food [19]. BC and smart contracts can handle this transaction in an SC process without a central control entity.

According to [55], BC-based solutions for food SCs could be crucial in pandemic times, as complex and lengthy overseas SCs made it challenging for agricultural exporters to get the same guarantees and maintain cashflow. On the example of Australia's surplus of seafood and agriculture, that Chinese market used to order, [55] explain that BC-based solution could give an ability for every participant of an SC to confirm the type of products shipped, track where it is at the real-time, and whether it has been stored under required conditions (e.g. temperature, humidity etc.).

The food transportation process is essential to be the focus on the safety, quality, and the certification of producers in a global market driven by profit—the rising number of problems related to food safety and contamination risks [56]. Product traceability from the origin producer to the final consumer is an essential problem to solve. BC disruptive technology can give solutions to this problem by managing identity of process stakeholders and associate immutable transaction block of product transactions [57]. BC and smart contracts can handle this transaction in a SC process without a central control entity.

Attributing food traceability as part of logistics management highlights the fact that quality assurance, food safety and overall efficiency of SC depend highly on logistics operations [49].

3   Use of Blockchain in Portugal

The European Commission recognizes a potential that BC technology is able to offer to improve European industry; like this, any type of company, from start-ups to giant corporations could transform their operations towards decentralized and transparent digital services [58]. In December 2019, the European Commission launched an open market consultation that is looking for improved and innovative BC solutions for the future evolution of the procurement process [58]. Governments should keep on creating a firm grasp of legal and regulatory issues for BC, at the same time supporting use cases of this technology in SC context [59].

Since BC technology still resides in its infancy, Portuguese companies that are working with this technology have been formed mainly by young graduates. Examples of these are companies such as:

Public Mint Inc. - presented as: "the first fiat-native blockchain settlement layer for programmable money" [60].

Genesis studio - created for the full adoption of BC and modern distributed accounting technology (DLT) [61].

Taikai - a start-up that creates challenges between large companies and BC start-ups. Taikai is a challenge platform that uses BC; it has raised 350 thousand euros and is headed by Mário Alves, who left the bank to lead the project [62].

WalliD - this Portuguese BC start-up received an investment of 600 thousand euros. Among the investors is the National Press - Casa da Moeda. WalliD developed an identity registration and management tool in the Ethereum BC platform. Through the WalliD tool, a user can store his/her identification documents in a BC-based digital wallet. This information can then be used to validate the person's entity in the services of companies and organizations that adopt the WalliD system [63].

Bitcliq - this Portuguese startup is the first worldwide BC market for fish trade, connecting fishing fleets with buyers and allowing the purchase of fish when they are caught at sea by retailers and restaurant owners. In addition to connecting fishers to buyers, the platform also allows full traceability from the catch location to the table, which is becoming essential for an ecosystem with ever lower prospects due to illegal fishing practices and ocean pollution [64].

Zenithwings - is developing a BC solution to help protect wine producers and consumers by allowing digital certification and product traceability [65].

As in the rest of the world, there are no known companies in Portugal that have yet implemented BC technology in its broad spectrum; it is mainly used for initial coin offerings (ICO) nevertheless it is expected to bring drastic change to both public and private entities [66] and disrupt SCM.

4   Methodology

This research aims to develop a tentative framework of how to assess the level of success of BC use in SC. The novelty of the topic justifies that it is addressed using a case study approach [16]. Hereafter, the case study will be called the pilot.

Following [16]'s recommendations, the quality of the results produced from the case study depends on the process of conducting it. Consequently, in our research focus is on defining the process, which will respect the guidelines suggested by [16].

For confidentiality reasons, the name of the focal company of the SC considered in the pilot will not be disclosed; it will be addressed as "Company X".

Data for the different stages of the case study was collected using semi-structured interviews to key flow managers of fish in Company X. These interviews were conducted at the location of the central processing point of the company. These were followed by a detailed guided visit of the processing facilities and the end-to-end process during working hours, which added observation as a data collecting tool for building the case. Several visits (four) to the retail points to observe final customers allowed identifying what they read and ask about the product before buying it (in all the selling points there was both pre-packed fresh fish and fish to be sold in bulk).

5   A Pilot in the Fish Sector in Portugal

5.1   Overall Approach for Adopting Blockchain Technology in Company X Supply Chain

Following recommendations of [16] and [12] framework, the pilot should start with the analysis of the relevance of the use of BC in the specific SC, therefore there should be an initial approach to the SC under analysis and the product to be addressed. Prior to the extension [12] introduced to [13] proposal based on [6], this overview can be achieved with a simple mapping of the supply such as the one provided in Fig. 1.

This mapping is relevant to identify the stakeholders in the SC process. A stakeholders analysis matrix should be conducted to identify their power and interest in being part of the SC and adopting BC. This would allow identifying the potential fragilities in the project but also potential allies. Those who recognize the potential in BC use to leverage the SC objectives should be identified for initial use cases. Interviews with decision-makers at each stakeholder should be the main data source to conduct the data collection for this stage. From this point forward, the approach to the critical SC objectives and the criticality of each stakeholder would be linked.

With the ever-growing challenges of global warming and scarcity of natural resources, it is very likely that not many years from now the origin of the fresh fish might change. New fishing companies, new fishing markets, or movements, such as aquaculture, are likely to consequently enter the SC, adding or replacing the current ones. These changes in the SC need to be considered as well as the new elements of the SC might have different approaches to the use of BC in SC and lead to a shift in the SC strategic goals.

The second stage would relate to the engagement with technology not only in the overall SC, but mainly at each stakeholder. BC technology will allow traceability if the different elements are linked, available and willing to share information, so their technological engagement needs to be considered. This approach will be conducted with an assessment of the technological options used by each stakeholder, its ability to communicate to other stakeholders, and their willingness to conduct the necessary adjustments.

Stakeholders, according to [13] and [12] proposals, need to develop reasoning to the adoption of BC technology. Without it and the shared knowledge of its impact on the SC goals, commitment might decrease. Technology adoption process itself lies in engagement from executives and main stakeholders' proposals [12]. Meetings are a method to assure this step of the process. It can be conducted at more than one level: initially with promoters of use cases and later with the remaining stakeholders, using the results of the use cases as an argument.

By conducting the previous step at two levels, first with use cases to show the potential of BC and then involving all stakeholders in the impact, the fourth step of [12] proposal is anticipated and conducted along with the third one. Differences of context between stakeholders will need to be addressed as the impact of BC can differ. For instance, the reception of fish from the vessels and transportation, by their nature, show more exposure to traceability fragilities while the processing and the retail points might be less exposed.

Next step in this framework is to make sure that BC technology is the best solution. If alternative technologies show the potential to produce better results for the SC in terms of its strategic goals, those should be considered. Nonetheless the decentralized nature of BC should be considered as a relevant safety issue in a fish SC such as the one in this pilot.

The technology landscape is evolving and alterations to technology need to be anticipated [13]. The use cases in the pilot need to consider these possible adjustments. Alternative solutions need to be planned as to assure SC resilience.

5.2   Addressing the Use of Blockchain

Fish as all products in the SCM process changes owners, and several companies are involved. One big issue among different stakeholders is that they have different information systems, and data exchange is complicated because of trust issues and the security process. BC can be a solution to overtake this problem, and thus creating a solution of traceability. We based this pilot on a concept proof of Hyperledger Fabric's framework to keep track of each part of this process. Commercial BC can also be used, but for this concepts proof, open sources create flexibility, and available libraries created flexibility towards our proof of concept implementation. So, we implement a simplified Hyperledger with associated channels (chains) that take data from different information systems and creates the possibility of transaction visibility. From this, a set of independent chains of transaction blocks containing only transactions for that particular channel is created.

Smart Contract allows defining conditions for transactions process and the fish asset changes ownership, and this result in changes to the ledger. The ledger contains the current performed transactions signed to each stakeholder. This is a network that is responsible for maintaining a consistently replicated ledger. This data is stored in a database for efficient access. Currently supported databases are LevelDB and CouchDB. Membership Service Provider (MSP) manages identity and permissioned access for clients and peers.

Since we have data from the fish SC in Portugal, which is no different from company to company in this market due to regulatory restrictions, we use this data to create a laboratory simulation of all fish SC in Portugal, which will be described in this chapter.

Company X is one of the leading retail groups in Portugal. This exercise complies the SC of Company X from the fishing vessels all the way through different parties that support the physical flow of the fish to the end-user. The global structure of this SC is shown in Fig. 1.

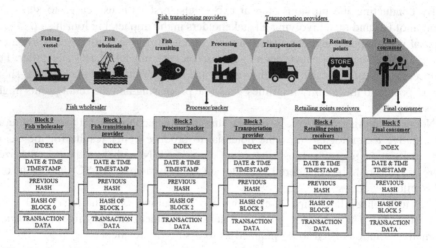

Fig. 1. Overall fish sector SC and BC architecture for Company X (based on [49, 67])

The fresh fish is captured in the ocean and brought to land in fishing vessels. The place and origin of the fish need to be clearly identified to assure quality, so the traceability of the product needs to start at the fishing moment. Traceability needs to be assured to the point of product availability, so all the entities that support the physical flow of the fish are considered. Additionally, every link in the SC can be a source of disruption.

– The BC traceability system is based on a set of signed transactions performed by the stakeholders from:

- **Fishermen (fishing vessels)** have a Vessel Monitor System (VMS) that registers GPS position at sea. From a Portuguese project SeaItAll a National project from a Portuguese company Xsealence [68], it is possible to identify the fish type using video cameras. This information with date and time is transmitted to a central management control system.
- **The fish wholesaler (Docapesca)** receive fresh fish from vessels and fish trade is performed. This is specific for Portugal. In other countries, equivalent processes and institutions are involved. The BC proposal starts here as Block 0, as can be seen in Fig. 1, and allows traceability, creates interoperability among different information system involved, establishes trust and security and provides control to avoid illegal

fishing. VSM (GPS position of the fishing process), fish type, vessel plate, date and time are associated. At the selling process weight and any other particular information is associated to the transaction. This information is collected from this central management system and associated in BC to the fish buyer key in the BC chain. This is the first register in the BC, and it is also where the *traceability process* starts. Example of this information is as follows:

```
var sardine = { id: '0001', holder: 'DocaPesca', location: {
latitude:     '40.40238',    longitude:     '2.145328'},     when:
'20190630123546', weight: '20Kg', vessel : '9523E' }
```

- **Fish transitioning providers** are responsible for receiving fresh fish from Docapesca and transit it to further processing and packaging. These are the transportation providers. The information that should be recorded at this stage is the receiving date, storage details, processing, sampling, analysis of the bulk fish and the dispatch date/time. If the bulk distributor performs the combination process, the information also must be recorded in the chain. This can be the output of the smart contract negotiation, but for this validation purpose, we only check the fish ownership change in the BC and associated transaction with price, date and other relevant information. This transaction generates a new block linked to the previous through the hash.
- **Processors/packers** are responsible for actions like splitting fish (e.g. big fish like tuna could be divided in smaller parts) and pack then. The initial fish product can be split here, and again a new chain is created and signed by processor entity (if the fish division occurs). A new register is raised. Taking into account the previous example, this block could be the sardine bulk of 20 kilos divided into packs of 1 Kg. New data stamp is associated with information about the packing company.
- **Transportation providers,** as before, are responsible for further movement of goods, and again, a new transaction is raised and linked to the previous one by the hash. Information includes date, time, transportation conditions, start and endpoints, number of km of transportation, stakeholder intervenient, type of vehicle used.
- **Retailing points receivers** get product and then create a new block of transaction that is linked to the previous block. Date, time, location and, entity is all crucial information to insert in the system at this point.
- **Final consumer** when buying the product, the new transaction is generated, and the end customer is able to trace back the whole process of the product that he is intending to buy.

5.3   Key Management and Identity Management – Building the Blocks

Each stakeholder should identify and keep secure a key to sign its transaction. Firstly, to ensure confidentiality, a common secret key is distributed among all entities in the system. Each participant in the system needs to generate a pair of the public and private key before starting its operation. Thus, the transaction block may contain information in the form of both plain text and ciphertext. The SC starts at the fishing vessel, and the fisherman generates the genesis block and adds the required information to the product.

Initial block (Block 0) is generated at the selling process in Docapesca. This entity signs with its key and certifies that this is a legal fishing process. The block is verified by the majority number of participants in the system before the next block is added to the chain. An ID number certifies the transaction order. This procedure is followed by the party that transits the fish to the processing point, the processor/packer, the transportation entity that provides logistics to retailing points, and in each retailing point, in order to include their own transactions in the chain.

This basic BC is a chain of blocks with the following data: 1) Index; 2) Timestamp with date and time; 3) Previous Hash to link to the previous block; 4) Current hash; 5) Data about the transaction (see in Fig. 1).

Consequently, BC is a set of information about transactions, secured by hash (a string of numbers and letters) and connected to the previous hash (order in it), and approved by all. Each time there is a need, the stakeholders can browse for chain block information and with the appropriate key that can check the product history under a controlled decentralized process.

5.4 Assessing the Impact of BC Used in the Pilot SC

Even following [13] and [12] proposals, there is no guarantee that the internal customers and the final customers will recognize the impact of the use of BC. The technology will not be recognized as valuable by these customers unless their own goals are met. Thus, the goals for both the SC parties and the final customers need to be identified. If for the SC parties those were already identified under the scope of [12]'s first step for the consideration of adopting BC, the relevant criteria for the final customers' needs still to be assessed.

Although it is easier to guess the final customers relevant criteria, the real criteria can differ from what the provider expects. As so, conducting an inquiry on what is relevant to them and the relative importance of those aspects is required. For Company X and the fresh fish pilot, it could be, for instance, the origin of the fish, the date of fishing, the continuity of the cold chain, among other issues that the end customers value.

Company X set as goals for the fish SC the reduction of time to market, improvement of quality (of the service provided to customers, of the physical quality of the product, of the reliability of the information - trust) and reduction of operational costs, which are goals difficult to fulfil at the same time. From the SC parties' perspective (excluding the final customers), the pilot needs to be assessed based on the improvements it produces at these several levels: operational costs, time to market reduction, freshness of the product, reliability of the information available, all assessed at each party in the SC. If the first two criteria can be assessed quantitatively, the last two require a more qualitative approach. As so, the success of the adoption of BC in SC for fresh fish, due to the fragile nature of the product, needs both a qualitative and a quantitative approach.

To conduct this assessment, each fish assembly package should have a unique identification number (ID number) that would be attributed at the vessel. After certifying the fish (or fish batch), it would be the unit that would flow through the SC down to the retail point and sell to a final client. All the parties involved in this chain can verify the validity of the organic certificate issued by querying the BC. When the fish changes ownership, this is recorded in the BC as well, and this enables anyone to check the provenance chain of the fish and all product information. By being recorded on the BC, every party validating the certificate is able to access this information. An auditor is also able to revoke accreditations on the level of an accreditation-body.

Although trust is difficult to assess, especially at the level of the end customer, a BC app could be developed to provide the traceability of the product (its origin, where it passed through to get to the retail point, where it stopped, how long it was at each link of the SC etc.) as well as to collect data on the satisfaction level of the customer with that availability of data and the improved trust the customer has on the SC. As this improved trust can dictate choosing one retail chain over another one, this proposed approach can provide additional information about the success of the BC initiative.

According to [69] on the international scale, seafood SC is one of the most complex and sensitive; using DNA barcoding, they revealed that as much as half of investigated food services establishments sold mislabeled seafood. With this study we claim, that BC is able to overcome this issue and provide suppliers throughout the chain as well as end-customers, with the veridical data and information of each product, by making it possible to trace backwards all the events occurring for each particular product. This opens a new frontier for future researches that could empirically investigate and provide new insights on achieving traceability for stakeholders using BC technology.

6 Conclusion

In the light of the current pandemic state, stricter measures are needed at each stage of SCs [70] for food provenance and safety. By initiating BC-based traceability process, SC actors can avoid fraudulent actions and potential corruptions, at the same time building trust with the end-customer by providing health and safety, that can be confirmed by the customer himself/herself. BC will allow stakeholders to analyze data on the travel path and duration [6], in order to be sure about location, storage conditions and each specific product lifetime information. Such a disruptive solution has the potential to significantly reduce illegal fishing, thus keeping and even driving business value. Current risks in the SC that are associated with a lack of supplier accountability and transparency of processes, could be overcome by the implementation of a BC-based traceability solution.

Being able to monitor events, processes and important data associated with a product, BC thus enables a full backward trace audit of data and creates a permanent encrypted platform for transaction and record-keeping throughout SC [71].

Regarding the BC impact assessment for SC context, the extension of traceability relevance for each element of the SC needs to be further developed. Since it is complicated to assess trust at the level of the end customer, a BC app could be developed in the future in order to provide the traceability of the product for the final consumers. However, [14] claims, that smartphones and BC alone are not enough for reliable tracking and monitoring of caught and processed fishes, thereby, other types of sensors and trackers, including IoT devices, remote sensors, and handheld DNA sequencers, could potentially help in overcoming this concern.

A possible extension of the [13] and [12] was detected as a consideration of BC adoption, as being a relevant and value-adding criterion for the final customer. Therefore, a research on the importance of the traceability feature that BC is able to provide for the end-customers could be a focus for future studies.

This pilot highlighted once again the emergence of the BC technology as a traceability and safety provider for operations and movements throughout SC's product lifecycle. At the same time, literature gaps and paths for future research were detected.

The use of a case study approach has some limitations, such as the difficulty to generalize findings. Nonetheless, the case is an example to support the development of the framework. Consequently, in further pilots or case studies with similar SC structure, the overall framework could be attempted.

References

1. Tapscott, D., Tapscott, A.: Blockchain solutions in pandemics - a call for innovation and transformation in public health. A Blockchain Research Institution Special Report (2020).
2. Tapscott, D., Tapscott, A.: Blockchain Revolution - How the Technology Behind Bitcoin and Other Cryptocurrencies is Changing the World, 2nd edn. Penguin Business, London (2019)
3. Nayak, G., Dhaigude, A.S.: A conceptual model of sustainable supply chain management in small and medium enterprises using blockchain technology. Cogent Econ. Financ. 7(1), 1667184 (2019)
4. Allen, M.: How blockchain could soon affect everyday lives (2017). https://www.swissinfo.ch/eng/joining-the-blocks_how-blockchain-could-soon-affect-everyday-lives/43003266. Accessed 18 May 2020
5. Sharma, T.: How blockchain can benefit you in your daily life (2018). https://www.blockchain-council.org/blockchain/how-blockchain-can-benefit-you-in-your-daily-life/. Accessed 06 May 2020
6. Kshetri, N.: 1 Blockchain's roles in meeting key supply chain management objectives. Int. J. Inf. Manag. 39, 80–89 (2018)
7. Rejeb, A., Keogh, J.G., Treiblmaier, H.: Leveraging the internet of things and blockchain technology in supply chain management. Future Internet 11(7), 161 (2019)
8. Sachdev, D.: Enabling data democracy in supply chain using blockchain and IoT. J. Manag. 6(1), 66–83 (2019)
9. van Hoek, R.: Exploring blockchain implementation in the supply chain. Int. J. Oper. Prod. Manag. 39(6/7/8), 829–859 (2019)
10. Montecchi, M., Plangger, K., Etter, M.: It's real, trust me! Establishing supply chain provenance using blockchain. Bus. Horiz. 62(3), 283–293 (2019)
11. Dobrovnik, M., Herold, D.M., Furst, E., Kummer, S.: Blockchain for and in logistics: what to adopt and where to start. Logistics 2(3), 18 (2018)
12. Van Hoek, R.: Developing a framework for considering blockchain pilots in the supply chain – lessons from early industry adopters. Supply Chain Manag. Int. J. 25(1), 115–121 (2020)
13. Verhoeven, P., Sinn, F., Herden, T.T.: Examples for blockchain implementations in logistics and supply chain management: exploring the mindful use of a new technology. Logistics 2(3), 20 (2018)
14. Howson, P.: Building trust and equity in marine conservation and fisheries supply chain management with blockchain. Marine Policy 115, 103873 (2020)

15. Hastig, G.M., Sodhi, M.S.: Blockchain for supply chain traceability: business requirements and critical success factors. Prod. Oper. Manag. **29**(4), 935–954 (2020)
16. Yin, R.K.: Case Study Research and Applications: Design and Methods, 6th edn. Sage Publications Inc., Thousand Oaks (2018)
17. Qian, X., Papadonikolaki, E.: Shifting trust in construction supply chains through blockchain technology. Eng. Constr. Archit. Manag. **28**(2), 584–602 (2020)
18. O'Leary, D.E.: Configuring blockchain architectures for transaction information in blockchain consortiums: the case of accounting and supply chain systems. Intell. Syst. Account. Financ. Manag. **24**(4), 138–147 (2017)
19. Wang, Y., Han, J.H., Beynon-Davies, P.: Understanding blockchain technology for future supply chains: a systematic literature review and research agenda. Supply Chain Manag. **24** (1), 62–84 (2019)
20. Li, D., Du, R., Fu, Y., Au, M.H.: Meta-key: a secure data-sharing protocol under blockchain-based decentralized storage architecture. IEEE Netw. Lett. **1**(1), 30–33 (2019)
21. Liu, J., Li, B., Chen, L., Hou, M., Xiang, F., Wang, P.: A data storage method based on blockchain for decentralization DNS. In: IEEE Third International Conference on Data Science in Cyberspace (DSC 2018), pp. 189–196. IEEE (2018)
22. Queiroz, M.M., Telles, R., Bonilla, S.H.: Blockchain and supply chain management integration: a systematic review of the literature. Supply Chain Manag. Int. J. **25**(2), 241–254 (2019)
23. Wang, J., Wu, P., Wang, X., Shou, W.: The outlook of blockchain technology for construction engineering management. Front. Eng. Manag. **4**(1), 67–75 (2017)
24. Chang, S.E., Chen, Y.C., Lu, M.F.: Supply chain re-engineering using blockchain technology: a case of smart contract based tracking process. Technol. Forecast. Soc. Change **144**, 1–1 (2019)
25. Kim, J.S., Shin, N.: The impact of blockchain technology application on supply chain partnership and performance. Sustain. (Switz.) **11**(21), 6181 (2019)
26. Cole, R., Stevenson, M., Aitken, J.: Blockchain technology: implications for operations and supply chain management. Supply Chain Manag. Int. J. **24**(4), 469–483 (2019)
27. Schuetz, S., Venkatesh, V.: Blockchain, adoption, and financial inclusion in India: research opportunities. Int. J. Inf. Manag. **52**, 101936 (2020)
28. Huang, Y., Han, W., Macbeth, D.K.: The complexity of collaboration in supply chain networks. Supply Chain Manag. **25**(3), 393–410 (2020)
29. Kshetri, N., Voas, J.: Supply chain trust. IT Prof. **21**(2), 6–10 (2019)
30. Ferreira, J., Martins, A., Gonçalves, F., Maia, R.: A blockchain and gamification approach for smart parking. In: Ferreira, J.C., Martins, A.L., Monteiro, V. (eds.) INTSYS 2018. LNICSSITE, vol. 267, pp. 3–14. Springer, Cham (2019). https://doi.org/10.1007/978-3-030-14757-0_1
31. Choi, T.M.: Blockchain-technology-supported platforms for diamond authentication and certification in luxury supply chains. Transp. Res. Part E Logist. Transp. Rev. **128**, 17–29 (2019)
32. Chalmers, D., Matthews, R., Hyslop, A.: Blockchain as an external enabler of new venture ideas: digital entrepreneurs and the disintermediation of the global music industry. J. Bus. Res. **125**, 577–591 (2019)
33. Ferreira, J.C., Martins, A.L.: Building a community of users for open market energy. Energies **11**(9), 2330 (2018)
34. Martins, J.P., Ferreira, J., Monteiro, V., Afonso, J.A., Afonso, J.L.: IoT and blockchain paradigms for EV charging system. Energies **12**, 2987 (2019)

35. Rue, H., Martino, S., Chopin, N.: Approximate Bayesian inference for latent Gaussian models by using integrated nested Laplace approximations. J. R. Stat. Soc. Ser. B Stat. Methodol. **71**(2), 319–392 (2009)
36. Caro, M.P., Ali, M.S., Vecchio, M., Giaffreda, R.: Blockchain-based traceability in agri-food supply chain management: a practical implementation. In: IoT Vertical and Topical Summit on Agriculture - Tuscany (IOT Tuscany), Tuscany, pp. 1–4 (2018)
37. Figorilli, S., et al.: A blockchain implementation prototype for the electronic open source traceability of wood along the whole supply chain. Sensors **18**, 3133 (2018)
38. Tian, F.: A supply chain traceability system for food safety based on HACCP, blockchain & Internet of Things. In: International Conference on Service Systems and Service Management, Dalian 2017, pp. 1–6 (2017)
39. Dujak, D., Sajter, D.: Blockchain applications in supply chain. In: Kawa, A., Maryniak, A. (eds.) SMART Supply Network. Springer, Cham (2019). https://doi.org/10.1007/978-3-319-91668-2_2
40. Biswas, K., Muthukkumarasamy, V., Tan, W.L.: Blockchain based wine supply chain traceability system. In: Future Technologies Conference (FTC 2017), pp. 56–62. The Science and Information Organization, UK (2017)
41. Sun, H., Fang, Y., Zou, H.: (Melody): Choosing a fit technology: understanding mindfulness in technology adoption and continuance. J. Assoc. Inf. Syst. **17**, 377–412 (2016)
42. Langer, E.J.: The Power of Mindful Learning. Addison-Wesley, Boston (1997)
43. Kamble, S.S., Gunasekaran, A., Sharma, R.: Modeling the blockchain enabled traceability in agriculture supply chain. Int. J. Inf. Manag. **52**, 101967 (2020)
44. Zhang, J.: Deploying blockchain technology in the supply chain. In: Blockchain and Distributed Ledger Technology (DLT) [Working Title], p. 16 (2019)
45. Zhao, G., et al.: Blockchain technology in agri-food value chain management: a synthesis of applications, challenges and future research directions. Comput. Ind. **109**, 83–99 (2019)
46. Liu, Z., Li, Z.: A blockchain-based framework of cross-border e-commerce supply chain. Int. J. Inf. Manag. **52**, 102059 (2020)
47. Sternberg, H.S., Hofmann, E., Roeck, D.: The struggle is real: insights from a supply chain blockchain case. J. Bus. Logist. **2020**, 1–17 (2020)
48. Higginson, M., Nadeau, M.C., Rajgopal, K.: Blockchain's Occam Problem (2019). https://www.mckinsey.com/industries/financial-services/our-insights/blockchains-occam-problem#. Accessed 29 May 2020
49. Behnke, K., Janssen, M.F.W.H.A.: Boundary conditions for traceability in food supply chains using blockchain technology. Int. J. Inf. Manag. **52**, 101969 (2020)
50. Hald, K.S., Kinra, A.: How the blockchain enables and constrains supply chain performance. Int. J. Phys. Distrib. Logist. Manag. **49**(4), 376–397 (2019)
51. Lu, Q., Xu, X., Liu, Y., Weber, I., Zhu, L., Zhang, W.: uBaaS: a unified blockchain as a service platform. Futur. Gener. Comput. Syst. **101**, 564–575 (2019)
52. Rejeb, A., Keogh, J.G., Treiblmaier, H.: How blockchain technology can benefit marketing: six pending research areas. Front. Blockchain **3**, 1–2 (2020)
53. Christopher, M.: Logistics & Supply Chain Management, 5th edn. FT Press, New Jersey (2016)
54. A Thematic Report by the European Union Blockchain Observatory and Forum: Blockchain in trade finance and supply chain (2019). https://www.eublockchainforum.eu/reports. Accessed 26 June 2020
55. Braue, D.: How blockchain could lead exports recovery (2020). https://ia.acs.org.au/article/2020/how-blockchain-could-lead-exports-recovery.html. Accessed 28 June 2020

56. Jing, Z.: Application of information technology in food storage and transportation safety management and establishment of information network integration platform for food storage and transportation safety management. In: International Conference on Information Management and Processing (ICIMP 2018), pp. 125–129. IEEE (2018)
57. Shi, P., Wang, H., Yang, S., Chen, C., Yang, W.: Blockchain-based trusted data sharing among trusted stakeholders in IoT. Softw. Pract. Exper. **2019**, 1–14 (2019)
58. European Commission – Shaping Europe's digital future (2020). https://ec.europa.eu/digital-single-market/en/blockchain-technologies. Accessed 28 June 2020
59. A Thematic Report by the European Union Blockchain Observatory and Forum: 2018–2020: Conclusions and Reflections (2020). https://www.eublockchainforum.eu/reports. Accessed 26 June 2020
60. Public Mint Homepage. https://publicmint.com/. Accessed 24 Apr 2020
61. Genesis Studio Homepage. https://genesis.studio/. Accessed 24 Apr 2020
62. Taikai Homepage. https://taikai.network/. Accessed 27 Apr 2020
63. WalliD Homepage. https://wallid.io/. Accessed 28 Apr 2020
64. Bitcliq Homepage. https://www.bitcliq.com/. Accessed 28 Apr 2020
65. Zenithwings Homepage. https://zenithwings.com/. Accessed 29 Apr 2020
66. Global Legal Insights Homepage. https://www.globallegalinsights.com/practice-areas/blockchain-laws-and-regulations/portugal#:~:text=Notwithstanding%2C%20in%20Portugal%2C%20blockchain%20technology,either%20private%20or%20public%20organisations.&text=Cryptocurrencies%20are%20thus%20not%20backed,Portugal%20(Portugal's%20central%20bank). Accessed 29 Apr 2020, Accessed 28 Apr 2020
67. SphereGen Technologies Homepage. https://www.spheregen.com/blockchain-technology-basics/. Accessed 30 Apr 2020
68. Sea Technologies, SA: https://www.xsealence.pt/. Accessed 30 Apr 2020
69. Pardo, M.Á., Jimenez, E.: DNA barcoding revealing seafood mislabeling in food services from Spain. J. Food Compos. Anal. **91**, 103521 (2020)
70. Rizou, M., Galanakis, I.M., Aldawoud, T.M., Galanakis, C.M.: Safety of foods, food supply chain and environment within the COVID-19 pandemic. Trends Food Sci. Technol. **102**, 293–299 (2020)
71. Delloite Homepage: When two chains combine supply chain meets blockchain. https://www2.deloitte.com/pt/pt/pages/consumer-industrial-products/articles/blockchain-supply-chain.html. Accessed 17 June 2020

An Integrated Lateral and Longitudinal Look Ahead Controller for Cooperative Vehicular Platooning

Enio Vasconcelos Filho[1]([✉])(iD), Ricardo Severino[1](iD), Anis Koubaa[2](iD),
and Eduardo Tovar[1](iD)

[1] CISTER Research Centre, ISEP, Rua Alfredo Allen 535, 4200-135 Porto, Portugal
{enpvf,rarss,emt}@isep.ipp
[2] Prince Sultan University, Riyadh, Saudi Arabia
akoubaa@psu.edu.sa

Abstract. Cooperative Vehicular Platooning (CoVP), has been emerging as a challenging Intelligent Traffic Systems application, promising to bring-about several safety and societal benefits. Relying on V2V communications to control such cooperative and automated actions brings several advantages. In this work, we present a Look Ahead PID controller for CoVP that solely relies upon V2V communications, together with a method to reduce the disturbance propagation in the platoon. The platooning controller also implements a solution to solve the cutting corner problem, keeping the platooning alignment. We evaluate its performance and limitations in realistic simulation scenarios, analyzing the stability and lateral errors of the CoVP, proving that such V2V enabled solutions can be effectively implemented.

Keywords: Cooperative platooning · Safety · V2V

1 Introduction

Cooperative Vehicular Platooning (CoVP) is an emerging application among the new generation of safety-critical automated vehicles that hold the promise to potentiate several benefits such as increasing road capacity and fuel efficiency and even reducing accidents. These benefits arise from groups of vehicles traveling close together, supported by vehicle-to-vehicle communication (V2V), vehicle-to-infrastructure (V2I) communication, or both (V2X). This challenging application encompasses different topics, such as cooperative control models [9], V2V and V2I communication [7], energy efficiency [13], safety, interaction with other vehicles and platoons, among others. The V2V and V2I has an important role in increasing the performance of the resulting platoons, comparing to

This work was partially supported by National Funds through FCT/MCTES (Portuguese Foundation for Science and Technology), within the CISTER Research Unit (UIDB/04234/2020).

those obtained without communication between the vehicles [10, 19]. Actually, in some cases, the AVs implementation with no communication, mixed with human driven vehicles can even decrease the traffic speed, given the acceleration profile of the AVs [1, 15]. Thus, the complexity of these systems of systems is naturally high.

Regarding the CoVP controller alone for instance, its development integrates several control areas. The error amplification and disturbance propagation in a platoon is studied in [2], where the authors analyze the problem of controlling a string of vehicles moving in a straight line. This study shows that even with a constant speed, the disturbance is propagated through the platoon, causing instability in the spacing error. Another important challenge is on how to manage the *cutting corner problem* [3], where the vehicles have the same orientation but do not follow the leader's trajectory. This is particularly important, since interestingly, several of the CoVP control models do not address lateral control, and those that do, ignore the advantage of relying upon V2X communications. A compromise is found in the work presented in [17], by proposing an integrated longitudinal and lateral controller which integrates an on-board radar sensor with V2V communication.

In [12], the authors propose an integrated lateral and longitudinal controller using the preceding vehicle acceleration, keeping the platooning safety with three main controllers. These controllers are: a feed forward controller for the string stable longitudinal control, a Corrective constraint controller and a MPC controller for the lateral problem. However, the error propagation through the platoon and the cutting corner problem are not addressed. A solution to it was proposed in [4] with a Look Ahead Controller (LAC). In this work, the controller estimates a trajectory between each leader trajectory point. However, there is a lack of research that focuses solely on V2V communications to accomplish CoVP control. This possibility is becoming increasingly scalable and viable with the advent of 5G integrated communications, and can be useful, particularly in scenarios where vehicle sensors can become impaired and provide incorrect readings, providing an extra layer of safety. In addition, relying upon V2V makes these applications more flexible and cheap, as they are not so dependant on expensive vehicle sensors. However, to enable such approach, more research is needed to fully understand its potential and limitations, for instance, on the impact of the network Quality of Service (QoS) upon the CoVP safety and performance. Nevertheless, to support such research, one needs to rely upon functional cooperative control models enabled by V2V communications in the first place. It is mostly with this in mind, that we decided to take this first step in this work.

In this paper, we propose a V2V-enabled CoVP Look Ahead Controller (LAC) with low complexity, that is able to provide good results in keeping the platoon distance, alignment and safety, reducing the impacts of the errors though the platoon and solving the cutting corner problem. The use of a well know base controller as a PID reduces the system complexity, in order to increase the system implementation in real life scenarios. The main simulator view can be observed in Fig. 1. The main contributions proposed in this work are: (1)

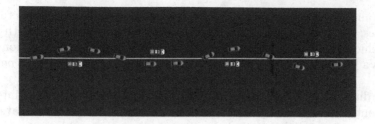

Fig. 1. Platooning view

The development of a longitudinal and lateral CoVP controller that relies only in V2V communications; (2) Improvement of the lateral controller to solve the cutting corner problem; (3) The development of a LAC strategy to increase the platoon's stability even with a large number of vehicles, reducing the disturbance propagation problem, presented in [14]; and (4) a safety analysis of the CoVP controller in a realistic scenario, with trajectory changes of the leader and obstacle avoidance. All the scenarios rely upon a robotics simulator, demonstrating that this controller and proposed mechanisms can be implemented in reality.

In the remaining of this paper, we present a problem formulation in Sect. 2, describing the platoon model. In Sect. 3, we describe the control models that were implemented and the simulation environment is presented in Sect. 4. In Sect. 5, we present the designed scenarios for the control model evaluation and an analysis about each one. The Conclusions and the suggestion for future works are presented in the last section.

2   Problem Formulation

Table 1. Definition terms

Abreviation	Meaning
i	Vehicle Identification
SV_i	Subject Vehicle i
$m_{SV_i, SV_{i+1}}$	Exchanged Messages Between The vehicles
$D_{SV_i, SV_{i+1}}$	Inter Vehicles Distance
d_{ref}	Objective Range
SD	Safety Distance
ε_i	Distance Error
$\theta_{e,i}$	Lateral Error
b_i	Bearing Error
SA_i	Steering Angle
$e\theta_{i+1}$	Lateral Error (with Bearing)

2.1   Basic Platoon Model and Stability Analysis

This work presents a CoVP model based on the ITS european standard [6], where a V2V communication model called Predecessor-Follower [11] is defined. Seeking to facilitate the understanding of the formulation proposed here, the Table 1 presents the main terms used and their nomenclatures. Each vehicle is modeled as unicycle in a Cartesian coordinate system. The platoon is composed of $i \in \mathbb{N}$ vehicles. The full set of vehicles can be defined as $SV_i = \{i \in \mathbb{N} | 0 \leq i \leq n\}$, with a set of *Subject Vehicles*, where SV_0 is the first vehicle and the platoon's Leader. Each SV_i can be a local leader of SV_{i+1} and a follower of SV_{i-1}. The platoon's model is exemplified in Fig. 2.

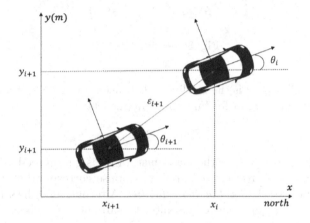

Fig. 2. Platoon model

Each SV_{i+1} receive data from SV_i, containing: the global position of SV_i - $(x_i(t), y_i(t))$, speed $(v_i(t))$, acceleration $(a_i(t))$, steering angle $(SA_i(t))$ and Heading $(\theta_i(t))$. The messages can be defined as $m_{SV_i,SV_{i+1}}(t)$, where SV_i is the sender and SV_{i+1} is the receiver. Once the vehicle SV_{i+1} receives $m_{SV_i,SV_{i+1}}(t)$, it performs the control process to accomplish the tracking goal. The SV_{i+1} should gather it's own orientation, θ_{i+1} and the inter distance between SV_i and SV_{i+1}, $d_{SV_i,SV_{i+1}}(t)$.

The inter vehicles spacing methodology is the *constant time-headway policy* (CTHP) [5], that uses the current speed of the vehicle to define the safety distance. In CTHP, the objective range (d_{ref}) in this policy is $d_{ref}(t) = SD + T_h v_i(t)$, where $SD > 0$ is the safety distance, T_h is the defined time headway, generally between 0.5 and 2 s, and $v_i(t)$ is the followers speed.

The platoon stability is defined as the spacing error between the real and the desired inter-vehicle spacing [14]. The spacing error between SV_i and SV_{i+1} can be determined using

$$\varepsilon_i(t) = d(SV_i(t), SV_{i+1}(t)) - d_{ref}, \tag{1}$$

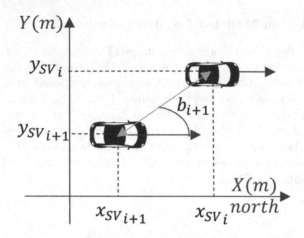

Fig. 3. Bearing error

where $d(SV_i(t), SV_{i+1}(t))$ is the Euclidian distance between $SV_i(t)$ and $SV_{i+1}(t)$. The steady state error transfer function is defined by

$$H(s) = \varepsilon_i / \varepsilon_{i-1}, \tag{2}$$

Based on the $\mathcal{L}_2$ norms, where the platoon stability is guaranteed if $\|H(s)\|_\infty \leq 1$ and $h(t) > 0$, where $h(t)$ is the impulse response corresponding to $H(s)$ [19]. This equation defines the *local platoon stability*. Alternatively, the string stability can be defined as $\mathcal{L}_\infty$, in order to guarantee the absence of overshoot for a signal while it propagates throughout the platoon. This performance metric is the same as characterized in [18], which defines the worst case performance in the sense of measuring the peak magnitude of the spacing distance between the vehicles, defining a *global platoon stability*.

2.2 Lateral Error

In a CoVP, the SV_{i+1} should perform the same path as the SV_i, based only on the received information. However, as $d_{ref}(t) \geq SD$, when SV_i is in position $(x_i(t), y_i(t))$, SV_{i+1} is in position $(x_{i+1}(t), y_{i+1}(t))$, with a speed of $(v_{i+1}(t)\cos(\theta_{i+1}(t)), v_{i+1}(t)\sin(\theta_{i+1}(t)))$, there is a *delay* between the current position of SV_{i+1} and the *desired* position of SV_i. Then, the SV_{i+1} controller will receive and store the messages $m_{SV_i, SV_{i+1}}$ from time $t - T_0$ until t, when SV_{i+1} reach the same position as SV_i in time t. The lateral error $\theta_{e,i+1}$ in the , refers to the difference between the heading of $SV_i(t - T_0)$ and $SV_{i+1}(t)$. This error is defined by

$$\theta_{e,i}(t) = \theta_{SV_i}(t - T_0) - \theta_{SV_{i+1}}(t) \tag{3}$$

The time of actuation over the SA_{i+1}, provided by $\theta_{e,i}(t)$, is responsible for the cutting corner error, since there is a difference between $(x_i(t - T_0), y_i(t - T_0))$ and $(x_{i+1}(t), y_{i+1}(t))$. This error can cause a bad alignment between SV_i and

SV_{i+1}, even with a $\theta_{e,i}(t) = 0$, given that the follower can start to perform a curve at a different instant as the leader. This bad alignment is called *bearing error*, $B_i(t)$, and can be seen in Fig. 3. The bearing error rises from accumulated lateral errors of SV_{i+1} while following SV_i particularly in curves and should be calculated when $\theta_{e,i}(t) \approx 0$. In our work, we defined this threshold as $0.15rad$. This limit was defined to indicate that the desired SV position is ahead of the current SV_i position, at a maximum angle of up to 16°. This value prevents Bearing performance from causing a correction beyond the vehicle's limits, causing instability, namely in sharp turns. The Bearing error is defined as:

$$b_i(t) = \arctan(\frac{x_i - x_{i+1}}{y_i - y_{i+1}}). \tag{4}$$

3   Control Models

We divide the implemented control methods for the SV_is in Longitudinal and Lateral controllers. Both were defined with as a low complexity PID controller model. In this work, we also propose a LAC that modifies both longitudinal and lateral controllers, increasing the platoon safety.

3.1   Longitudinal and Lateral Controllers

The longitudinal controller is responsible for ensuring the safety of the platoon, maintaining the inter distance between SV_i and SV_{i+1}, adjusting v_{i+1}. The main PID controller equation for SV_i in time t is:

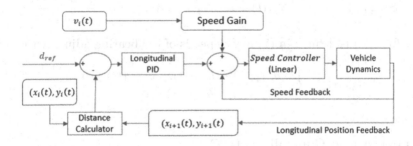

Fig. 4. Longitudinal controller model

$$v_{i+1}(t) = K_P * \varepsilon_{i+1}(t) + K_I * \int \varepsilon_{i+1}(t) + K_D * \frac{\Delta\varepsilon_{i+1}(t)}{dt}, \tag{5}$$

where K_P, K_I and K_D denote respectively the Proportional, Integrative and Derivative gain constants. The full controller is presented in Fig. 4, where we assume that the time constant of the actuator is much bigger then the time constant of the motor.

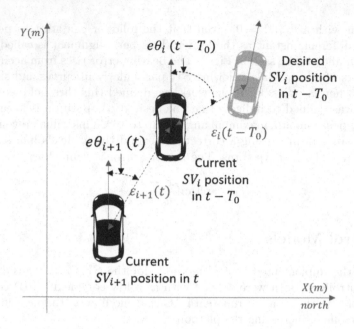

Fig. 5. The LAC consider the difference between the current position of SV_{i-1} and the desired position

The lateral controller is responsible for the vehicle's heading. The main equation of the PID controller is presented in Eq. 6.

$$SA_{i+1}(t) = K_P * e\theta_{i+1}(t) + K_I * \int e\theta_{i+1}(t) + K_D * \frac{\Delta e\theta_{i+1}(t)}{dt}, \qquad (6)$$

Where $E\theta_{i+1}(t)$ is defined in (7) and depends of the bearing adjust actuation.

$$e\theta_{i+1}(t) = \begin{cases} \theta_{e,i+1}(t) + B_{i+1}(t), & \theta_{e,i+1}(t) \le 0.15 \\ \theta_{e,i+1}(t), & \theta_{e,i+1}(t) > 0.15 \end{cases} \qquad (7)$$

3.2   Look Ahead Controller - LAC

The PID controller is typically reactive, thus, when facing a abrupt change of setpoint, the adjustment can saturate the actuator and cause oscillations or instability. In the CoVP, this effect is observed particularly after closed curves and in quick re-adjustments of speed with a cumulative effect throughout the platoon. In many situations, this effect is reduced given the nature of the test track, particularly when using only long straight roads with few curves. However, in a more realistic scenario, the oscillations of the platooning can cause instability and decrease the system's safety.

The proposed LAC adds an error information about $SV_i, i > 0$ in the controller of SV_{i+1}. This information is transmitted to SV_{i+1} in order to reduce the disturbance propagation, allowing SV_{i+1} to compare its position with SV_{i-1} position, keeping the main reference in the SV_i. This approach also avoids the need for the leader to send messages to all platoon cars, which allows the increase of the platoon's size.

As demonstrated in [4], analysing the platooning, the disadvantage from the common LAC is that the SV_{i+1} lateral position is correct only in a straight line, compared with SV_i. This leads the system to the cutting corner problem, since there is no information about the trajectory of the leader. There is also the increasing error provided by the difference between the current position of SV_{i+1} and the desired position, provided by the path performed by SV_i. Assuming that this error exist, are greater then 0 and are denoted by $\varepsilon_{i+1}(t)$ and $E\theta_{i+1}(t)$, the error between the SV_i and SV_{i+2} increases in each curve. So, the proposed look ahead incorporates the difference between the current position of SV_{i+1} and its desired position, increasing the correction to be performed by SV_{i+2}. In this case, the LAC reduces the difference between the path provided by the platoon's leader and the rest of the followers, as depicted in Fig. 5. The new errors can be defined, $\forall SV_i, i > 1$, as:

$$\varepsilon_{i+1}(t) = \varepsilon_{i+1}(t) + \varepsilon_i(t - T_0) \tag{8}$$

$$e\theta_{e,i+1}(t) = e\theta_{i+1}(t) + e\theta_i(t - T_0) \tag{9}$$

4 Simulation Environment

Given the complexity and safety-critical nature of these CoVP systems of systems, one must carry out extensive validation before any real deployment in vehicles. However, to achieve this, one must rely upon realistic simulators, that can effectively replicate the behaviour of the vehicles as close as possible. Some simulators have been presented, such as [16], where the microscopic characteristics of the CoVP can be analyzed together with the enabling communications. Also robotic testbeds [8] can enable their validation in platforms quite close to a real vehicle. In this work, we implemented the CoVP controller and associated mechanisms over the CopaDrive simulator, so that after the controller's performance evaluation, we could easily shift focus into the communications' impact as a future work. This simulation environment was built using the Robotic Operating System (ROS) in tight integration with the robotics simulator Gazebo. Vehicular communications are emulated via ROS topics using its flexible publish/subscribe middle-ware. The vehicle model is based on Toyota Prius, as used in [16], which replicates the real car main characteristics, such as acceleration, breaking, friction and weight. This model enabled us to simulate in a realistic fashion the behavior of the platooning agents in a microscopic way, analyzing issues such as wheel angles, skidding, among others. Similarly, it was also possible to analyze each vehicle's lateral deviation in detail, allowing the evaluation and improvement of the lateral controller.

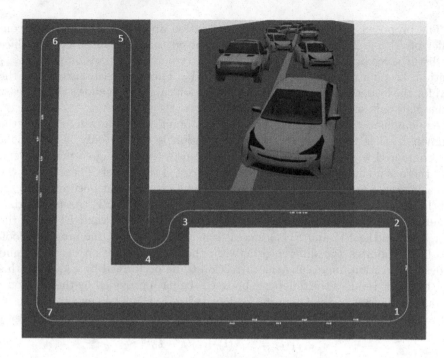

Fig. 6. City circuit

In this work, V2V communication is simulated using the ROS topics, as presented in Fig. 7, in a Linux Ubuntu 18.04.6 Bionic, with Gazebo 9.0 and ROS Melodic. The running PC has a Intel® Core® i7-975H CPU, with 16 MB RAM memory and a NVIDIA Geforce GTX 1650. Every vehicle in the platoon publishes its own information in the $car_i/TXNetwork$ in a frequency of 33 Hz - the maximum frequency proposed in [6].

Those topics are all republished by a ROS topic $Network\_Simulation$ in another topic called $car_i/RXNetwork$. So, the SV_i subscribes to the respectively $car_i/RXNetwork$ topic and perform the defined control actions. As the proposed V2V communication uses a broadcast model, every vehicle receives all the data from other vehicles in the network but only uses the corresponding SV_{i-1}. This architecture was built in order to allows the use of a network simulator in future works to represent the communications in a more realistic way.

5   Simulation Scenarios

In order to evaluate the proposed controllers four scenarios were designed, with two circuits - an Oval and a City circuit, presented in Fig. 6. Scenarios 01 and 02 present each controller feature, namely the bearing controller and the LAC, comparing the platoon safety performance with and without these controllers. Scenarios 03 and 04 presents a more realistic scenario, in a city circuit with and

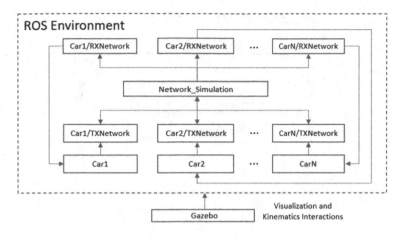

Fig. 7. Simulation architecture

without obstacles. All the scenarios represent a full lap in the designed circuit, finishing with a braking action by the platoon leader, without any crash, as visible in the video presented in https://youtu.be/Gjpg-yV0tDc. The principal scenarios parameters are presented in Table 2:

Table 2. Model parameters

Parameters	Definition
Vehicles	4 to 11
Max Steering	0.52 rad
Safety Distance (SD)	5.5 m
Time Headway (T_H)	0.5 s
Leader Speed	50 Km/h
Longitudinal: K_P, K_I, K_D	2.0, 0.005, 2.0
Lateral: K_P, K_I, K_D	2.5, 0.001, 1.0
Time between Messages	0.03 s

5.1 Scenario 01 - Bearing Test

The first scenario was designed to test the bearing adjustment of the lateral controller in an oval circuit. We performed a full lap with 4 SVs, with and without the bearing controller. The vehicles' path in each test is presented in Fig. 8. in this figure, it is possible to observe that even though with a similar trajectory, the vehicles without the bearing controller, does not follow exactly the same path in some parts of the circuit. The error is reduced in the curvature sections, but

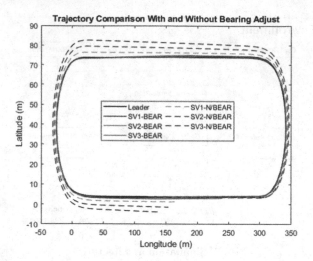

Fig. 8. Scenario 01 - bearing test

increases afterwards. As previously explained, this occurs because the heading of the $\theta_{e,i}(t)$ is near to zero, even with the cars in the wrong alignment. With the Bearing controller correction however, results are clearly much better, and the path of SVs is very close to the one performed by the Leader. In order to evaluate this performance, we can compare the average distance error for SV_3 in each test. Without the bearing controller, $\varepsilon_3 = 0.9863$ m, while using the bearing controller, this error was reduced to $\varepsilon_3 = 0.4931$ m, that indicates 50.01% improvement.

5.2 Scenario 02 - LAC

In order to evaluate the LAC performance, we carried out several laps with a 9 vehicles CoVP without the LAC. Then, we rebuilt the test using the LAC with a 11 vehicles CoVP. Figure 9 compares the trajectory of the vehicles in both situations in one lap. Without the LAC, where the SVs were able to follow the Leader, but with oscillations in the tail vehicles, namely in SV_6, SV_7 and SV_8. This oscillation is caused by the back propagation of the abrupt adjustments in the Leader's trajectories, which increases considerably with the number of vehicles in the platoon. The LAC, as depicted in Fig. 9, deals with this problem, reducing the error propagation throughout the platoon and reducing the oscillation in the vehicles' trajectory. The LAC performance can be demonstrated considering the average distance error $(AVG(\varepsilon))$ in SV_8. Without the LAC, $AVG(\varepsilon_8) = 1.523$ m, while using LAC, this error is reduced to $AVG(\varepsilon_8) = 0.7079$ m. Another improvement provided by the LAC implementation is the possibility to increase the platoon size, given that the $AVG(\varepsilon_{10}) = 1.207$ m, also reducing the error from the last vehicle in the test without the LAC in 16%.

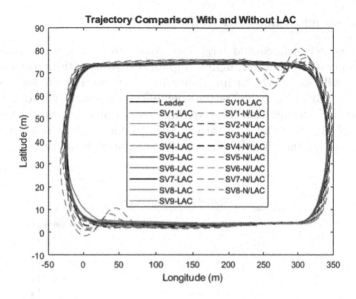

Fig. 9. Scenario 02 - Look Ahead Controller (LAC)

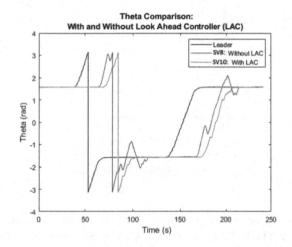

Fig. 10. Scenario 03 - Platooning curve performance

Comparing to the Leader, the lateral adjust in the last vehicles in each test also demonstrate the improvement provided by the LAC, as presented in Fig. 10, with a comparison between the SV_8 in the test without LAC and SV_{10} using the LAC. It is possible to observe that SV_{10} lateral adjusts are more smooth and have less oscillation in comparison with SV_8.

5.3 Scenario 03 - Complex Circuit

The CoVP is well defined and largely analysed in long straight roads, with easy or no curvature. However, more complex scenarios, with harder curvature, can cause oscillation and even instability in many controllers, decreasing the platoon's safety. In order to analyse our controller, using the longitudinal, lateral, bearing and LAC, we performed several laps with a platoon with 11 vehicles in the circuit of Fig. 6, without obstacles. This circuit presents some interesting challenges, namely the different direction curves, straight sections and a quite hard bend.

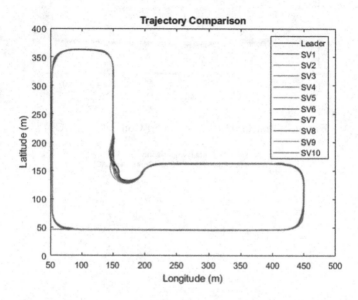

Fig. 11. Scenario 03 - vehicles path

The vehicle's trajectory is presented in Fig. 11 and demonstrated in the video in https://youtu.be/Gjpg-yV0tDc. All the SVs were able to closely copy the same path as of leader, with just a small oscillation in curve 4. Figure 12 shows the average error between the desired distance of SV_i and SV_{i+1} during the lap. As this distance never gets close to the defined SD, the platoon's safety is guaranteed, thus avoiding any collisions between the vehicles. Figure 12 also demonstrates that the average error of the vehicle's distances is close to zero, although it varies in different situations, like curves. However, even with those changes, the errors are reduced after the curves. In the selected scenario, the local stability of the platoon cannot be guaranteed by the strict criteria proposed in Sect. 2, since $\varepsilon_4/\varepsilon_3 > 1$, for instance. However, the *global* stability of the platoon can be guaranteed, since $\forall \varepsilon_i/\varepsilon_1 < 1$, for $i > 1$.

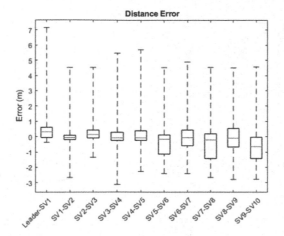

Fig. 12. Scenario 03 - vehicles inter distances

5.4   Scenario 04 - Obstacle Avoidance

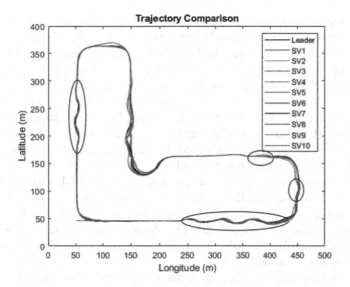

Fig. 13. Scenario 04 - vehicles path

To further push the limits of the CoVP controller, in this last scenario we included a slalom section. The Leader uses sonars to avoid 14 vehicles distributed in the circuit, as presented in Fig. 6. The path carried out by the vehicles is depicted in Fig. 13, where the blue circles indicates the track obstacles. Again, it is possible to observe that all the *SV*s closely copied the same path as the

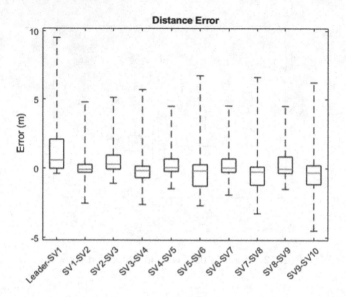

Fig. 14. Scenario 04 - vehicles inter distances

Leader, even with the many and quick shifts in orientation. A presentation of this scenario is given in https://youtu.be/4ysgAFnvWpI. In Fig. 14 it is possible to observe that even with these imposed oscillations of the Leader, the mean of the distance errors of the platoon vehicles is close to zero. However, it is also possible to observe that SV_{10} gets closer to SV_9, since the distance error increases in the negative way. This means that as the vehicles perform closed curves in sequence, the SV_{i+1} are getting closer tho the SV_i, decreasing the platoon's safety. This occurs because the desired speed is constant. So, in a sequence of turns in different directions, while the SV_i linear speed decreases, SV_{i+1} linear speed is bigger, reducing the distance between the vehicles.

Since the Leader reduce it's linear speed in curves 3 and 4, this effect is propagated through the platoon. Even with this approximation, none of the vehicles have come near to the SD. It is also possible to observe that the global platoon stability was guaranteed. This scenario also demonstrates the importance of having the lateral controller working together with the bearing adjust mechanism, in order to avoid collisions.

The platooning efficiency in this scenario also can be evaluated by the distance that the vehicles pass from the obstacles. In this case, the safety distance to the obstacles was defined as 0.5 m. The minimal, maximum and average distance between the vehicles and the obstacles are show in Fig. 15. This one also demonstrates that the average distance between the vehicles in the platoon to the obstacles is almost the same, which shows the efficiency of the algorithm and the ability of the vehicles to follows the leader's path.

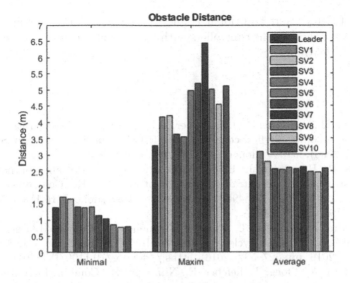

Fig. 15. Scenario 04 - obstacles distances

6   Conclusions and Future Work

In this work, we presented a V2V-enabled Look Ahead PID controller, together with a method to reduce the disturbance propagation in the platoon. The proposed platooning controller also implements a solution to solve the cutting corner problem, keeping the platooning alignment. We evaluated the performance of these mechanisms over a robotics simulator, showing that this low complexity V2V-enabled CoVP controller can be effectively implemented and its maintains its stability under several different and challenging scenarios.

The bearing adjustment mechanism and the LAC were shown to be most important to increase the stability and decrease the lateral error along the platoon, mitigating the cutting corner problem and the disturbance propagation. We believe this controller can indeed represent an excellent stepping stone towards further research, particularly to support further investigations on the communications' impact in CoVP applications. These controllers were analysed in this work under several conditions, increasing the challenges and showing the controller reliability.

The implementation of an integrated controller for the platooning based purely in V2V communications avoid some costs like the necessity of any change in the infrastructure of the road, demanding only the presence of an On Board Unity in order to transmit the measured data between the vehicles. However, the analysis about the packet loss impact should be implemented as a future work. The implemented architecture was designed in order to facilitate integration with an network simulator, like OMNET, using the ROS.

As future work, we will extend the analysis of these CoVP control mechanisms to analyze the communication's impact over the CoVP controller, in particular the effect of delays and additional traffic upon the CoVP behavior. We also aim to compare the current controllers with a machine learning approach, using reinforcement learning.

References

1. van Arem, B., van Driel, C.J.G., Visser, R.: The impact of cooperative adaptive cruise control on traffic-flow characteristics. IEEE Trans. Intell. Transp. Syst. **7**(4), 429–436 (2006). https://doi.org/10.1109/TITS.2006.884615
2. Barooah, P., Hespanha, J.: Error amplification and disturbance propagation in vehicle strings with decentralized linear control. In: IEEE Conference on Decision and Control 2005, pp. 4964–4969 (2005). https://doi.org/10.1109/CDC.2005. 1582948. ISSN: 0191-2216
3. Bayuwindra, A., Aakre, O.L., Ploeg, J., Nijmeijer, H.: Combined lateral and longitudinal CACC for a unicycle-type platoon. In: IEEE Intelligent Vehicles Symposium (IV) 2016, pp. 527–532 (2016). https://doi.org/10.1109/IVS.2016.7535437
4. Bayuwindra, A., Ploeg, J., Lefeber, E., Nijmeijer, H.: Combined longitudinal and lateral control of car-like vehicle platooning with extended look-ahead. IEEE Trans. Control Syst. Technol. **28**, 1–14 (2019). https://doi.org/10.1109/TCST. 2019.2893830
5. di Bernardo, M., Salvi, A., Santini, S.: Distributed consensus strategy for platooning of vehicles in the presence of time-varying heterogeneous communication delays. IEEE Trans. Intell. Transp. Syst. **16**(1), 102–112 (2015). https://doi.org/ 10.1109/TITS.2014.2328439
6. European Telecommunications Standards Institute: ETSI TR 103 299 V2.1.1 Intelligent Transport Systems (ITS); Cooperative Adaptive Cruise Control (CACC); Pre-standardization study. Technical report, European Telecommunications Standards Institute (2019)
7. Fernandes, P., Nunes, U.: Platooning with IVC-enabled autonomous vehicles: strategies to mitigate communication delays, improve safety and traffic flow. IEEE Trans. Intell. Transp. Syst. **13**(1), 91–106 (2012). https://doi.org/10.1109/TITS. 2011.2179936
8. Filho, E.V., et al.: Towards a cooperative robotic platooning testbed. In: IEEE International Conference on Autonomous Robot Systems and Competitions (ICARSC), Ponta Delgada, Portugal, pp. 332–337 (2020). https://doi.org/10.1109/ ICARSC49921.2020.9096132
9. Gong, S., Du, L.: Cooperative platoon control for a mixed traffic flow including human drive vehicles and connected and autonomous vehicles. Transp. Res. Part B: Methodol. **116**, 25–61 (2018). https://doi.org/10.1016/j.trb.2018.07.005
10. Jia, D., Lu, K., Wang, J.: A disturbance-adaptive design for VANET-enabled vehicle platoon. IEEE Trans. Veh. Technol. **63**(2), 527–539 (2014). https://doi.org/10. 1109/TVT.2013.2280721
11. Karoui, O., Khalgui, M., Koubâa, A., Guerfala, E., Li, Z., Tovar, E.: Dual mode for vehicular platoon safety: simulation and formal verification. Inf. Sci. **402**, 216–232 (2017). https://doi.org/10.1016/j.ins.2017.03.016
12. Kianfar, R., Ali, M., Falcone, P., Fredriksson, J.: Combined longitudinal and lateral control design for string stable vehicle platooning within a designated lane. In: IEEE Conference on Intelligent Transportation Systems (ITSC) 2014, pp. 1003–1008 (2014). https://doi.org/10.1109/ITSC.2014.6957819. ISSN: 2153-0017

13. Luo, F., Larson, J., Munson, T.: Coordinated platooning with multiple speeds. Transp. Res. Part C: Emerg. Technol. **90**, 213–225 (2018). https://doi.org/10.1016/j.trc.2018.02.011
14. Seiler, P., Pant, A., Hedrick, K.: Disturbance propagation in vehicle strings. IEEE Trans. Autom. Control **49**(10), 1835–1841 (2004). https://doi.org/10.1109/TAC.2004.835586
15. Talebpour, A., Mahmassani, H.S.: Influence of connected and autonomous vehicles on traffic flow stability and throughput. Transp. Res. Part C: Emerg. Technol. **71**, 143–163 (2016). https://doi.org/10.1016/j.trc.2016.07.007
16. Vieira, B., Severino, R., Filho, E.V., Koubaa, A., Tovar, E.: COPADRIVe - a realistic simulation framework for cooperative autonomous driving applications. In: IEEE International Conference on Connected Vehicles and Expo - ICCVE 2019, Graz, Austria, pp. 1–6 (2019). https://doi.org/10.1109/ICCVE45908.2019.8965161
17. Wei, S., Zou, Y., Zhang, X., Zhang, T., Li, X.: An integrated longitudinal and lateral vehicle following control system with radar and vehicle-to-vehicle communication. IEEE Trans. Veh. Technol. **68**(2), 1116–1127 (2019). https://doi.org/10.1109/TVT.2018.2890418
18. Zhao, Y., Minero, P., Gupta, V.: On disturbance propagation in leader-follower systems with limited leader information. Automatica **50**(2), 591–598 (2014). https://doi.org/10.1016/j.automatica.2013.11.029. https://linkinghub.elsevier.com/retrieve/pii/S0005109813005463
19. Öncü, S., van de Wouw, N., Heemels, W.P.M.H., Nijmeijer, H.: String stability of interconnected vehicles under communication constraints. In: IEEE Conference on Decision and Control (CDC) 2012, Maui, HI, USA, pp. 2459–2464 (2012). https://doi.org/10.1109/CDC.2012.6426042. ISSN: 0743-1546

Impact of Charging Infrastructure Surroundings on Temporal Characteristics of Electric Vehicle Charging Sessions

Milan Straka[1]([✉])(iD), Ľuboš Buzna[1,2](iD), and Gijs van der Poel[3](iD)

[1] Department of Mathematical Methods and Operations Research,
Faculty of Management Science and Informatics, University of Žilina,
Univerzitná 8215/1, Žilina, Slovakia
{milan.straka,lubos.buzna}@fri.uniza.sk

[2] Department of International Research Projects - ERAdiate+,
University of Žilina, Univerzitná 8215/1, Žilina, Slovakia

[3] ElaadNL, Utrechtseweg 310 (bld. 42B), 6812 AR Arnhem (GL), The Netherlands

Abstract. In this paper, we apply a data-driven approach to analyse the temporal characteristics of charging sessions performed at a slow charging infrastructure. By using the variable selection ability of the Lasso method, combined with the bootstrap driven post-selection inference, we evaluate measures quantifying the potential impacts of charging infrastructure surroundings. We derive the description of the surroundings of the charging infrastructure from several publicly available datasets, representing social, demographic, business and physical environments. From the temporal characteristics, we focus on the average and standard deviation of the connection and charging time. We uncover a non-linear relationship between the connection time and the charging time. The main driving factors behind the connection time are linked with the employment-related predictors and certain types of traffic influencing the variation of the connection time. The charging time is mainly affected by the economic wealth of residents. This study extends the knowledge about the electric vehicle driver charging behaviour and can be used to inform charging infrastructure deployment strategies.

Keywords: Electric vehicles · Smart charging · Data analysis · Temporal characteristics

This document is a result of the Operational Program Integrated Infrastructure 2014–2020 "Innovative solutions for propulsion, power and safety components of transport vehicles" code ITMS313011V334, co-financed by the European Regional Development Fund. It was partly supported by the research project VEGA 1/0089/19 "Data analysis methods and decisions support tools for service systems supporting electric vehicles", APVV-19-0441 "Allocation of limited resources to public service systems with conflicting quality criteria" and by Slovak Research and Development Agency under the contract no. SK-IL-RD-18-005.

A. L. Martins et al. (Eds.): INTSYS 2020, LNICST 364, pp. 160–174, 2021.
https://doi.org/10.1007/978-3-030-71454-3_10

1   Introduction

It is expected, that the electrification could contribute to the decarbonisation of transport and energy systems. With potentially zero emissions, electric vehicles (EVs) are an alternative to internal combustion engine (ICE) vehicles, additionally decreasing the noise pollution [1].

Charging behaviour of EV drivers is not aligned with the refuelling patterns of ICE vehicles. The fast charging stations, primarily used for long trips, are not as well utilised as slow charging stations [2]. According to [3], 95% of public charging infrastructure will be slow charging stations in 2030, compared to the current 70%. Hence, more research is required to better understand the charging patterns observed at a slow charging infrastructure.

1.1   Previous Relevant Work

Slow charging stations, compared to fast charging stations, offer higher flexibility to the electrical grid, as often just a fraction of the time that an EV is plugged into a station, is really used for charging. The length of the period when an EV is plugged into a charging station is here referred to as connection time. The part of this period during which is the EV receiving energy is denoted as the charging time. The difference between the connection and the charging time, called an idle time, may take longer than the charging time, e.g. due to the use of free parking at charging stations, forcing other EV drives to search for charging opportunities elsewhere, while decreasing the utilisation of charging infrastructure.

Although there have already been studies utilising GIS data, typically they do not use a broad range of predictors and are limited to datasets with a small number of charging events. Often, data-driven studies use GPS data from vehicles with a combustion engine to build the EV charging infrastructure [16], but this can lead to inaccurate results as the behaviour of EV users may differ. In recent years, also data-driven studies utilising larger EV charging datasets have emerged [31], proposing how to expand the existing charging infrastructure while aiming at its efficient use. A review paper [9], explores the preferences of EV users in relation to charging infrastructure while reporting on papers that include socio-economic and GIS data which are utilised to improve the location of public charging infrastructure. Among the first publications utilising socio-economic data for charging station placement is Ref. [8], where authors aim at covering the night- and day-charging demand. A GIS based charging station location approach, considering a few GIS criteria mostly related to risk, is provided in [7]. Another GIS data-based study proposing a methodology on how to locate EV charging stations at both, low-and high-level spatial scales, was provided in [5].

In [17] authors addressed the problem of estimating idle times while applying the Random Forest, Gradient Boosting and XGBoost methods using characteristics of charging sessions as predictors. The most influential predictors turned out to be start time of charging sessions, ID of EV drivers identification card, and total charged energy. The only predictor used in the study that is describing the surroundings of charging infrastructure was the type of the closest road segment. A similar analysis including more factors characterising the vicinity of charging infrastructure was conducted by Pevec et al. [25]. Authors use historical charging data, GIS data as points of interests and driving distances between charging stations to predict the utilisation of charging infrastructure and provide recommendations where to deploy charging stations.

Prediction of the EV charging infrastructure popularity with GIS data and charging infrastructure parameters by logistic regression with l_1 regularisation, Gradient Boosted Regression Trees and Random Forests methods was performed in [28]. Together with the predictive ability of the methods, authors also evaluated the influence and significance of individual predictors using the logistic regression with l_1 regularisation, where the largest impact was attributed to the residential areas and charging infrastructure parameters such as the roll-out strategy, maximum charging power and the number of other charging stations located in the proximity. Authors in [30] performed a similar study to explore the relationship between the energy consumption of charging infrastructure using the Lasso method and the GIS data describing the charging infrastructure environment. The most influential factors identified by this study are pointing at the economic prosperity of inhabitants living and working in the proximity of the charging infrastructure. Authors also applied various stratification of the charging infrastructure, where the city size returned the most promising results.

1.2 Our Contribution

In this paper, we extend the previous studies [28,30], by analysing the temporal characteristics of charging sessions. We use the Lasso method combined with the post-selection inference to identify the predictors characterising the surroundings of the charging infrastructure that are potentially influencing the temporal properties of charging sessions, specifically the connection and the charging time and their variability. Moreover, the identified features are interpreted and compared with the previous studies.

2 Data

2.1 Terminology

A document [21], issued by the Dutch authorities, proposes a unified terminology for the electromobility field. It states that a charging station may consist of several charging points. A charging point must be equipped by at least one connector, where only one connector can be used at time to charge an EV. The term charging pool denotes a set of charging stations, which share the same address and the same operator. Since we are interested to investigate the influence of surroundings of charging infrastructure, we consider charging pools as the study objects.

2.2 EVnetNL Dataset

The EVnetNL dataset contains over one million charging transactions, performed on around 1700 charging pools, by more than 50000 EV drivers. The charging pools are spread across the whole Netherlands. The first transaction was recorded in January 2012 and the most recent one in March 2016. The dataset consists of two database tables, the first is named Charging transactions. The second, named Meterreadings, contains meter reading records collected with a frequency of 15 min. All the charging pools offer slow charging, with the maximum charging power of 11 kW. In the analysis we consider only transactions performed in 2015, as this is the first and the only complete year, contained in the EVnetNL dataset when the number of EV drivers and charging pools was relatively stable. A more detailed description of the dataset can be found in Ref. [30].

2.3 Geospatial Datasets

We gathered open GIS data from various sources to model the surroundings of charging pools. Table 1 provides a brief overview of the used datasets. More elaborated descriptions are available in Ref. [30].

Table 1. Overview of collected GIS datasets.

Dataset	Brief description	Source
Population cores	Detailed population data at the resolution of municipalities	[20]
Neighbourhoods	Population data aggregated to the level of statistical units called neighbourhoods	[19]
Land use	Land use data (organised in 25 categories) modelled by high resolution polygons	[18]
Energy	Aggregated natural gas and electricity consumption of companies and households	[6]
Liveability	General index describing the quality of living in 5 categories (housing, residential area, services, safety, and living environment) at the level of neighbourhoods	[13]
Traffic flows	Database of traffic volumes (cars, buses and trucks) on individual road segments	[26]
LandScan	Ambient population density in the raster format	[15]
OpenStreetMap	OpenStreetMap (OSM) points of interest (POI)	[23]
Charging pools 2015	Locations of charging pools in 2015	[22, 24]

3   Methods

3.1   Data Processing

The GIS data were processed using circular buffers with 350 m radius centred at the locations of charging pools. Predictors were extracted from the data in vector and raster formats using attribute values and estimating their values for the buffer areas by applying the methodology which is detailed in [29]. From the POI data, the minimum distance from the charging pool to the POI and the number of POIs inside the buffer were calculated. From the GIS data, we obtained a matrix with 195 predictors.

The following response vectors were extracted from the EVnetNL dataset: average connection time, standard deviation of connection time, average charging time and the standard deviation of charging time. To obtain these quantities we grouped the charging transactions by charging pools and calculated the elements of response vectors, one for each charging pool.

Based on [4,12,14] we formed a data processing procedure displayed in Fig. 1. First, we excluded from further analysis predictors with more than 95% zero values, i.e. those which carry a small information value [14, p. 44]. To mitigate the multicollinearity we at first removed the predictors with Pearson's correlation coefficient $\rho \geq 0.95$, and in the next step iteratively removed predictors with highest variance inflation factor (VIF) value, until all the VIF values were below 10. After exploring the basic transformations from the set $\sqrt{\boldsymbol{y}}, \log(\boldsymbol{y}), \boldsymbol{y}^2, \boldsymbol{y}^3$ to the response vector $\boldsymbol{y}$ with the ordinary least squares (OLS) model, we found out the transformation $log(\boldsymbol{y})$ returned the highest R^2. So from now on, we will consider the response variable $\boldsymbol{y}$ to be log transformed. After the processing, the data matrix has 1256 rows (observations) and 119 columns (predictors).

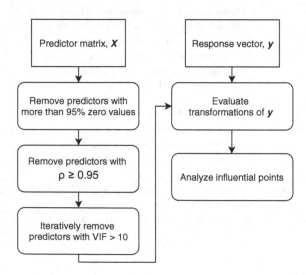

Fig. 1. Data processing procedure.

3.2   The Lasso Method and Statistical Inference

For the collection of n observations of predictor and response variables $\{(\boldsymbol{x}_i, y_i)\}_{i=1}^n$, the Lasso method [12, p. 219] solves the following optimisation problem

$$\underset{\beta_0, \beta}{\text{minimize}} \left\{ \frac{1}{2n} \sum_{i=1}^n (y_i - \beta_0 - \sum_{j=1}^p x_{ij}\beta_j)^2 + \lambda \sum_{j=1}^p |\beta_j| \right\}, \qquad (1)$$

where $\lambda \geq 0$ is the hyperparameter, the scalar β_0 (intercept) and the vector β are optimisation variables, also called regression coefficients. The first term represents the least squares objective function and the second is the penalty function. Hence, the parameter λ determines a trade-off between the goodness of the fit and the number regression coefficients with non-zero value (variable selection).

We determine the value of the hyperparameter λ in Eq. (1) using the k-fold cross-validation [10], where we select the λ with the smallest MSE, denoted as λ^{CV} and the corresponding coefficients we denote as $\hat{\beta}_0^{CV}$ and $\hat{\beta}^{CV}$.

Due to the adaptive nature of the Lasso method, it is difficult to estimate the p-values. From the available approaches, we selected the bootstrap [10, p. 142], which was also recommended as a suitable method for assessing the stability of coefficient after the application of the Lasso method in [11]. With the bootstrap, we create a number samples of the original dataset and we apply k-fold cross-validation to each of them. This gives us an estimate of the distribution of regression coefficients $\hat{\beta}^{CV}$. For each coefficient, we evaluate the number of cases when the coefficient took a non-zero value and the consistency of its sign to assess the significance of the corresponding predictor [10, p. 153].

4   Results

4.1   Software Libraries and Settings

The data were processed in R language with packages *sf*, *raster* and *osmar* and we used the implementation of the Lasso method in the *glmnet* package. The number of folds in the cross-validation was set to 10. To determine the value of the hyperparameter λ by the cross-validation procedure combined with the Lasso method, we searched through the values 10^i, for i ranging from -4 to 0, in steps of 0.02. To sample the distribution of regression coefficients, we used 1000 bootstrap samples of the data as the input for the Lasso method.

4.2   Preliminary Analyses

We examined the distribution of all four response vectors, which we display in Fig. 2. It should be noted that the connection time is longer and varies more than the charging time. When looking at individual charging sessions, the charging time is similar to connection time mostly in cases when the connection time is short. This can be seen in Fig. 3, which shows a nonlinear relationship between the connection time and the charging time. To improve the readability of the scatter plot, we used the log-normal scale. Different charging rates of EVs and a simple fact that afterwards an EV is fully charged the connection time grows while the charging time does not, shape the nonlinear relationship.

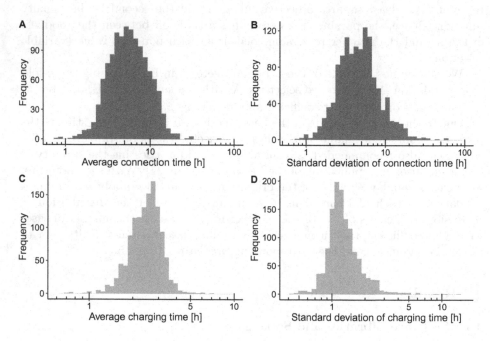

Fig. 2. Histograms of considered response variables attributed to charging pools after applying the function $log_{10}(y)$. **A** The average connection time. **B** The standard deviation of the connection time. **C** The average charging time. **D** The standard deviation of the charging time.

In Table 2 we show the coefficient of determination R^2 of the fit between the individual response vectors and the predictor matrix using the ordinary least squares method. It is notable that with the available data the connection time is better explainable than the charging time.

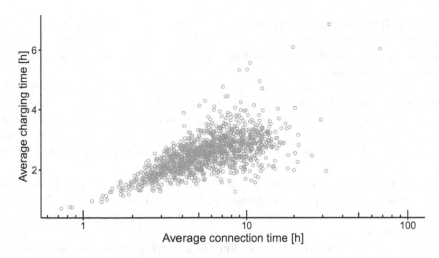

Fig. 3. Scatter plot of the average charging time vs. the average connection time at charging pools after applying the function $log_{10}(y)$. The log-normal scale improves the readability of the plot and emphasises a nonlinear relationship between these two quantities.

Table 2. The R^2 obtained by regressing the response vectors with the predictor matrix using the ordinary least squares method.

Response vector	R^2
Average connection time	0.327
Standard deviation of connection time	0.304
Average charging time	0.252
Standard deviation of charging time	0.163

4.3 Explaining the Temporal Characteristics of Charging Sessions with the Surroundings of the Charging Pools

To be able to compare multiple regression coefficients and to evaluate the influence of individual predictors, we standardised each element of $\hat{\beta}^{CV}$ by dividing it by the sample standard deviation of the corresponding predictor bootstrap sample. Standardised coefficients value shows, how much does the response changes if a predictor changes by one standard deviation. With the absolute value of a standardised coefficient increases the corresponding predictor's potential impact on the response variable [27, p. 372].

The sign of some regression coefficients tends to change across samples, which can be attributed to the low significance of the corresponding predictors and the simultaneous selection of correlated predictors [10, p. 144]. Therefore, we consider as significant those predictors, where the number of cases when the coefficient is equal to zero is less than 5% of all samples and the number of samples with the opposite sign to the sign of the median is negligible. To get a broader view on results, in Fig. 4–5 we show predictors having value zero at maximum in 10% of samples ordered descendingly by the median value of bootstrap realisations.

We can see that the number of significant coefficients is decreasing with R^2, presented in Table 2. It is worth noting that if predictors representing the minimum distance of certain objects from a charging pool have a positive coefficient, the proximity of the object has a negative impact on the response vector and the response value increases with the distance of the object from the charging pool.

For easier understanding, we divide significant predictors into three categories, namely demographics, businesses and physical environment. The minus sign in the brackets $(-)$ indicates the negative impact of the feature on the response variable.

For the average connection time we find the following predictors as significant:

- *Demographics:* percentage of employed residents working in the wholesale, ICT, finance, and non-commercial sector, net number of immigrants,
- *Businesses:* number of financial and real estate businesses, density of the work-related OSM amenities, density of food OSM amenities $(-)$,
- *Physical environment:* area taken by the open wet natural terrain and water, railway, terrain for retail and catering industry $(-)$, area taken by roads $(-)$, area taken by sports fields $(-)$, density of OSM amenities related to education $(-)$.

The largest positive impact on the average connection time has the area taken by the open natural terrain and water, which spreads primarily over the more developed western parts of the Netherlands, where also the four biggest Dutch cities are located. Residents employed in well-paying working sectors, and the work-related OSM amenities, which are not too close to the charging pool, have both positive influences, as well as the financial and real estate businesses. It points to the longer connection times observed at charging pools situated at locations where EV drivers tend to charge during the work. From the view of the physical environment, a positive impact has the proximity of the railway infrastructure. The negative impact has the presence of educational OSM amenities, sport fields, and terrain for retail and catering industry, i.e. locations where EV drivers tend to park for a short time and thus are not suitable for slow charging. Moreover, the negative impact is also associated with charging pools surrounded by the dense road infrastructure.

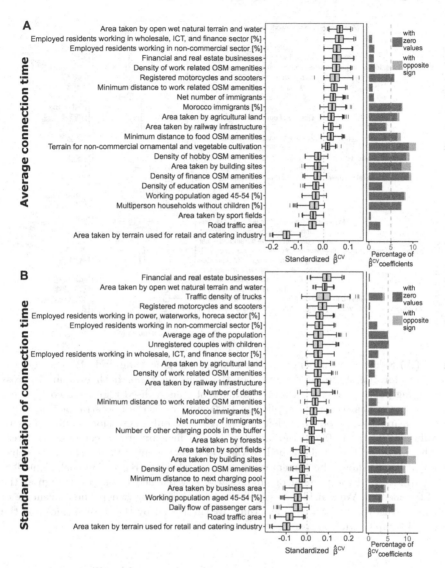

Fig. 4. (**A**) Selected regression coefficients for the average connection time and (**B**) the selected coefficients for the standard deviation of the connection time, both evaluated across the charging pools. The empirical distributions of standardised regression coefficients, obtained by the Lasso method applied to 1000 samples of the bootstrapped data, are displayed using Tukey's box plot (left panel). We show only regression coefficients with zero value in less than 10% of the samples. The coefficients are descendingly ordered, from the largest to the smallest median value of a coefficient sample. The stacked bar plot (right panel) shows the percentage of samples when the regression coefficient $\hat{\beta}^{CV}$ was set to zero and the number of samples where it reached the opposite sign as the sign of the median. We consider as significant those predictors where the percentage of coefficients with the zero value is less than 5% (indicated by the dashed line) and the number of samples with opposite sign is small.

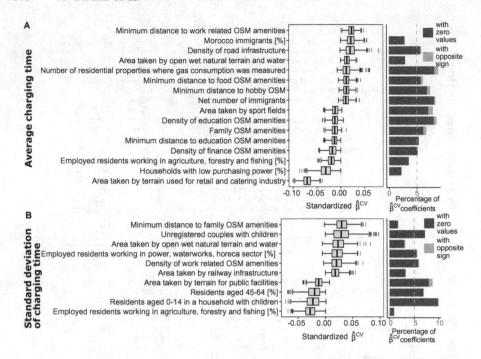

Fig. 5. (**A**) Selected coefficients for the average charging time and (**B**) the selected coefficients for the standard deviation of the charging time, both evaluated across the charging pools. The empirical distributions of standardised regression coefficients, obtained by the Lasso method applied to 1000 samples of the bootstrapped data, are displayed using Tukey's box plot (left panel). We show only regression coefficients with zero value in less than 10% of the samples. The coefficients are descendingly ordered, from the largest to the smallest median value of a coefficient sample. The stacked bar plot (right panel) shows the percentage of samples when the regression coefficient $\hat{\beta}^{CV}$ was set to zero and the number of samples where it reached the opposite sign as the sign of the median. We consider as significant those predictors where the percentage of coefficients with the zero value is less than 5% (indicated by the dashed line) and the number of samples with opposite sign is small.

For the standard deviation of the connection time, we identified the following predictors as significant:

- *Demographics:* percentage of employed residents working in the wholesale, ICT, finance, non-commercial, power, waterworks, and horeca (hotel/ restaurant/ cafe) sector, the number of registered motorcycles and scooters, average age of the population, net number of immigrants, percentage of working population aged 45–54 (−),
- *Business:* number of financial and real estate businesses, density of the work-related OSM amenities,

– *Physical environment:* area taken by agricultural land, railway, terrain for retail and catering industry (−), roads (−), businesses (−) and the minimum distance to the work-related OSM amenities.

For the standard deviation of the connection time we find similar coefficients as for the average connection time. In addition, we got the number of registered motorcycles and scooters and traffic density of trucks, indicating that higher intensity of certain type of road traffic in the proximity of charging pools, increases the variance of the connection times. The size of the area taken by businesses, terrain for retail and catering industry tend to decrease the variability in the connection times, representing locations where EV drivers typically park for a specific time, which does not vary much across different cases.

Analysis of the average charging time revealed the following predictors as significant:

– *Demographics:* percentage of Morocco immigrants, residents employed in agriculture, forestry and fishing sector (−), percentage of households with low purchasing power (−),
– *Business:* minimum distance to the work-related OSM amenities (−), density of finance OSM amenities,
– *Physical environment:* area taken by open wet natural terrain and water, area taken by terrain for retail and catering industry (−).

In difference to the connection time, the charging time has larger variance (see Fig. 2), what is most likely caused by different battery capacities and different state of charge when the charging of EVs is initiated. Surprisingly, the highest impact have the percentage of Morocco immigrants and area taken by open wet natural terrain and water. Obviously, both these predictors represent a proxy for some other hidden effects that get expressed through them. For example, higher presence of the open wet natural terrain and water is in the western part of the Netherlands, where also the largest cities are located. Considerable negative impact has area taken by terrain for retail and catering industry and proximity of the work-related OSM amenities. Here, we also see the possible impact of the wealth of residents, represented by the percentage of households with low purchasing power, and the percentage of residents with less paid occupation (agriculture, forestry and fishing).

For the standard deviation of the charging time the following predictors are significant:

– *Demographics:* residents working in agriculture, forestry and fishing industries,
– *Business:* the minimum distance to the work-related OSM amenities (−), density of finance OSM amenities,
– *Physical environment:* area taken by the open wet natural terrain and water, area taken by railway infrastructure, the minimum distance to family OSM amenities (−).

Similar predictors are linked with the standard deviation of the charging time as with the average charging time. Besides, the standard deviation gets influenced by the proximity of a railway.

4.4   Comparison with the Previous Studies

In this study, we evaluated the response vectors expressed per one charging transaction, providing a different point of view on EV charging compared to Ref. [30]. For the charging time, we found only a few significant predictors that are similar to those observed for the consumed energy and connection time. Noteworthy, the connection time is associated with a few additional predictors, e.g. the minimum distance to work or family related OSM amenities.

5   Conclusions and Discussion

In this study, we applied the Lasso method together with the post-selection inference to identify characteristics of charging infrastructure surroundings (described by predictors) that are potentially influencing the temporal characteristic of EV charging sessions.

We found out, that the connection time and charging time on charging pools exhibit a nonlinear relationship, possibly caused by the fact that battery is often fully charged long before an EV departure. The arithmetic average and the standard deviation of the connection time, are mostly affected by the working sector of residents and the work-related amenities, as well as the road density. In particular, a certain type of traffic flows present in the vicinity of charging pools appear to be influencing the variation of the connection time. In the case of the arithmetic average of the charging time at charging pools, significant predictors point to the wealth of individuals. The standard deviation of the charging times exhibits only four significant coefficients. By looking at the selected coefficients and the values of R^2 for individual variables in Table 2, we can conclude that the connection time can be better explained than the charging time from the surroundings of the charging infrastructure. This suggests that the parking behaviour, which is to large extent determining the connection time, is more influenced by the surroundings of the charging infrastructure than the state of charge at the time when an EV charging is initiated, which is strongly driving the charging time.

This study not only extends the available knowledge about the charging behaviour of EV drivers but can be also used to improve charging infrastructure deployment strategies, e.g. by utilising the information about the significant predictors in the design of predictive and prescriptive data analytic models. As future work, we recommend to identify of clusters of charging pools, e.g. to capture occasional, home and work charging and to study for them more precisely how the surroundings of charging infrastructure influence the charging behaviour of EV drivers.

References

1. Cazzola, P., Gorner, M., Schuitmaker, R., Maroney, E.: Global EV outlook 2016. Technical report, International Energy Agency, France (2016)
2. Cazzola, P., Gorner, M., Schuitmaker, R., Maroney, E.: Global EV outlook 2017: Two million and counting. Technical report, International Energy Agency (2017)
3. Cazzola, P., Gorner, M., Schuitmaker, R., Maroney, E.: Global EV outlook 2019: scaling-up the transition to electric mobility. Technical report, International Energy Agency (2019)
4. Chatterjee, S., Hadi, A.S.: Regression Analysis by Example. Wiley, Hoboken (2015)
5. Csiszár, C., Csonka, B., Földes, D., Wirth, E., Lovas, T.: Urban public charging station locating method for electric vehicles based on land use approach. J. Transp. Geogr. **74**, 173–180 (2019)
6. Nationale EnergieAtlas: Energy Atlas. https://www.pdok.nl/introductie/-/article/cbs-aardgas-en-elektriciteitsleveri-1. Accessed 16 Oct 2018
7. Erbaş, M., Kabak, M., Özceylan, E., Çetinkaya, C.: Optimal siting of electric vehicle charging stations: a GIS-based fuzzy multi-criteria decision analysis. Energy **163**, 1017–1031 (2018)
8. Frade, I., Ribeiro, A., Gonçalves, G., Antunes, A.P.: Optimal location of charging stations for electric vehicles in a neighborhood in Lisbon, Portugal. Transp. Res. Rec. **2252**(1), 91–98 (2011)
9. Hardman, S., et al.: A review of consumer preferences of and interactions with electric vehicle charging infrastructure. Transp. Res. Part D: Transp. Environ. **62**, 508–523 (2018)
10. Hastie, T., Tibshirani, R., Wainwright, M.: Statistical Learning With Sparsity: The Lasso And Generalizations. Chapman and Hall/CRC, Boca Raton (2015)
11. Hsu, D.: Identifying key variables and interactions in statistical models of building energy consumption using regularization. Energy **83**, 144–155 (2015). https://doi.org/10.1016/j.energy.2015.02.008
12. James, G., Witten, D., Hastie, T., Tibshirani, R.: An Introduction to Statistical Learning: With Applications in R. Springer, New York (2014). https://doi.org/10.1007/978-1-4614-7138-7
13. Koninkrijksrelaties, M.v.B.Z.e.: Liveability Meter. https://data.overheid.nl/dataset/leefbaarometer-2-0---meting-2016. Accessed 15 Oct 2018
14. Kuhn, M., Johnson, K.: Applied predictive modeling. Springer (2013)
15. ORN Laboratory: Landscan Datasets. https://landscan.ornl.gov/landscan-datasets. Accessed 20 May 2018
16. Liu, Q., Liu, J., Le, W., Guo, Z., He, Z.: Data-driven intelligent location of public charging stations for electric vehicles. J. Clean. Prod. **232**, 531–541 (2019)
17. Lucas, A., Barranco, R., Refa, N.: EV idle time estimation on charging infrastructure, comparing supervised machine learning regressions. Energies **12**(2), 269 (2019)
18. Netherlands CBS: CBS land cover. https://www.pdok.nl/introductie/-/article/statistics-netherlands-land-use-2015. Accessed 14 Nov 2017
19. Netherlands CBS: Neighbourhoods Dataset 2015. https://www.cbs.nl/nl-nl/dossier/nederland-regionaal/geografische-data/wijk-en-buurtkaart-2015. Accessed 20 Aug 2018
20. Netherlands CBS: Population cores in the Netherlands. https://www.cbs.nl/nl-nl/achtergrond/2014/13/bevolkingskernen-in-nederland-2011. Accessed 17 Nov 2017

21. Netherlands Enterprise Agency: Electric vehicle charging - definitions and explanation (2019). https://bit.ly/2LehwPk. Accessed 19 June 2019
22. OpenChargeMap. https://openchargemap.org. Accessed 10 Jan 2019
23. OpenStreetMap. https://www.openstreetmap.org. Accessed 13 Feb 2019
24. OplaadPalen. https://www.oplaadpalen.nl/. Accessed 20 Feb 2019
25. Pevec, D., Babic, J., Kayser, M.A., Carvalho, A., Ghiassi-Farrokhfal, Y., Podobnik, V.: A data-driven statistical approach for extending electric vehicle charging infrastructure. Int. J. Energy Res. **42**(9), 3102–3120 (2018)
26. National Institute for Public Health and the Environment: Traffic flows database. http://www.rivm.nl/. Accessed 07 Jan 2019. The database was provided for research purposes by the National Institute for Public Health and Environment
27. Siegel, A.: Practical Business Statistics. Academic Press, Cambridge (2016)
28. Straka, M., et al.: Predicting popularity of electric vehicle charging infrastructure in urban context. IEEE Access **8**, 11315–11327 (2020). https://doi.org/10.1109/ACCESS.2020.2965621
29. Straka, M., Buzna, L.: Preprocessing of GIS data for electric vehicle charging stations analysis and evaluation of the predictors significance. Transp. Res. Proc. **40**, 1583–1590 (2019)
30. Straka, M., Carvalho, R., van der Poel, G., Buzna, L.: Explaining the distribution of energy consumption at slow charging infrastructure for electric vehicles from socio-economic data. arXiv preprint arXiv:2006.01672 (2020)
31. Yang, Y., Zhang, Y., Meng, X.: A data-driven approach for optimizing the EV charging stations network. IEEE Access **8**, 118572–118592 (2020)

Deployment of Electric Buses: Planning the Fleet Size and Type, Charging Infrastructure and Operations with an Optimization-Based Model

Teresa Cardoso-Grilo[1,2(✉)], Sofia Kalakou[1], and João Fernandes[1]

[1] Business Research Unit (BRU-IUL), Instituto Universitário de Lisboa
(ISCTE-IUL), Avenida das Forças Armadas, 1649-026 Lisboa, Portugal
teresa.sofia.grilo@iscte-iul.pt
[2] Centre for Management Studies of Instituto Superior Técnico,
Universidade de Lisboa, Av. Rovisco Pais 1, 1049-001 Lisboa, Portugal

Abstract. The current awareness about climate change creates the urgency in adjusting the services provided in public transport towards more sustainable operations. Recent studies have shown that the integration of electric vehicles into existing fleets is an alternative that allows reducing CO_2 emissions, thus contributing to a more sustainable provision of services in the sector. When the aim is to achieve a full electrification of a bus fleet, several decisions need to be planned, such as i) the number of buses that are required, ii) the types of batteries used in those vehicles, iii) the charging technologies and strategies, iv) the location of the charging stations, and v) the frequency of charging. Nevertheless, although several planning studies have focused on the full electrification of a bus fleet, no study was found considering all these planning decisions that are deemed as essential for an adequate planning. Our study thus contributes to this gap in the literature, by proposing an optimization-based planning model that considers all these planning dimensions in the decision-making process related to the integration of electric buses in a public bus transport system – the *MILP4ElectFleet* model. All these decisions are evaluated while ensuring the minimization of investment and operating costs. The *MILP4ElectFleet* model is applied to the Carris case study, a Portuguese public transport operator in the metropolitan area of Lisbon.

Keywords: Electric bus fleet · Public transport · Optimization

1 Introduction

As concerns about climate change are increasing, governing agents are implementing strategies and adopting measures with the potential to mitigate greenhouse gas emissions (GHG) and especially CO_2 emissions. According to the International Energy Agency (IEA), the energy, industry, construction and transport sectors are the main contributors to global emissions. In 2019 the transport sector, in particular, was responsible for 24% of direct CO_2 emissions, out of which approximately 75% came

A. L. Martins et al. (Eds.): INTSYS 2020, LNICST 364, pp. 175–193, 2021.
https://doi.org/10.1007/978-3-030-71454-3_11

from road transport (cars, trucks, buses and motorcycles) (IEA 2020), indicating the need for more radical actions in road transport management and policies.

In the European Union, in order to enhance sustainable development, the European Guidelines for Developing and Implementing a Sustainable Urban Mobility Plan (SUMP) bring together the stakeholders of a city and aim to implement mobility measures aligned with the Paris Agreement (Rupprecht Consult 2019). One well-established initiative has been the implementation of Low Emission Zones that serve the objective of reducing emissions and mobility-associated environmental impacts. In this context, transport management actions related to improvements in the emissions efficiency of vehicles arise, and the evolution of electromobility has been strongly stimulated worldwide in the use of both light and heavy vehicles such as buses. Hence, the need to efficiently integrate electric buses in the fleet of current bus operators of public transport emerges, and so do the challenges for transport operators. Cities such as Paris, London, Los Angeles, and Copenhagen follow the C40 Fossil Fuel Free Street Declaration that pledges to procure only zero emission buses from 2025 and ensure to operate emission-free fleets by 2030 (C40 Cities). Planning and management strategies are required to determine technical and economic aspects of the transition to fleet electrification.

Operating bus networks is per se a complex process that involves a variety of decisions ranging from strategic to operational ones. Particularly, when the aim is to achieve full fleet electrification, key decisions involve the location of charging stations (conditioned or arbitrary), the choice of charging technologies and strategies, the typology of vehicle powering batteries and the frequency of charging. And to ensure the economic viability of the electrification of bus network operations, the costs of fleet size, battery typology and charging systems need to be addressed and eventually minimized.

From a business perspective, electrifying bus fleets imposes additional costs to both cities and operators, worldwide, who are still having cost barriers and are using grants to cover the expenses of all the stages of electric bus integration ranging from procurement to operation (Li et al. 2018b). The purchasing cost of electric buses is higher than the corresponding of the conventional ones (Rothgang et al. 2015). At the operational phase, the costs of movement and charging infrastructure need to be considered. Decisions on the type of charging infrastructure to be employed is determinant for the resulting operating costs, which depending on the service frequency, the circulation length and the speed of a transit system, may have a great impact on the performance of different charging infrastructures (charging stations, charging lanes – via charging-while-driving technologies – and battery swapping stations) (Chen et al. 2017). As the charging process can follow different strategies, namely be slow or fast, energy consumption varies in accordance to vehicle's weight, weather conditions and route's characteristics. The costs of purchasing a battery bus for slow charging are quite high, but its operating costs are generally lower compared to other charging strategies (Lajunen 2018). Overall, several operational aspects influence the total costs incurred by the adoption of electric vehicles.

Profitable choices of bus fleets are not obvious and thorough consideration of the total costs is vital in making decisions on the battery type to be employed, the charging infrastructure to be installed, the charging network to be designed and the frequency of charging to be planned. Previous work has focused on the full substitution of conventional bus fleet from electric buses to make decisions on the fleet management (Wang et al. (2017); Tang et al. (2019)). Nevertheless, while several studies aimed at planning the full electrification of a bus fleet while considering the minimization of costs and identifying the dimension of the fleet, battery types, charging infrastructure and frequency of charging, none of them considers simultaneously all these four planning aspects. This study aims to fill in this gap in the literature.

In the context of electrifying transport, this paper aims to contribute to the electrification of public transport with the proposal of an optimization-based model that can be used to support the decision-making process of transport operators on the selection of electric bus types, location of charging stations, and also on the frequency of charging. The proposed model is based on a Mixed Integer Linear Programming (MILP) model, hereafter called *MILP4ElectFleet*, which allows determining the minimum number of electric buses with the minimum charging requirements to secure the routes currently offered by the public transport operator. As far as loading is concerned, this model makes it possible to identify the need for investment in charging stations with different charging strategies, as well as the required frequency of charging. The model also makes it possible to identify the required investment in vehicles with different battery types. To illustrate the applicability of the model, it is applied to the operation of a public transport operator (Carris) in the metropolitan region of Lisbon.

The remainder of this article is organized as follows. Section 2 presents a brief literature review on bus fleet electrification. Background information on the problem under analysis is explored in Sect. 3. Section 4 presents the mathematical details of the optimization-based model proposed in this study. The results obtained are explored in Sect. 5, and key conclusions and future research are presented in Sect. 6.

2 Literature Review on Bus Fleet Electrification

This section is focused on the review of studies that analyze technical and economic aspects related to bus fleet electrification and aim to support the decision-making process of integrating electric buses in the bus fleet of public transport companies. A review of the methods is summarized at the end of the section and the contribution of this paper is presented.

2.1 Electric Bus Battery Types, Charging Infrastructure and Strategies

Battery characteristics (size and useful life among others) are determinant aspects for the design of electric transport networks. For instance, the requirements in recharging activities of electric buses decrease fast as the maximum driving range increases (Wang et al. 2017). Hence, battery performance has direct impacts on the costs and the performance of electric fleets as well. The most common batteries in electric mobility are lithium ion batteries, and there are three types to cover different operational requirements (Carrilero et al. 2018):

- *Lithium Iron Phosphate - LiFePO4 (LFP):* a common technology in electric buses with the advantages of having a high cycling-life, good power parameters, high thermal stability and competitive price but comparing with other types of batteries, the technology has a low nominal voltage (3.2 V), low capacity (90–120 Wh/kg) resulting into larger and heavier batteries that charge slower degrade faster.
- *Lithium Nickel Manganese Oxide Cobalt - LiNiMnCoO2 (NMC):* has a capacity of 150–220 Wh/kg which allows greater autonomy and smaller size, aspects that constitute it suitable for smaller buses but is more expensive than LEP and entails safety risks (is environmentally dangerous) in case of an accident.
- *Lithium Titanate - Li4Ti5O12 (LTO):* has excellent thermal stability and can be charged frequently with no impacts on its lifecycle but is more expensive than the others and it has a low voltage rating (2.4 V) and a reduced power capacity resulting in larger and heavier batteries.

The charging infrastructure types (battery swapping stations, plug-in charging stations and wireless charging facilities (Chen et al. 2017)) may be employed for recharging all battery types. Depending on the transport system, different infrastructure types might be advantageous. For bus rapid transit corridors, the use of charging lanes enabled by currently available inductive wireless charging technology might be appropriate. On the other hand, for transit systems, swapping stations can result into a lower total cost than charging lanes and charging stations, but when there are low service frequencies and short circulations, swapping stations might be the proper choice (Chen et al. 2017).

The charging mode can also vary and six charging strategies can be considered by bus operators (Carrilero et al. 2018): (1) *Slow charging*, in which charging is performed in about 6 h; (2) *Fast charging or opportunity charging*, with larger power charges; (3) *Regenerative braking,* with energy independence due to the exploitation of the energy generated while braking but with faster battery degradation compared to fast charging; (4) *Combination of fast charging and opportunity charging* for buses that use slow charging at the end of the route and fast charging during the route; (5) *Moving charge (trolley bus)* for buses charged through overhead cables in sections of a route; (6) *Physical exchange of batteries* when batteries are replaced at battery exchange stations when batteries reach low levels.

2.2   Operational Aspects of the Electrification of Bus Fleets

The passage from conventional vehicles to electric ones in the business of public transport entails several challenges and comprises of several phases that could gradually lead to full electrification.

At a first stage, different scenarios of battery sizing and charging can be employed to analyse the feasibility and efficiency of electric bus implementation. Analysis of the energy requirements of a bus network in the city of Aachen in Germany, showed that charging at certain bus stops results into higher infrastructure costs compared to charging at bus terminals (Sinhuber et al. 2010). This happens because batteries don't store enough energy to complete their operation. By simulating the life cycle cost of a bus fleet using 4 routes in Finland and California, Lajunen (2018) explored the potential of three types of charging: slow (overnight), end of route and opportunity charging. The authors found that while the initial costs of opportunity charging costs are quite high, they are quite flexible in terms of operation. Considering a 12-year lifespan for buses and comparing them with a diesel model, charging at the terminal becomes the most efficient, having only 7% more costs, while overnight charging has 26% more and opportunity charging has 35% more costs. However, simulation tests have demonstrated that while overnight charging implies a lower investment, allows greater schedule flexibility and longer useful life of batteries, it requires bigger batteries, more space, more energy and less passenger seats (Rothgang et al. 2015).

The use of different batteries introduces flexibility in the charging system. Based on real data of the operation of a bus fleet for a full year, further work indicated the need for flexibility in the charging system of the bus fleet. Employing multiple battery configurations and flexible battery swapping practices in electric buses, could result into the use of smaller batteries with shorter charging events (e.g., at a designated bus stop at the end of the route) through ultrafast charging for both short and long routes increasing in the case the battery degradation rate (Gao et al. 2017). Such flexibility, however, implies that the bus fleet satisfies similar demand volumes along all the network.

The cost of battery charging activities is part of the total cost of the fleet electrification which can be assessed through the estimation of Total Cost of Ownership (TCO) and the analysis of the viability of an investment made in infrastructure to support electric mobility and the costs of vehicle acquisition, operation and maintenance. Göhlich et al. (2013) presented a financial forecasting method for innovative urban transport systems, employing a Monte Carlo simulation in order to respond to future uncertainties related to technology and market aspects. Applying the TCO methodology for the Berlin bus system, including vehicle costs, financial costs, operating costs, infrastructure costs and emissions costs, they introduced the concept of charging buses while performing routes in addition to charging only at night, which requires larger batteries and consequently higher weight and consumption of buses. Due to technical limitations, the long-range electric buses are limited, considering the batteries range capacity and size, implying a higher investment. Laurikko et al. (2015) presented the TCO to obtain the equivalent annual cost incurred in owning and operating a fleet of electric buses considering drivers' labour costs, capital costs of the vehicle (including battery), maintenance and fuel costs. Rogge et al. (2018) analysed the viability of electric fleets in the city of Aachen (Germany) and the connection of Roskilde-Copenhagen (Denmark) from a TCO perspective based on an optimization model that considered investment costs in the fleet and infrastructure, operating costs, energy consumption, schedules, distances and availability of charging station in order to the fleet size, fleet models, optimization of the loading process and minimization of TCO.

It is evident that there are many parameters to consider when making decisions on the design of an electric bus network and the focus should lie on both technical and economic aspects. Depending on the network design, different configurations might be appropriate. In this line, several studies have attempted to find the optimal network design focusing on costs minimization and following operational restrictions. The combination of electric charging infrastructure, batteries and energy consumption is a major theme in the deployment of an electric bus fleet in order to both reduce emissions and increase energy efficiency, as well as to guarantee the operation carried out by bus fleets minimising infrastructure costs wherever possible. In this context, Kunith et al.

(2014) developed a MILP model to minimize the cost of implementing charging stations for an infrastructure with opportunity charging type serving a route (15-h service, length of 28.5 km, 30 stops) by determining the minimum number and location of charging stations required based on certain operational and technological constraints (battery consumption). Different energy consumption scenarios representing different traffic volumes and different weather conditions, with different battery capacities and charging infrastructures were analysed. Further on, they employed opportunity charging for the complete substitution of the diesel fleet in Berlin and as an alternative to its existing electric trolley-bus fleet that need to be continuously connected to the electric grid in order to define the infrastructure requirements when employing different battery types (Kunith et al. 2017). Advancing on this MILP model, the cost of batteries was additionally considered to cater for the electrification cost (Kunith et al. 2016).

Previous work on operations' optimization has also aimed to minimize total costs and energy consumption. A case study in Stockholm determined the location of bus charging points considering the availability of two charging options: (a) points in the main public transport stops (eg. Next to train stations) and (b) at the beginning and the end of bus routes (Xylia et al. 2017). For the city of Padova, investments on batteries and operating costs on a ten-year time horizon were minimized in order to determine the location of the battery recharging/replacement points in a bus network and assess the sustainability performance of the bus fleet (Andriollo and Tortella 2015). Focusing on the employment of fast-charging infrastructure, flexible battery sizes and the addition of demand charges to total costs, the results of total cost minimization model for a bus fleet in Salt Lake City (Utah) highlighted that bus operators need to consider the trade-off between fast-charging station cost and bus battery cost as properly deployed fast-charging stations have the potential to reduce both the battery cost and the total costs (He et al. 2019).

Focusing on total operational costs, an optimum mix of battery electric and diesel hybrid bus operated in Connecticut was reached in Islam and Lownes (2019) by minimizing the purchasing, operating and maintaining costs of the entire fleet including costs of charging infrastructure, fuel cost, salvage value, and emission costs. Following the same perspective of objectives, Rinaldi et al. (2020) explored the optimum fleet size of hybrid and electric buses in order to minimize the total costs occurred considering the charging requirements.

2.3   Concluding Remarks

The literature review has shown that optimization techniques have been widely employed in studies that aim to determine the optimal integration of electric bus in the fleet of bus operators based on costs (both operating and investment costs) and considering operational constraints related to the route length, bus capacity and bus schedules. Table 1 provides an overview of the afore-mentioned optimization studies aiming at planning the integration of electric buses in existing fleets of public transport. This table makes it clear that no study jointly considers all the planning decisions that are considered as essential for an adequate planning (number of vehicles, location of charging stations, frequency of charging and selection of charging technology and battery types). Also, few studies consider the minimization of both operating and investment costs, with investment costs being related to investments in different vehicles with different types of batteries as well as with investments in charging infrastructure. Within this setting, there is scope to develop more comprehensive planning models that jointly consider all these dimensions. The current paper aims to fill this gap in the literature.

Table 1. Key planning decisions and objectives within optimization studies focused on the integration of electric buses in public transport fleets (X depict the features considered in each study).

Study	Planning decisions					Cost-oriented objectives
	Location of charging stations	Frequency of charging	Charging strategy	Battery type	Fleet dimension	
Kunith et al. (2014)	X					Costs with infrastructures
Kunith et al. (2017)	X					
Andriollo and Tortella (2015)		X				Total operating costs
Kunith et al. (2016)						
Xylia et al. (2017)	X		X		X	
Houbbadi et al. (2019)						
Rogge et al. (2018)		X			X	
He et al. (2019)	X		X	X		
Islam and Lowens (2019)				X	X	Investment and total operating costs
Pelletier et al. (2019)		X		X	X	
Rinaldi et al. (2020)		X		X		
MILP4ElectFleet	X	X	X	X	X	

3   Electrification of a Public Bus Operator in Portugal

The Roadmap for carbon neutrality 2050 (RNC2050 2020) in Portugal has imposed the objective of reducing GHG by 50% to 60% by 2050, compared to the corresponding levels of 1990. In order to keep up with world trends, Portugal has also defined some strategies that allow to adapt to world developments, and a series of measures have been defined for the use of more efficient vehicles, namely electric vehicles. In particular, there is the example of the Action Plan for Electrical Mobility, Methodology for

Locating New Loading Points and Financial and Tax Incentives (Ministry of Environment, Spatial Planning and Energy 2015). Also, at the level of the Major Options of the Plan for 2018, the government has registered mandatory loading points in new houses and garages starting from 2019, among others.

Carris, a Portuguese public transport operator focusing its activity in the metropolitan area of Lisbon, is used as a case study in this paper. Carris aims at providing an urban surface passenger transport service by making available buses, trams, lifts and elevators. Following the national guidelines, Carris is currently evolving towards a more sustainable provision of its services, and one of the strategies followed by the company involves the integration of electric buses within its fleet. The company owns a variety of buses – standard, articulated, medium, and mini-buses – but for the moment, the investment in electric vehicles is only focused on standard buses. Accordingly, a key challenge faced by Carris involves planning the investment in additional electric standard buses while also ensuring the most efficient integration of these electric buses in its fleet. This efficient integration implies ensuring the minimum operating and investment costs (with costs varying with the number of electric buses, type of batteries used in the vehicles, as well as with the charging technologies and strategies and frequency of charging) while ensuring part of the routes currently offered by Carris in the metropolitan area of Lisbon. Particularly, the company aims at achieving the full electrification of the routes in the central area of Lisbon (a total of 17 routes), and this mainly due to the higher expected impact in the environmental quality of all the city of Lisbon.

Within this setting, the *MILP4ElectFleet* will support the following decisions:

   i. How many buses are required to ensure the full electrification of the routes in the central area of Lisbon? And which types of batteries should be used in those routes?
  ii. How much should be invested in different charging technologies and strategies? And where should those charging stations be located (terminal and/or stops)?
 iii. What is the minimum frequency of charging for the different charging technologies and per electric bus?

4   Methodology

This section presents the mathematical details of the *MILP4ElectFleet* model.

4.1   Assumptions Used for Building the *MILP4ElectFleet* Model

Several assumptions are used so as to build the *MILP4ElectFleet* model:

   i. Each bus can only be used in one single route;
  ii. All the routes should be ensured for all the shifts, i.e., the minimum number of buses should be enough to ensure all those routes;
 iii. A single type of battery can be used by all the buses of each route;
 iv. Each bus can be charged at the terminal and/or at the stops of routes;

v. A set of route stops is selected for installing charging technologies, if needed, and multiple charging strategies can be followed;

vi. A maximum number of charges at the terminal is imposed per day;

vii. A maximum number of charges at the stops is imposed per shift, with this maximum number depending on the number of trips per route of each shift;

viii. The first shift of the day starts with all the buses fully charged.

4.2   Notation

Indices and Sets

$r \in R$	Routes
$s \in S$	Shifts
$p \in P$	Batteries
$q \in Q = Q^{TN} \cup Q^{TD} \cup Q^S$	Charging strategies, including charging during the night (Q^{TN}) and during the day (Q^{TD}) in charging stations installed in the terminals, and also in the route stops (Q^S)
$j \in J = J^T \cup J^S$	Terminals (J^T) and route stops (J^S) selected for installing a charging system (if required)
$h \in H = \{(q,j) : q \in Q, j \in J\}$	Charging strategy $q \in Q$ the technology of which can be installed in terminal/route stop $j \in J$
$u \in U = \{(r,s) : r \in R, s \in S\}$	Routes $r \in R$ performed during shift $s \in S$
$v \in V = V^T \cup V^S = \{(r,j) : r \in R, j \in J^T\}$ $\cup \{(r,j) : r \in R, j \in J^S\}$	Routes $r \in R$ with terminal $j \in J^T$, and routes $r \in R$ with route stop $j \in J^S$

Parameters

N_s^{shift}	Duration (in hours) of shift $s \in S$
N_r^{route}	Number of minutes required to complete route $r \in R$
NR_{rs}	Number of times each route $r \in R$ must be completed (i.e., number of trips) over shift $s \in S$ by each bus
NB_{rs}	Number of buses required for route $r \in R$ and shift $s \in S$
Cap_r^{Trip}	Capacity (kW) required to complete each trip of each route $r \in R$
Cap_p^{Bat}	Capacity (kW) of each battery $p \in P$
CC_{qp}	Charging capacity (kW) for the charging strategy $q \in Q$ when using battery $p \in P$
C_{qp}	Energy hourly cost (€/kW) for charging strategy $q \in Q$ using battery $p \in P$
I_q	Investment (€) required per charging strategy $q \in Q$
I_p	Investment (€) required per bus using battery $p \in P$
M_q^T	Maximum number of charges allowed per day using charging strategy $q \in Q^{TD}$

M_{rsq}^S Maximum number of charges allowed per bus for route $r \in R$ during shift $s \in S$ using charging strategy $q \in Q^S$

K Minimum capacity (kW) for buses

L High auxiliary value

Variables

X_{prsq} Equal to 1 if a bus using battery $p \in P$ required for route $r \in R$ during shift $s \in S$ is charged using the charging strategy $q \in Q$

Z_{qjr} Equal to 1 if charging strategy $q \in Q$ involves installing a charging technology at stop $j \in J$ belonging to route $r \in R$

Z'_{qj} Equal to 1 if charging strategy $q \in Q$ involves installing a charging technology at stop $j \in J$

T_{pr} Equal to 1 if a bus using battery $p \in P$ is required for route $r \in R$

B_{pr}^T Total number of buses using battery $p \in P$ required for route $r \in R$

B_{prs}^{Shift} Number of buses using battery $p \in P$ required for route $r \in R$ during shift $s \in S$

Y_q Number of infrastructures installed for charging strategy $q \in Q$

W_{rs} Available capacity (kW) for a bus with battery $p \in P$ used in route $r \in R$ at the end of shift $s \in S$

4.3 Objective Function

The key objective of the model is the minimization of total costs, including i) charging cost for different charging strategies (first term of Eq. (1)), ii) investment cost for different charging strategies (second term of Eq. (1)) and iii) investment cost for buses with different batteries (third term of Eq. (1)).

$$Min \sum_{p \in P} \sum_{r \in R} \sum_{\substack{s \in S \\ r:(r,s) \in U}} \sum_{q \in Q} C_{qp} X_{prsq} + \sum_{q \in Q} I_q Y_q + \sum_{p \in P} \sum_{r \in R} I_p B_{pr}^T \quad (1)$$

4.4 Constraints

A key constraint of the model is given by Eq. (2). Equation (2) imposes that each bus should have capacity (in kW) to complete all the trips of each route $r \in R$ for all the shifts $s \in S$ to which it is assigned. If the capacity available at the beginning of each shift (Cap_p^{Bus} for the first shift and W_{rs} for shifts other than the first) for a given bus is not enough to complete all the trips of the route, there is need to charge that bus using the available charging strategy.

$$NR_{rs} Cap_r^{Trip} \le \begin{cases} \sum_{p \in P} \left[T_{pr} Cap_p^{Bat} + \sum_{q \in Q^S} X_{prsq} CC_{qp} \right], \forall (r,s) \in U, s = 1 \\ W_{r(s-1)} + \sum_{q \in Q^{TD} \cup Q^S} \sum_{p \in P} X_{prsq} CC_{qp}, \forall (r,s) \in U, s > 1 \end{cases} \quad (2)$$

On the other hand, the capacity available at the end of each shift $s \in S$ for all the buses allocated to a given route $r \in R$ is computed based on Eq. (3).

$$W_{rs} = \begin{cases} \sum_{p \in P} \left[T_{pr} Cap_p^{Bat} + \sum_{q \in Q^s} X_{prsq} CC_{qp} \right] - NR_{rs} Cap_r^{Trip} \forall (r,s) \in U, s = 1 \\ W_{r(s-1)} + \sum_{q \in Q^{TD} \cup Q^s} \sum_{p \in P} X_{prsq} CC_{qp} - NR_{rs} Cap_r^{Trip} \forall (r,s) \in U, s > 1 \end{cases}$$

(3)

Equation (4) imposes that each bus cannot not goes below a minimum capacity.

$$W_{rs} \geq K \, \forall (r,s) \in U \tag{4}$$

The number of buses using each type of battery $p \in P$ for route $r \in R$ is determined based on Eqs. (5–6).

$$B_{pr}^T \geq B_{prs}^{Shift} \forall (r,s) \in U, p \in P \tag{5}$$

$$B_{prs}^{Shift} = NB_{rs} TP_{pr} \forall p \in P, (r,s) \in U \tag{6}$$

Equations (7–8) are related to the selection of batteries for each bus. Equation (7) defines that only one type of battery can be used for buses used in each route $r \in R$. Equation (8) defines that buses can only be operating using the selected type of battery.

$$\sum_{p \in P} T_{pr} = 1 \quad \forall r \in R \tag{7}$$

$$X_{prsq} \leq T_{pr} \forall p \in P, (r,s) \in U, q \in Q \tag{8}$$

Equation (9) ensures that charging only takes place for buses required to perform routes required in a given shift. L is used as a high auxiliary value to allow for a high number of charges during each shift, if needed. On the other hand, a maximum number of charges is imposed per bus and per day (if the charging takes place at the terminal; Eq. (10)) or per shift (if the charging takes place at the stops; Eq. (11)).

$$X_{prsq} \leq \begin{cases} L \, \forall p \in P, (r,s) \in U, q \in Q \\ 0 \, \forall p \in P, (r,s) U, q \in Q \end{cases} \tag{9}$$

$$\sum_{s \in S} \sum_{\substack{r \in R \\ r:(r,s) \in U}} X_{prsq} \leq M_q^T \, \forall p \in P, q \in Q^{TD} \tag{10}$$

$$\sum_{\substack{r \in R \\ r:(r,s) \in U}} X_{prsq} \leq \sum_{\substack{r \in R \\ r:(r,s) \in U}} M_{rsq}^S \, \forall p \in P, s \in S, q \in Q^S \tag{11}$$

Equation (12) imposes that at least one charging strategy should be available for each route $r \in R$, in order to ensure the charging of the buses serving those routes.

$$\sum_{q \in Q} \sum_{\substack{j \in J \\ j:(r,j) \in V \\ j:(q,j) \in H}} Z_{qjr} \geq 1 \quad \forall r \in R \tag{12}$$

Equations (13–15) establish the link between decision variables related to the charging strategies. Particularly, Eq. (13) defines that no bus can be charged using a charging strategy involving a technology that is not installed, and Eqs. (14–15) define the maximum number of infrastructures that should exist for each charging strategy $q \in Q$.

$$X_{prsq} \leq \sum_{\substack{j \in J \\ j:(r,j) \in V \\ j:(q,j) \in H}} Z_{qjr} \; \forall p \in P, (r,s) \in U, r \in R, q \in Q \tag{13}$$

$$Y_q = \sum_{\substack{j \in J \\ j:(q,j) \in H}} Z'_{qj} \; \forall q \in Q \tag{14}$$

$$Z'_{qj} \geq Z_{qjr} \; \forall (r,j) \in V, (q,j) \in H \tag{15}$$

Finally, Eqs. (16–23) define variable domains.

$$X_{prsq} \in \{0, 1\} \; \forall p \in P, r \in R, s \in S, q \in Q \tag{16}$$

$$Z_{qjr} \in \{0, 1\} \; \forall j \in J, r \in R, q \in Q \tag{17}$$

$$Z'_{qj} \in \{0, 1\} \; \forall j \in J, q \in Q \tag{18}$$

$$T_{pr} \in \{0, 1\} \; \forall p \in P, r \in R \tag{19}$$

$$B^T_{pr} \in [0; +\infty[\; \forall p \in P, r \in R \tag{20}$$

$$B^{Shift}_{prs} \in [0; +\infty[\; \forall p \in P, r \in R, s \in S \tag{21}$$

$$Y_q \in [0; +\infty[\quad \forall q \in Q \tag{22}$$

$$W_{rs} \geq 0 \; \forall r \in R, s \in S \tag{23}$$

5   Case Study

We herein present the results obtained through the illustrative application of the *MILP4ElectFleet* model to the case of Carris. For this application, the model was implemented in the General Algebraic Modeling System (GAMS) 23.7 and was solved with CPLEX 12.0 on a Two Intel Xeon X5680, 3.33 Gigahertz computer with 12 Gigabyte RAM.

5.1   Dataset and Assumptions Used for the *MILP4ElectFleet* Model Application

The model is applied to support decisions related to the investments in electric buses by Carris, so as to ensure the electrification of the routes in the central area of Lisbon. This area comprises a total of 17 routes $\{r_1, \ldots, r_{17}\}$, and these routes share the same terminal (*Pontinha*) and are organized in four different shifts – starting at 9am, 1pm, 6pm and 11pm. Several assumptions are used for this application:

i. Two types of lithium ion batteries are considered as possible investments by Carris: smaller 150 kW batteries $[p = 1;\ Cap^{Bat}_{p=1} = 150]$ and larger 300 kW batteries $[p = 2; Cap^{Bat}_{p=2} = 300]$;

ii. Three charging strategies are considered as possible by Carris:
   a. Slow charging during the night at the *Pontinha* terminal $[q = 1]$ - charging during a 6-h period with a charging capacity of 300 kW, corresponding to a full load of the buses $[CC_{(q=1)(p=1)} = 150;\ CC_{(q=1)(p=2)} = 300]$;
   b. Slow charging during the day at the *Pontinha* terminal $[q = 2]$, between shifts – charging during a 4-h period with a charging capacity of 200 kW $\left[CC_{(q=2)(p=1)} = 150; CC_{(q=2)(p=2)} = 200\right]$;
   c. Fast charging during the day at selected stops, i.e., final stops for all the routes $[q = 3]$ - charging during a 5 min period with a charging capacity of 75 k W $\left[CC_{(q=3)(p=1)} = CC_{(q=3)(p=2)} = 75\right]$.

iii. All the buses are fully charged during the night, and only one charging can take place at the *Pontinha* terminal during the night and also during the day (if needed) $\left[M^T_{q=1} = M^T_{q=2} = 1\right]$;

iv. Fast charging can take place after completing each trip of each route (if needed), i.e., fast charging can take place as many times as the number of trips of each route of a given shift:

$$M^S_{rs(q=3)} = NR_{rs} \forall (r, s) \in U \tag{24}$$

v. Slow charging system is already installed at *Pontinha*, meaning that no investment should be considered ($I_{q=1} = I_{q=2} = 0; Y_{q=1} = Y_{q=2} = 1$). Consequently, charging during the night takes place for all the buses ($Z_{(q=1)r} = 1$);

vi. Fast charging systems can be installed at the final stops of all the 17 routes, with an investment of 350 000€ per system ($I_{q=3}$ = 350 000) (Kunith et al. 2017). These 17 routes share 12 final stops (J^S).

In addition to these assumptions, the model application also required the use of the data shown in Table 2.

Table 2. Dataset in use.

Parameters	Values
N_s^{shift}	$\{4; 5; 5; 3\}$ h
N_r^{route}	$\{44; 44; 46; 38; 29; 50; 54; 44; 1; 41; 48; 42; 69; 38; 23; 41; 24\}$ min
NR_{rs}	Between 2 and 11 trips per bus, depending on the route and shift[a]
Cap_r^{Trip}	Between 18 and 45 kW, depending on the route[a]
C_{qp}	22,5€ (q = 1, p = 1), 45€ (q = 1, p = 2), 22,5€ (q = 2, p = 1), 30€ (q = 2, p = 2) and 11,25€ (q = 3, p = 1 and p = 2) – total cost per charge considering 0,15 €/kW (EDP, 2020)
I_p	350 000€ (p = 1) and 500 000 € (p = 2) (Rogge et al. 2018)
θ_q	$\{1; 1; 12\}$
K	50 kW

[a]More details about this data are available upon request to the authors.

5.2 Results

Planning Results: Number of Buses and Types of Batteries

Table 3 shows the results obtained for the number of buses required to ensure the electrification of the 17 routes in the central area of Lisbon, as well as for the type of batteries that should be used for those routes. Accordingly, if Carris aims at electrifying all the central area of Lisbon, a total of 141 buses are required – 97 with lower capacity batteries and 44 with higher capacity batteries -, which corresponds to an investment of 55 950 000€ (third component of cost in Eq. (1)).

Table 3. Number of buses and types of batteries in use for the 17 routes in the metropolitan area of Lisbon.

Routes	Number of buses		
	150 kW batteries	300 kW batteries	Total
r_1	–	9	9
r_2	7	–	7
r_3	8	–	8
r_4	7	–	7
r_5	–	8	8
r_6	10	–	10
r_7	10	–	10
r_8	–	7	7
r_9	6	–	6
r_{10}	–	7	7
r_{11}	17	–	17
r_{12}	6	–	6
r_{13}	16	–	16
r_{14}	5	–	5
r_{15}	–	4	4
r_{16}	–	9	9
r_{17}	5	–	5
Total number of buses	97	44	141

Planning Results: Investment in Charging Strategies

Since Carris already have a slow charging system at the *Pontinha* terminal, no investment in this type of technology is needed. On the other hand, a significant investment is required in fast charging systems – 11 out of the 12 final stops should have a fast charging system, with a total investment of 3 850 000€ (second component of cost in Eq. (1)). Routes r_3 and r_4 share the only stop (*Alameda*) in which it is not necessary to have a charging system – this happens because buses used in these routes can be charged at the *Pontinha* terminal with enough capacity to complete all the trips of the routes of each shift.

Planning Results: Frequency of Charging

Table 4 shows the results obtained for the frequency of charging, both fast and slow charging, per route. This frequency should be read as the number of charges required for the set of buses needed per route – for instance, if 9 buses are needed in a given route, and if each bus needs two charges, the frequency shown in the table is 18.

As previously mentioned, all the buses start the first shift with full charge, meaning that all the buses use the slow charging system at the *Pontinha* terminal during the night (Table 4, second column). On the other hand, since no fast charging is needed for routes r3 and r4, all the buses used in these routes need to charge once at the *Pontinha* terminal during the day (Table 4, third column). Also, part of the buses used in the first and second shift are not required for the second and third shift, respectively. For that reason these buses leave to the *Pontinha* terminal and use the slow charging system before being in use again during the third and fourth shift, respectively (Table 4, third column).

Considering the frequency of charging shown in Table 4, and also considering the costs presented in Table 2, a total daily cost of around 11 700€ (first component of cost in Eq. (1)) should be supported by Carris with such charging.

Table 4. Frequency of charging per route.

Routes	Slow charging		Fast charging			
	Night	Day	Shift 9am	Shift 1pm	Shift 6pm	Shift 11pm
$r1$	9	3	–	12	12	–
r_2	7	3	7	10	12	1
r_3	8	10	–	–	–	–
r_4	7	13	–	–	–	–
r_5	8	7	–	12	15	1
r_6	10	2	10	16	22	–
r_7	10	3	10	21	27	2
r_8	7	–	–	10	10	–
r_9	6	3	6	8	17	–
r_{10}	7	–	–	10	10	–
r_{11}	17	2	17	22	26	3
r_{12}	6	2	6	10	16	–
r_{13}	16	1	16	24	32	–
r_{14}	5	2	5	12	14	–
r_{15}	4	–	–	9	6	–
r_{16}	9	6	–	15	18	–
r_{17}	5	4	5	6	15	–
Total	141	61	82	197	252	7

Computational Results

The application of the model to the case of Carris resulted in a model with 1 701 equations and 756 variables (out of which 540 are binary variables). The solution detailed above was obtained in 0.12 s with an optimality gap of 0%.

6 Conclusions

This study arises within the current context of an increasing awareness about climate change, where there is clearly the need to adopt strategies to reduce CO_2 emissions, with the transport sector arising as a key sector to be explored. Accordingly, being focused on a more sustainable provision of services in the public transportation sector, this study proposes a planning model to support the decision-making process related to the integration of electric buses in a public bus transport system.

Literature in the area shows a wide variety of studies proposing methods to support the full electrification of a bus fleet. Nevertheless, according to the authors knowledge, no study has jointly considered all the planning decisions that are considered as essential for an adequate planning, such as decision related to the number of vehicles, selection of battery types, location of charging stations, frequency of charging and selection of charging technologies and strategies.

This study fills this gap in the literature by proposing an optimization model, the *MILP4ElectFleet* model, aiming at providing guidance on: i) the number of buses required to ensure the full electrification of a bus fleet; ii) the types of batteries that should be used in those vehicles; iii) the charging technologies and strategies that should be made available; iv) the location of the charging stations; and v) the frequency of charging. And all these decisions should be made while ensuring the minimization of investment and operating costs.

Carris, a Portuguese public transport operator focusing its activity in the metropolitan area of Lisbon, is used as case study to illustrate the usefulness of the proposed model. In particular, the model is used to support the decisions related to the full electrification of the routes in the central area of Lisbon (a total of 17 routes).

Results show that 141 electric buses are required to ensure the routes in the central area of Lisbon, out of which 70% should have lower-capacity lithium ion batteries. It is also possible to conclude that a high investment in fast charging systems is required – 15 out of the 17 routes will need to ensure the charging of buses using fast charging stations, either due to the low capacity of the batteries in use, or due to the extension of the routes. Consequently, ensuring the operation of the 17 routes will imply a combination of slow charging (either overnight and during the day) and fast charging, with a daily charging cost of around 11 700€.

Several lines of further research should be pursued. First, the proposed model should be extended for a mix-fleet planning model aiming to plan a fleet including not only electric buses, but also gas and diesel buses. Such a model would be essential for planning the transition to an electric fleet for cases in which a full electrification is not possible or even desired. Secondly, the proposed model should also be extended for a multi-period model, thus allowing for a long-term planning of the electrification of the bus fleet. This long-term planning would allow exploring the impact of fast and slow charging on battery life span, as well as to quantify the costs of such an electrification in the long-term. Thirdly, other planning objectives should be included in the analysis. Particularly, the minimization of CO_2 emissions should also be included thus allowing to explore the trade-off between cost and emissions. Also, extending the application of the model to include for a higher variety of battery types and charging technologies and strategies would be more informative, as well as to account for the impact of the number of people per bus on the effective energy consumption of the bus. Finally, it will be relevant to apply the adjusted model to the entire fleet of Carris, and also to compare the results obtained for the Portuguese context with the current reality in other European countries.

Acknowledgments. The authors acknowledge the support from the Business Research Unit (BRU-IUL). The authors also acknowledge Carris for the data.

References

Andriollo, M., Tortella, A.: Sustainability evaluation of an electric bus fleet for the urban public transport system of Padova, Italy. In: Urban Transport XXI, vol. 146, pp. 533 – 545. WIT Press (2015).

C40 Cities. https://www.c40.org/other/green-and-healthy-streets. Accessed 21 July 2020

Carrilero, I., González, M., Anseán, D., Viera, J.C., Chacón, J., Pereirinha, P.G.: Redesigning European public transport: impact of new battery technologies in the design of electric bus fleets. Transp. Res. Procedia **33**, 195–202 (2018)

Chen, Z., Liu, W., Yin, Y.: Deployment of stationary and dynamic charging infrastructure for electric vehicles along traffic corridors. Transp. Res. Part C **77**, 185–206 (2017)

EDP. https://www.edp.pt/particulares/servicos/mobilidade-eletrica/carregar-fora-de-cas. Accessed 22 July 2020

Gao, Z., et al.: Battery capacity and recharging needs for electric buses in city transit service. Energy **122**, 588–600 (2017)

Göhlich, D., Spangenberg, F., Kunith, A.: Stochastic total cost of ownership forecasting for innovative urban transport systems. In: IEEE International Conference on Industrial Engineering and Engineering Management (2013). https://doi.org/10.1109/IEEM.2013.6962529

He, Y., Song, Z., Liu, Z.: Fast-charging station deployment for battery electric bus systemsconsidering electricity demand charges. Sustain. Cities Soc. **48**, article 101530 (2019)

Houbbadi, A., Pelissier, S., Trigui, R., Redondo-Iglesias, E., Bouton, T.: Overview of Electric Buses deployment and its challenges related to the charging - the case study of TRANSDEV. In: 32nd Electric Vehicle Symposium (EVS32), 11, hal-02148377v2, Lyon, France (2019)

International Energy Agency (IEA). https://www.iea.org/reports/tracking-transport-2020. Accessed 22 July 2020

Islam, A., Lowens, N.: When to go electric? A parallel bus fleet replacement study. Transp. Res. Part D **72**, 299–311 (2019)

Kunith, A., Goehlich, D., Mendelevitch R.: Planning and optimization of a fast-charging infrastructure for electric urban bus systems. In: Proceedings of the Second International Conference on Traffic and Transport Engineering, ICTTE, Belgrado, Sérvia, pp. 43–49 (2014)

Kunith, A., Mendelevitch, R., Goehlich, D.: Electrification of a city bus network: An optimization model for cost-effective placing of charging infrastructure and battery sizing of fast charging electric bus systems. Int. J. Sustain. Transp. **11**(10), 707–720 (2017)

Kunith, A., Mendelevitch, R., Kuschmierz, A., Goehlich, D.: Optimization of fast charging infrastructure for electric bus transportation – Electrification of a city bus network. In EVS29 International Battery, Hybrid and Fuel Cell Electric Vehicle Symposium (2016)

Lajunen, A.: Lifecycle costs and charging requirements of electric buses with different charging methods. J. Clean. Prod. **172**, 56–67 (2018)

Laurikko, J., et al.: Electric city bus and infrastructure demonstration environment in Espoo, Finland. In: EVS28 International Electric Vehicle Symposium and Exhibition, Korea (2015)

Li, X., Castellanos, S., Maasen, A.: Emerging trends and innovations for electric bus adoption—a comparative case study of contracting and financing of 22 cities in the Americas, Asia-Pacific, and Europe. Res. Transp. Econ. **69**, 470–481 (2018b).

Ministry of Environment, Spatial Planning and Energy: Approves the Electric Mobility Action Plan, Order n^{er} 8809/2015 (2015)

Pelletier, S., Jabali, O., Mendoza, J.E., Laporte, G.: The electric bus fleet transition problem. Transp. Res. Part C **109**, 174–193 (2019)

Rinaldi, M., Picarelli, E., D'Adriano, A., Viti, F.: Mixed-fleet single-terminal bus scheduling problem: modelling, solution scheme and potential applications. Omega **96**, 102070 (2020)

RNC2050.   https://www.portugal.gov.pt/download-ficheiros/ficheiro.aspx?v=aa27c4c9-dac3-47c3-96ae-4ca86183635d. Accessed 22 July 2020

Rogge, M., Hurk, E., Larsen, A., Sauer, D.U.: Electric bus fleet size and mix problem with optimization of charging Infrastructure. Appl. Energy **211**, 282–295 (2018)

Rothgang, S., Rogge, M., Becker, J., Sauer, D.: Battery design for successful electrification in public transport. Energies **8**, 6715–6737 (2015)

Rupprecht Consult: Guidelines for developing and implementing a sustainable urban mobility plan, Second Edition. https://www.eltis.org/sites/default/files/sump_guidelines_2019_interactive_document_1.pdf. Accessed 21 July 2020

Sinhuber, P., Rohlfs, W., Sauer, D.U.: Conceptional considerations for electrification of public city buses — Energy storage system and charging stations. In: 2010 Emobility - Electrical Power Train, Leipzig, pp. 1–5 (2010)

Tang, X., Lin, X., He, F.: Robust scheduling strategies of electric buses under stochastic traffic conditions. Transp. Res. Part C **105**, 163–182 (2019)

Xylia, M., Leduc, S., Patrizio, P., Kraxner, F., Silveira, S.: Locating charging infrastructure for electric buses in Stockholm. Transp. Res. Part C: Emerg. Technol. **78**, 183–200 (2017)

Wang, Y., Huang, Y., Jiuping, X., Barclay, N.: Optimal recharging scheduling for urban electric buses: a case study in Davis. Transp. Res. Part E: Logist. Transp. Rev. **100**, 115–132 (2017)

Logistics Infrastructure of Automobile Industry Between Germany and Poland

Adeel Ali Qureshi(✉)

Poznan University of Economics and Business, Al. Niepodległości 10,
61-875 Poznań, Poland
adeel84@gmail.com

Abstract. This study reviews the logistical infrastructure of the automotive industry of Germany and Poland; to be specific, the factories in Poland which are run by German automobile companies are studied, in order to assess the benefit in the movement of factories from Germany to Poland. Quantitative data of Poland's logistical structure, German and Polish economies, production output figures and values, etc. are studied under scholarly literature for qualitative assessments. Critical analysis has been made with comparison to each other and Czech Republic as well which is a neighbor and strong competitor of Poland in the industry. Furthermore, data is restructured to assess the economic benefits of German companies and the effect on Polish economy to ascertain the feasibility to produce in a neighboring country in order to save on wages and continue to pay for transportation, rather than producing in the home country of the companies. Findings are drawn in conclusion and a tentative benefit of savings has been noted. Manufacturing volume, vehicular exports, automotive parts exports as well as railway density, carriage of goods and road transport has been analyzed during the process.

Keywords: Logistics · Automobile transportation · Production · Manufacturing

1 Introduction

The purpose of this study is to analyze the logistical infrastructure of automobile industry, comparing case studies from Germany and Poland. The paper provides an encompassing review of the literature, as well as a quantitative analysis. Combined, these approaches allow us to draw some qualitative conclusions about the logistics and infrastructure on automobile industry between those two countries.

The collection of processes involving the management of acquiring resources, storage, and transportation to destination is known as logistics. For manufacturing firms, logistics management includes transportation of goods, identification of distributors, finding most effective solution for accessing destinations and cost effectiveness [1]. Moreover, research shows that the performance of logistical operations is directly related to volume of trade [2]. Naturally, with a smoother transportation of manufactured goods, trade will not be hindered by unneeded disruptions.

© ICST Institute for Computer Sciences, Social Informatics and Telecommunications Engineering 2021
Published by Springer Nature Switzerland AG 2021. All Rights Reserved
A. L. Martins et al. (Eds.): INTSYS 2020, LNICST 364, pp. 194–207, 2021.
https://doi.org/10.1007/978-3-030-71454-3_12

In 2018, with 82.7 million inhabitants, the German GDP per capita was 47,501 USD [3], whereas, Poland's GDP per capita was 15,418 USD for 2018 with 38 million inhabitants [4]. German-Polish border, the Oder-Neisse line is 467 km long [5]. Sharing borders and amicable relationships, capitalizing on each other's advantages is advantageous for both. According to Financial Observer [6], Polish-German trade in 2016 exceeded 100 billion euros [6]. Motivation for both parties remains economical; German companies reach economies of scale by growth in manufacturing considering lower wages in Poland, while Poland receives increased FDI and employment.

German companies such as Volkswagen Group, Opel and Daimler AG produce ready cars and parts in Poland relying on hefty logistical processes for transporting them to various destinations. One quick example can be that Daimler AG recently invested 500 million euro in a manufacturing plant in Poland [7], another could be the Volkswagen manufacturing in Poland as well. However, in order to understand the transportability of goods, manufacturing data based on each factory as well as the industry as a whole must be analyzed.

Research question that this study tends to answer is whether is it beneficial for German automobile companies to move their production plants in Poland, or not, in order to gain economic benefits based on the advantage the logistical infrastructure of the two countries provide between the shared land border.

This paper is organized as follows. After this section of Introduction, Literature Review discusses scholarly work regarding logistics, transportation costs, trade, etc. related to the subject. Afterwards, the methodology is detailed of how this study has been performed. Next is Quantitative Analysis of the German-Polish automobile industry. Results follow showing my findings restructuring aforementioned data for further analysis. Discussion section ensues where a critical analysis of quantitative results is done under the light of scholarly works for qualitative assessment of the German-Polish automotive industry. Among other things, the rationale is also discussed behind German companies' continuous decision of utilizing Polish factories instead of home-based production solutions. All this is concluded in the last section therein, namely Conclusion.

2 Literature Review

Logistics plays a crucial role for a well-functioning business. As Mallik [8] stresses in her 2010 study on page 104, "having the right item in the right quantity at the right time at the right place for the right price in the right condition to the right customer" [8]. Narrowing it down, business logistics and management of supply chain is the process of material flow of goods from the producer to the end user [9]. According to Nyhuis and Wiendahi Hans-Peter [10], logistics, especially related to production is an ever changing process that offers the opportunity of constant improvements. Since this study covers automobile manufacturing plants, therefore, production logistics is mentioned. Nyhuis and Wiendahi [10] elaborate furthermore that new production plants require allocation of machinery and logistical transport of product. Existing plants face recurring renewal of machinery and the routine transport of product [10].

Of transport costs, Limao and Venables [11], in 2001, suggest that while international trade fundamentally relies on logistics affecting countries and companies, many studies focus on geographical characteristics or those regarding the product, instead of added transportation costs [11]. To encompass it all, I discuss Polish volume of goods, transport cost as well as added transport costs in the form of toll taxes and the ownership of heavy duty vehicles (HDVs). Interestingly, the same point about added transport cost has been raised by W. F. Wong [12] in 2017 as well, that in trade based studies, cost is usually exhibited exogenously and is understood based on distance [12].

It must be noted that according to research, the ownership taxes are actually paid on the route itself [13] while adding to the benefit of Polish economy, but increasing in German companies' transport cost. According to Limao and Venables [11], transport costs may reach up to 60% of landlocked countries with poor logistical infrastructure. For countries connected to sea, Martínez-Zarzoso et al. in 2014 [14] suggest that transport cost and aggregate trade value is inversely proportional; trade value includes volume and variety of products [14]. Limao and Venables [11], in 2001, state the same but from another semantic that countries with coastal lines but poor infrastructure of logistics may see a hike of transport costs for as much as 40%. Since Poland is not landlocked, however, the trade between Germany and Poland and most of the Europe (except Scandinavia) is done through land, therefore, the rail and road based infrastructure is of utmost importance.

According to the report by Arvis, Ojala, Wiederer and Shephard [15], logistics infrastructure is of crucial value for cross-border trade, the same report also stresses on the importance of scheduling and timely deliveries based on their study and rankings of Logistics Performance Index (LPI). High LPI score countries in top quintile report that shipments almost always reach on time. Poor LPI score countries in low quintile report only half of the shipments to be on time [15]. Barbero et al. [13] also emphasize on distance and time related costs (e.g. maximum speed, traffic lights, curvature of roads, etc.) that affect delivery scheduling directly [13]. Another hindrance may be the customs and delays caused by processes or complicated regulations. According to the 2016 study by Martincus, Carballo and Graziano [16], delays caused by customs in arrival of goods may be accumulated in trade costs for the particular transaction [16]. The same study states that, if each exported item is checked and takes up to 2 days, then all 2011 exports would have been reduced down 16.4%. The same would be reduced 8.4% provided that Ordinary Least Squares (OLS) methodology is used [16].

Based on LPI data in the 2018 report by Arvis et al. [15], countries in top and bottom quintile scored almost the same (62% and 61% respectively) for Customs as the determinant, but the middle countries (3rd quintile) scored the least, (44%) [15]. It shows that while laws have not dramatically changed in either the top or bottom countries group, they still exhibit improvement in logistics environment (since 2015), but not as such in 3rd quintile [15]. Poland has 83.5% highest performance, and Germany has 100%, therefore, both fall in the 1st quintile.

Zarzoso and Suarez-Burguet [17] in their 2015 study state that trade, based on the gravity model is directly proportional to the economic size of the countries and negatively to the geographical distance between them [17]. Similar to Germany and Poland, using Spain and France as neighbors' example, Matinez-Zarzoso et al. [17]

indicate that Spanish regions near France export more to it. Distance effect is further validated with comparatively lesser export volume from Spanish regions to third countries. However, according to Barbero et al. [13], tolls, which add up to transport costs, are also directly proportional to the geographical distance, and since Poland and Germany use roads that require tolls, such transport costs are added.

3 Methodology

In order to assess the logistical infrastructure of German automobile companies that manufacture their products (vehicles or vehicular parts) within Poland for economic benefits, Volkswagen is used as a sample case study. Nevertheless, since Poland also houses factories of other companies as well, therefore, general automobile industry's manufacturing in Poland are considered as well. In order to ascertain the volume of automobile products, production volume is also recorded. Data has been collected of total production, passenger cars, commercial vehicles, etc. as well as of production of German companies namely Opel and Volkswagen. This is corresponded to export of Polish goods to the rest of Europe and contrasted with Germany only as well, in order to exhibit the share of automobile industry which may utilize land based logistical solutions such as truck fleets, railways, etc. The export volume to the said countries (and Russia) are noted as well. Furthermore, the logistics infrastructure of Poland is observed with land based solutions currently in the infrastructure, motorways and railways.

In order to assess the economic aspect of the collected data, freight transport costs in the region are collected for light and heavy duty vehicles as well as for the rail. Infrastructure of Germany and Poland is also noted for comparison. Based on factories' location within Poland, and the destination of products, the distance and cost ratio is assessed.

A tentative calculation is also performed in order to understand the savings made by the sample Volkswagen factory in Poland had it been Germany based instead of Poland, based on the minimum wage, production and employees' data. The savings made based on remuneration for employed labor is calculated. Next is the calculation for the transportation of cars from the Volkswagen Poznan to Berlin, as an example. The mode selected for transportation is HDV fleet and toll is also calculated. Later, the transportation cost is subtracted from the saving made through the difference in labor salaries in Germany and Poland, and a tentative figure is calculated. Naturally, learning business secrets would be impossible, therefore, a general idea is constructed to exhibit the usage of logistics and its effect on the logistical infrastructure.

Data has been collected from reliable sources such as Government of Poland's statistics office, Polish Automotive Industry Association's released data, European Commission's published reports, etc. Vehicles are considered to be used for public transport for at least ten persons seating capacity.

4 Automobile Industry Between Germany and Poland; A Quantitative Analysis

After examining the findings of the literature concerning the relationship between logistics and international trade, this section will focus on a preliminary data research based on the logistics of the automobile industry between Germany and Poland. With many German factories, Poland receives FDI from Germany and employment increases. In 2019, unemployment in Poland was 5.1%, coming from 12% in 2015 [18]. Minimum monthly wage in Poland is 523.09 EUR [19], whereas the minimum hourly wage in Germany is 9.19 EUR [20]. With 160 average working hours a month, it amounts to 1470.4 EUR/month; the difference (947.31 EUR) per employee might be highly beneficial for German companies.

Poland produced 662,000 cars in 2016 resulting in 3.5% market share of EU with 8th position in the production output ranking. (Czech had 7% market share and acquired the 5th position. Slovakia had 4.9% market share and acquired the 7th position, while Hungary acquired the 9th position). Between 2013–16, automotive sold production in Poland had an almost 26% increase, which amount to 71% if compared against 2008 (beginning of global crisis). This is one of the highest figure in Europe w. r.t. the 2008 crisis. In 2011, the value of produced car parts and accessories exceeded the value of manufactured ready cars. In 2016, 57% production output based on parts and accessories, coming up from 42% from 9 years ago [21].

Table 1. Production of motor vehicles in Poland (in thousands)

Year	Total	Type of vehicles				Selected German brands	
		Passenger cars	Commercial vehicles			Opel Poland	Volkswagen Poznan
			Total commercial	Lorries, tractors	Public transport		
2007	791.7	697.7	94	–	–	–	–
2008	947.1	841.7	105.4	–	–	–	–
2009	880.5	818.8	61.7	–	–	–	–
2010	871.3	785	86.3	–	–	–	–
2011	839.7	740.5	99.2	–	–	–	–
2012	647.8	540	107.8	–	–	–	–
2013	590.2	475	115.2	–	–	108.5	170.9
2014	593.5	472.6	120.9	115.9	5	88.9	175.5
2015	660.6	534.7	125.9	120.9	5	169	170.8
2016	681.8	554.6	127.2	–	–	201.2	187.4
2017	689.7	514.7	175	–	–	165.2	238
2018	659.6	451.6	208	–	–	106.5	266.8

Total (2nd column) = passenger + commercial vehicles. Public Transport = vehicles for of at least 10 persons

Sources: 2014/15 passenger and commercial vehicles: [22]. Selected German brands and Types of Vehicles: [23].

We see passenger cars leading against lorries/tractors; production of public transport vehicles remains minuscule in comparison. This data does not exhibit exports. Let us analyze Polish exports in general as well as to the EU and specifically to Germany (Table 2).

Table 2. Export of Polish Goods to EU, Germany and in total

2014		2015		Countries
Thousand tons	Million t-km	Thousand tons	Million t-km	
61075	53594	63601	53252	Total
56446	47346	60497	49229	European Union
23897	15447	25923	16125	Germany

t-km is ton kilometer – Data source: Road Transport in Poland [22]

8% of Polish GDP comes from automotive production which is 13% of Polish exports creating 1.1 million jobs [24]. Volkswagen has 1 factory in Wrzesnia, and another near Poznan [25]. Opel Manufacturing Poland, a subsidiary of the German company Opel Automobile GmbH in Rüsselsheim, Germany runs 2 factories in Poland. One in Gliwice to assemble passenger cars, the largest foreign investment in Silesia. It achieved a milestone building 1.5 million vehicles in 2011 [26]. Tychy factory, for engines only, achieved a milestone by producing 2 million engines in 2009. Engines from here are to be delivered to a factory in Trnava, Slovakia [27]. Daimler AG has a production facility in Warsaw [28]. Besides this, Mercedes-Benz Cars has been building a battery factory in Jawor [29]. Since there is a strong emphasis on the production of car parts, etc. as well, therefore, the following data is presented (Table 3).

Table 3. Exports of components, parts and accessories (EUR billion)

2010	2011	2012	2013	2014	2015	2016	2017	2018
12.6	14.5	14.5	15.8	16.8	18.2	19.7	21.1	22.3

Accessories include tires, glass, batteries, engines, electric equipment and mechanical parts of combustion engines – Source: KPMG Poland [23]

Table 4 presents Polish exports of the automobile branch. The value of exports to various destinations in Europe are presented and the production is subdivided between final products and components.

Table 4. Destination focused Polish exports (Vehicle, trailers and semi-trailers as well as components, parts and accessories) – 2018 (EUR billion)

Country	Vehicles, trailers and semi-trailers	Components, parts and accessories
Czech	0.33	2.34
Germany	3.4	7.03
France	0.81	1.44
Great Britain	0.94	1.37
Hungary	0.34	0.79
Italy	1.02	1.43
Russia	0.06	0.1

Source: KPMG Poland [23]

Railway lines, railway density and motorways are important for land logistics. Poland and Germany share Oder-Neisse line, and their logistics is mainly land based. Referring back to the study by Hausman et al. [2] published in 2012, logistical performance is directly related to the volume of trade [2]. Therefore, the following data is crucial to understand the network spread for land based logistics. Czech, being a neighbor and a strong CEE competitor of Poland in the EU automobile industry is kept for comparison.

Table 5. 2018 – Railway density, carriage of goods, total length of motorways and railway lines and toll cost.

Country	Railway density	Carriage of goods (million ton-kilometers)		Total length of motorways and railway lines (kilometers)		Toll cost (eur/km)
		Rail	Road	Motorways	Railway lines	
Poland	61.5	59388	315874	1637	19235	0.27
Germany	107.6	128816	316767	13141	38416	0.19
Czech	121.4	16564	41073	1252	9572	0.18

Unit for Railway Density: Kilometers of Lines Operated per 1000 km^2. Source for Railway Density, Carriage of Goods, Total Length of Motorways and Railway Lines: [30]. Source for Toll Costs: Estimating Road Transport Costs Between EU Regions by [13].

Table 6. Average freight transport operating costs in NSM-5 EU

Mode (t-km)	HDV	LDV	Rail freight
Cost (EUR)	0.07	1.81	0.06

Source: Schade et al. [31] – NSM-5 means nations newly added to EU; Czech Republic, Hungary, Poland, Slovenia, and Slovakia

In light of the average freight costs, it should also be noted that factories have been placed strategically for economic benefits of their owner companies. E.g. Opel's factory in Gliwice (Poland) and headquarters in Rüsselsheim (Germany) are 888 km away from each other (8 h by road, more by rail). And the factory in Tychy (Poland) which sends engines to Trnava (Slovakia) is 308 km away from it (less than 4 h by road and slightly more by rail). Such strategic placement may help control freight costs better. Based on data from Table 5 and Table 6, average HDV transport operation from Gliwice to Russelsheim would cost 62.16 and 239.76 for toll, amounting to a total of 301.92 euro. And from Tychy to Trnava would total to 104.72 euro. This calculation is tentative and naturally does not include additional practical costs.

5   Results

Poland's 662,000 automotive output in 2016 with 3.5% EU market share may not seem astounding at large scale, but Volkswagen Group with a big share in Polish automotive manufacturing industry curtails 24.5% EU market share between January and November of 2019 considering new registrations only [32]. The difference with predecessor PSA Group was almost 9%. This important because Volkswagen has two factories in Poland. The output of one of these is exhibited in the following chart (Fig. 1):

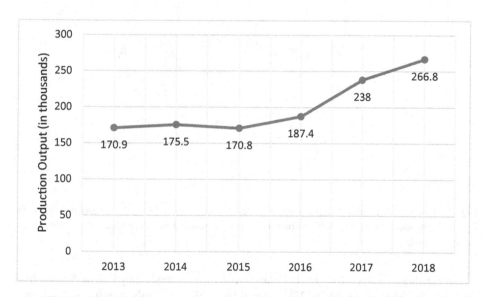

Fig. 1. Volkswagen Poznan production plant's production output (in thousands)

Increase in sold-production in the automotive industry in Poland (26% between 2013–16 and 71% in comparison to 2008) is promising for Germans to increase their manufacturing output in Poland, and useful for Polish economy. Similarly, the production of car parts exceeding ready cars is also hopeful for the same purpose, that componential production is as well equally promising. In 2015, in comparison to the previous year, total motor vehicles production had an 11.3% increase, passenger cars had a 13.1% increase, lorries/tractors saw a 4.4% increase and public transport vehicles had no change at all. Separately, Polish exported goods were unloaded in Germany amounting to 25,923,000 tons, 40.7% of all Polish exported goods unloaded everywhere.

In Volkswagen Poznan, 750 vehicles are produced daily; 1 every 2 min. Września plant can produce up to 420 vehicles a day. Recently, Volkswagen opened a new factory in Białężyce. Volkswagen Poland employs 11000 people [33] (Fig. 2).

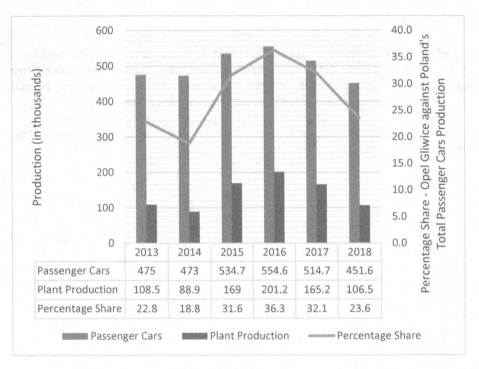

	2013	2014	2015	2016	2017	2018
Passenger Cars	475	473	534.7	554.6	514.7	451.6
Plant Production	108.5	88.9	169	201.2	165.2	106.5
Percentage Share	22.8	18.8	31.6	36.3	32.1	23.6

Fig. 2. Poland's total production of passenger cars with respect to Opel's production plant in Gliwice's production share (Self restructured data). Source: Own reproduction of data from Table 1's data

According to a study by KPMG Poland which was published by Polish Automotive Industry Association in 2019 [23], more than 7 billion euro's worth car parts and almost 3.4 billion euro's worth of vehicles were exported to Germany. Comparing to another neighbor of Poland, Russia (Poland-Russia border is 210 km long while Poland-Germany border is 467 km long [5]), we see that 0.1 billion euro's worth of car parts and 0.06 billion euro's worth of vehicles were exported to Russia.

Surprisingly, Polish railway density is almost half the size of Czech's, another major car manufacturer in Central and Eastern Europe. For logistics, carriage of goods, in 2018, Poland compounded to 59,388 million ton-kilometers in rail far above Czech and almost half that of Germany. For road, Poland and Germany stand very close to each other, surprisingly, at 315,874 for the former and 316,767 for the latter. Czech remains far below in this category. Poland has a more thorough spread out network of motorways and railways (exact figures in Table 5) compared to Czech but stands far below Germany. It may be noted that the land area of Poland is 312,679 km^2, of Germany is 357,386 km^2 and of Czech is 78,856 km^2.

Railroad, and motorways are also important because transportation industry used for logistics stands separate from automotive industry but together adds up to Polish economy, giving Poland a very strong economic intake from German investment besides direct foreign investment and direct job creation.

Table 7. Tentative savings calculation of Volkswagen Poland (Self restructured data)

Country	Monthly minimum wage	Salary for 11000 employees	Specification
Germany	1470.4	16,174,400	Salary in Germany
Poland	523.09	5,753,990	Salary in Poland
Difference	947.31	10,420,410	Savings in Poland

Source: Minimum wage: Germany [20], Poland [19]. Employees of Volkswagen employees: [33]. Calculation: Own reproduction of data

And as mentioned earlier, Volkswagen Poznan produces up to 750 cars per day. 5 days a week, 20 days a month, 15,000 cars would be produced. Poznan to Berlin is 272 km [34]. Considering the Poznan to Berlin distance bracket for the sake of the case example, and considering the more expensive cost for HDV transport operation and toll costs, the following table is generated (Table 8).

Table 8. Tentative Poznan to Berlin HDV transport operating cost

		Cost for 1 HDV operation	Cost of 15000 cars
Distance (km)	272	–	–
HDV (per km)	0.07	19.04	285600
Toll (per km)	0.27	73.44	1101600
Total			1387200

Subtracting this transportation total cost from the Difference (Savings) computed from Table 7.

$$10{,}420{,}410 - 1{,}387{,}200 = 9{,}033{,}210 \text{ (euro)}$$

A very tentative calculation suggests that producing cars in Poznan (Poland) and transporting them to Berlin (Germany) allows Volkswagen to save more than 9 million euro per month. Please note that this calculation does not cover additional costs of logistics, safety, taxation, legalities, insurance, administration, management, etc. Introducing such costs would reduce the savings significantly.

6 Discussion

In 2016, Polish-German Chamber of Commerce conducted a study for investment attractiveness among German companies interested in investment in CEE. Poland came 2nd, after leading for 3 previous years, replaced by Czech Republic at number 1 in the report. It is promising that Germans have not decided to step back in last 3 years, on the contrary, Daimler AG has recently invested 500 million euro in a factory in Lower Silesia, Poland [6]. This phenomenon probably works swiftly because it fits to Oliver and Webber's [9] material flows of goods theory; Polish subsidiaries producing goods that utilize Polish land network access to various destinations depicting a practical of business logistics and supply chain management.

With the aforementioned investment attractiveness drop of Poland, the contemporary situation brings to light Nyhuis and Wiendahi Hans-Peter's [10] concept that logistics of production changes constantly, constant improvements are needed [10]. As shown in Table 5, Czech's motorways and railway network is not much smaller than that of Poland's while Czech being one quarter to the size of Poland by land area.

The point raised by Limao and Venables [11], mentioned earlier, about added transport costs is seen in practice because within EU, due to lack of trade barriers, it is the characteristics regarding the product or the transport costs in the context of geographical distances that affect the logistics. Same as the suggestion by W. F. Wong [12], transport costs being exogenous. The study by Bensassi, Martínez-Zarzoso and Suárez-Burguet [14] suggest the relationship between transport costs and aggregate trade value to be inversely proportionate [14], which we see to be utilized by Opel in transporting the engines produced in the production plant in Tychy, Poland to Trnava, Slovakia by reduced costs and increased transport value.

The logistical infrastructure of railway density in Poland as shown by Table 5 is mediocre, when contrasted against that of Czech, primarily because Czech being significantly smaller than Poland comprises of a railway density of 121.4 kms/1000 km^2, as of 2018, whereas, Poland stands with 61.5 kms/1000 km^2. Not to forget that Germany comprising of a similar area than that of Poland surprisingly shows the railway density of 107.6 kms/1000 km^2 as depicted in Table 5 as well. And economic advancement of Germany may not stand as a strong reason alone if the economic condition of Czech is also considered for one variable such as railways density, per se.

This mediocrity of structure is contrasted by the report by Arvis et al. [15] where it is mentioned that infrastructure is very important for cross-border trade [15]. The report continues about scheduling, timely deliveries and so on, however, as for the infrastructure, and the aforementioned drop in CEE investment attractiveness ranking [6], Poland appears weak in the logistical infrastructure. Since land logistics are used by various industries, it must effect other industries as well.

Zarzoso and Suarez-Burguet [35] emphasize on the positive relationship of trade and economic size and the negative one of trade and distance [35]. We witness this between Germany and Poland (for distance), since they share Oder-Neisse line and many important cities lie very close to each other, for instance the distance between Berlin and Poznan is almost 270 km only [34], however, the economic size differs. Polish GDP per capita (15,418 USD [4]) is far less than that of Germany (47,501 USD [3]), however, trade has been positive, this phenomenon may be explained by the fact that the production facilities of German companies within Poland are direct subsidiaries of their German corporations. Trade, nevertheless, between Germany and Poland is quite high, for comparison, German-Polish trade is almost double than German-Russian trade [6], validating Zarzoso's and Suarez-Burguet's [35] distance based.

The minimum wage gap, as shown earlier, between German and Polish labor market is 947.31 euro/month. Volkswagen Poland employs 11,000 people. As earlier tentative calculation exhibited a profitable margin, we notice the German companies' motivation. For Poland, the increased employment, FDI, are crucial. Besides these, many industries are influenced positively, such as raw material suppliers, construction companies for factories and roads, even housing, stores or other small business near the factories, etc.

7   Conclusion

Logistics and logistical infrastructure are crucial to augment efficiency in production and returns to trade (both domestic and international). This study utilized economic, logistical and geographical data of automotive factories in Poland run by German companies producing ready vehicles as well as parts, etc., in order to understand the logistical infrastructure and gain some economic insight to the German-Polish auto-motive industry. Analyzing growth, recent competition with Czech, distinction between producing ready vehicles vs parts, etc., the comparisons are done over quantitative data and qualitative assessments have been made regarding scholarly work by various authors to understand the economic benefit of German companies in pro-ducing in Poland and economic benefit of Poland by German investments. Data has been restructured for comparisons in order to reach qualitative judgments backed by quantitative reasoning.

The research question for this study to investigate and see if it was beneficial for German automobile companies to movie their production plants in Poland in order to gain economic benefits based on the advantage the logistical infrastructure of the two countries provide between the shared land border is conclusively answered positively. German companies benefit in profit maximization by reallocating their production to where wages are lower and distance is not very far to be infeasible. Even adding transportation cost, they are still benefitting from the wage gap. The Polish automotive industry seems to run on the path like the automotive industry of UK and Spain where many local names were acquired by foreigners, however, Poland's automotive industry differs by manufacturing for others as of now, therefore, the strong requirement of logistics is of utmost importance. While the foreign investment seems to be growing and the industry continues to thrive creating employment and even allowing local entrepreneurs new opportunities. However, the infrastructure of rail and road has room for improvement, especially when compared against Czech, which is considerably smaller in geographical size but enjoys the same competitive advantage as Poland of having central location within the EU. Poland, nevertheless, has been called among the fastest growing economies of EU [4], and with the overall infrastructure, transportability and manufacturing outcome, the logistics infrastructure of automobile industry between Germany and Poland is successfully on the right track.

References

1. Kenton, W.: Investopedia. https://www.investopedia.com/terms/l/logistics.asp. Accessed 28 Sept 2020
2. Hausman, W., Lee, H., Subramanian, U.: The Impact of logistics performance on trade. Prod. Oper. Manag. Soc. **22**(2), 236–252 (2013)
3. Germany GDP per capita 2018 – Trading Economics. https://tradingeconomics.com/germany/gdp-per-capita. Accessed 13 Oct 2020
4. Poland Overview – World Bank. https://www.worldbank.org/en/country/poland/overview#1. Accessed 13 Oct 2020
5. Concise Statistical Yearbook of Poland 2013. https://stat.gov.pl/en/topics/statistical-yearbooks/statistical-yearbooks/concise-statistical-yearbook-of-poland-2013,1,14.html. Accessed 13 Oct 2020
6. Godlewski, A.: Obserwator Finansowy. https://www.obserwatorfinansowy.pl/in-english/macroeconomics/trade-between-poland-and-germany-reaches-record-levels/. Accessed 14 Oct 2020
7. Daimler Media. https://media.daimler.com/marsMediaSite/en/instance/ko/Investment-of-around-500-million-euros-Mercedes-Benz-builds-new-engine-plant-in-Jawor-Poland.xhtml?oid=22530538. Accessed 14 Oct 2020
8. Mallik, S., Bidgoil, H.: The Handbook of Technology Management: Supply Chain Management, Marketing and Advertising, and Global Management V2, 1st edn. Wiley, Chichester (2010)
9. Oliver, R., Webber, M., Christopher, M.: Logistics: The Strategic Issues, 1st edn. Chapman & Hall, London (1992)
10. Nyhuis, P., Wiendahl, H.-P.: Fundamentals of Production Logistics, 1st edn. Springer, Heidelberg (2009). https://doi.org/10.1007/978-3-540-34211-3
11. Limao, N., Venables, A.: Infrastructure geographical disadvantage and transport costs. World Bank Econ. Rev. **15**(3), 451–479 (2001)
12. Wong, W.: The Round Trip Effect: Endogenous Transport Costs and International Trade. https://freit.org/WorkingPapers/Papers/Transportation/FREIT1334.pdf. Accessed 14 Oct 2020
13. Persyn, D., Díaz-Lanchas, J., Barbero, J.: Estimating road transport costs between EU regions, JRC Working Papers on Territorial Modelling and Analysis. https://www.econstor.eu/bitstream/10419/202274/1/jrc-wptma201904.pdf. Accessed 14 Oct 2020
14. Martínez-Zarzoso, I., Suárez, C., Bensassi, S.: The effect of maritime transport costs on the extensive and intensive margins evidence from the Europe-Asia trade. Marit. Econ. Logist. **16**(3), 276–297 (2014)
15. Arvis, J., et al.: Connecting to Compete 2018 – Trade Logistics in the Global Economy. https://openknowledge.worldbank.org/bitstream/handle/10986/29971/LPI2018.pdf?sequence=1&isAllowed=y. Accessed 14 Oct 2020

16. Martincus, V., Jerónimo, C., Graziano, A., Schaur, G.: Customs. J. Int. Econ. **96**(1), 119–137 (2016)
17. Bensassi, S., Marquez-Ramosb, L., Martinez-Zarzoso, I., Suarez-Burguet, C.: Relationship between logistics infrastructure and trade: evidence from spanish regional exports. Transp. Res. Part A: Policy Pract. **72**, 47–61 (2015)
18. Poland Unemployment Rate – Trading Economics. https://tradingeconomics.com/poland/unemployment-rate. Accessed 14 Oct 2020
19. Poland Gross Minimum Monthly Wage – Trading Economics. https://tradingeconomics.com/poland/minimum-wages. Accessed 14 Oct 2020
20. Germany Gross Minimum Wages – Trading Economics. https://tradingeconomics.com/germany/minimum-wages. Accessed 14 Oct 2020
21. Traczyk, W., Klass, L.: Poland Good Results of the Automotive Industry. https://www.spotlightmetal.com/poland-good-results-of-the-automotive-industry-a-812409/. Accessed 14 Oct 2020
22. Road Transport in Poland in the Years 2014 & 2015. https://stat.gov.pl/download/gfx/portalinformacyjny/en/defaultaktualnosci/3323/5/4/1/road_transport_in_poland_in_the_years_2014-2015.pdf. Accessed 14 Oct 2020
23. Year Book 2019/2020 – Polish Automotive Industry Association. https://www.pzpm.org.pl/en/content/download/11068/67912/file/Rocznik_2019-2020_v3.pdf. Accessed 14 Oct 2020
24. Blum, M., Klass, L.: Strong Position of Poland's Automotive Producers. https://www.spotlightmetal.com/strong-position-of-polands-automotive-producers-a-815247/. Accessed 14 Oct 2020
25. European assembly plant map – Automotive News Europe, Interactive. https://europe.autonews.com/article/20140519/ANE/140429957/interactive-european-assembly-plant-map. Accessed 20 Sept 2020
26. Pressroom Opel Media. https://int-media.opel.com/en/taxonomy/term/5727. Accessed 21 Sept 2020
27. Revolvy – Opel Manufacturing Poland. https://www.revolvy.com/page/Opel-Manufacturing-Poland. Accessed 28 Dec 2019
28. Daimler Warszawa. https://www.daimler.com/career/about-us/locations/location-detail-page-5199.html. Accessed 14 Oct 2020
29. Global battery production network – Daimler.com. https://www.daimler.com/company/locations/battery-factory-jawor.html. Accessed 14 Oct 2020
30. Railway Density – United Nations Economic Commission for Europe. https://w3.unece.org/PXWeb/en/CountryRanking?IndicatorCode=47. Accessed 14 Oct 2020
31. Schade, W., et al.: Compete Final Report Analysis of the contribution of transport policies to the competitiveness of the EU economy and comparison with the United States. https://ec.europa.eu/ten/transport/studies/doc/compete/compete_report_en.pdf. Accessed 14 Oct 2020
32. Selected passenger car manufacturers' EU market share between January and November 2019 based on new registrations – Statista. https://www.statista.com/statistics/263421/market-share-of-selected-car-maunfacturers-in-europe/. Accessed 14 Oct 2020
33. Volkswagen Poznan Products. https://volkswagen-poznan.pl/en/products. Accessed 14 Oct 2020
34. Google Maps Poznan to Berlin. https://www.google.com/maps/dir/poznan/berlin/. Accessed 14 Oct 2020
35. Martínez-Zarzoso, I., Suárez-Burguet, C.: Transport costs and trade empirical evidence for Latin American imports from the European Union. J. Int. Trade Econ. Dev. **14**(3), 353–371 (2005)

Simulation and Prediction

Performance Evaluation of Object Detection Algorithms Under Adverse Weather Conditions

Thomas Rothmeier[✉] and Werner Huber

Ingolstadt University of Applied Sciences, Ingolstadt, Germany
{thomas.rothmeier,werner.huber}@thi.de

Abstract. Camera systems capture images from the surrounding environment and process these datastreams to detect and classify objects. However, these systems are prone to errors, often caused by adverse weather conditions such as fog. It is well known that fog has a negative effect on the camera's view and thus degrades sensor performance. This is caused by microscopic water droplets in the air, that scatter light, reduce contrast and blur the image. Object detection algorithms show severely worse performance and high uncertainty when exposed to fog. However, they need to work safe and reliable in all weather conditions to enable full autonomous driving in the future. This work focuses on the evaluation of several state-of-the-art object detectors in normal and foggy environmental conditions. It is shown that the detection performance deteriorates considerably when exposed to fog. Further, the results suggest that some algorithms are more robust towards fog than others.

Keywords: Object detection · Adverse weather · Autonomous driving

1 Introduction

One of the greatest challenges still remaining to enable fully autonomous vehicles, is the ability to drive safely and reliably even in low visibility conditions. Safety systems rely on data from surround sensors to correctly perceive their environment. Although most sensors perform well in good visibility conditions, their performance degrades extremely during adverse weather conditions such as rain, fog and snow. Hasirlioglu et al. showed that the effects of rain on camera, lidar and radar sensors degrade sensor performance [6,8]. Reway et al. evaluated camera-based object detection by simulating various environmental conditions [19].

Camera-based object detection is of high importance when it comes to vehicle safety. Currently, the camera is the only sensor that can reliably interpret a situation, due to its ability to recognize the semantic of an object. Early, accurate

This work is supported under the FH-Impuls program of the German Federal Ministry of Education and Research (BMBF) under Grant No. 13FH7I01IA.

A. L. Martins et al. (Eds.): INTSYS 2020, LNICST 364, pp. 211–222, 2021.
https://doi.org/10.1007/978-3-030-71454-3_13

and reliable detection results can prevent traffic accidents and thus save lifes. In the last few years huge progress has been made in the field of computer vision, mostly induced by the success of neural networks for object detection tasks. However, these novel algorithms are not yet able to completely mimic human perception. Furthermore, most of the algorithms have been trained under good weather conditions, which leads to problems and high uncertainty under poor visibility conditions.

Poor visibility can occur in fog, for example. Fog consists of microscopic water droplets in the air that scatter light and lead to reduced contrast, color saturation and less precision in contours and details. These effects grow with increasing distance to the object and lead to an overestimation of the distance to the object ahead [13, 21].

In this work we focus on performance evaluation of camera-based object detection under foggy weather conditions. We want to quantify the extent to which the uncertainty of the predictions and the localisation error change with increasing distance to the object. Furthermore we aim to give a comparison of different object detectors in dense fog. The evaluation is based on data recorded in the adverse weather chamber of CARISSMA on which a car attrap moves from the camera sensor.

Outline. This paper is organised as follows: Sect. 2 gives an overview of related work towards object detection in adverse weather. Section 3 describes our experimental setup, data preparation and evaluation methods. Section 4 shows the results of the object detectors on our test scenario, while Sect. 5 summarizes our contribution and discusses limitations and future work.

2   Related Work

In recent years, neural networks, especially Convolutional Neural Networks (CNNs), have increasingly emerged as the standard for object detection and object recognition. There is a large variety of object detectors that use different features and sensor data as input. However, most of them share similar basic concepts that can be roughly divided into one-stage-detectors and two-stage-detectors. The following section will give a short overview of object detectors and shortly summarize their underlying concepts.

An example for a two-stage-detector is Faster R-CNN [18]. In the first stage a feature map is given to a Region Proposal Network (RPN) that proposes regions of interest that might contain an object. In the second stage the proposed regions of the RPN are then classified by another network layer. Since two network passes are required, these detectors are slower than networks that predict location and class in a single step.

In order to address this issue other architectures were proposed that only require one network pass, so called one-stage-detectors. Well known examples are YOLOv3 [17], Single-Shot-Detector (SSD) [12] and RetinaNet [10]. They differ from two-stage-detectors as they omit the region proposal stage and therefore predict bounding boxes and object classes in a single network run. This leads to faster inference times than with two-stage-detectors. SSD uses multiple feature maps at different scales, to predict bounding boxes and classify objects at different size. Similarily YOLOv3 uses a feature pyramid to extract features from 3 different scales. It is trimmed for fast inference time. RetinaNet introduces a new focal loss, that aims to tackle to problem of class imbalance encountered during training of dense detectors.

Although there is lots of progress in the field of object detection, adverse weather conditions still pose a huge problem. In [1,5,23] techniques for fog removal in images were proposed in order to recover scene contrasts and thus improve the overall image quality as a pre-processing step for object detectors.

Furthermore, approaches for the detection of fog in images are being researched. The only reliable information in images with fog is loss of contrast and blurring of the image. However, information about presence and density of fog could help to decrease uncertainty in object detection. Pavlic et al. proposed an approach to detect the presence of fog in images and classify it using Gabor Filters [14,15].

Volk et al. present a method to improve object detection algorithms by augmenting training data with synthetic rain variations [22]. Hnewa et al. tested YOLOv3 and Faster R-CNN under clear and rainy weather conditions and gave an overview of promising approaches to improve object detection under rainy weather conditions [9].

Reway et al. showed the drop of camera sensor performance in different daytime and weather conditions using a virtual simulation [19]. Therefore a real camera is placed in front of a high resolution monitor that films the simulated environment. Hasirlioglu et al. evaluated in [7] the performance of a camera sensor mounted inside a car with raindrops on the windshield. They measured, how these raindrops affect the performance of two different object detectors in between one wiping action. They showed that false detections increase proportionally with the amount of raindrops on the windshield. In [8] the performance of camera, radar and lidar sensors were assessed. Here, an adverse weather facility was used which is capable of simulating reproducible rain with different intensities.

Object detection does not solely rely on the camera sensor for detecting objects. An automated vehicle e.g. is equipped with a set of different sensors like camera, lidar and radar. These redudant sensor data can be used in fusion architectures for object detection. Pfeuffer et al. introduced a data fusion architecture based on deep neural networks that unifies the sensor streams to improve detection capabilities [16]. Bijelic et al. [2] collected a large set of data for camera and lidar and proposed a deep multimodal sensor fusion approach for improving object detection in bad weather.

In this work we focus on the performance evaluation of camera-based object detection algorithms in dense fog, as automotive camera sensors are cheap and are already widely used in existing cars. In particular, the contribution of our work is to present a test method to measure the performance of object detectors in fog. Furthermore we contribute by evaluating several object detectors with the presented test method and show that the performance of different object detectors varies under the same environmental conditions.

3   Method and Materials

In this section we describe the experimental setup of our test scenario, the recorded dataset, the object detection algorithms and the evaluation metrics that were applied. We will speak of normal weather conditions when no fog is present.

3.1   Experimental Setup

In order to compare the performance of object detectors in different weather conditions we prepared a dynamic test scenario. Videos were recorded with a standard automotive camera with a resolution of 2 megapixels at a frame rate of 24 frames per second.

We recorded our test data in the indoor test facility of CARISSMA which is capable of simulating dense fog up to a human visual range of 20m. A standardized Euro NCAP Vehicle Target (EVT) [20] was positioned in front of the camera with a distance of 1m. The EVT is placed on a unmanned vehicle platform that is constantly moving away from the camera at a speed of 20 km/h over a distance of 50 m. Figure 1 shows the experimental setup with and without fog. The scenario mimics a highway scene with a car moving away from the camera sensor. The same scenario was recorded for five times under normal conditions and five times with dense fog. The EVT is the only object visible in the camera's field of view (FOV).

Fig. 1. Image sequence of the EVT moving away from the camera sensor. The sequence on top shows the test setup under normal conditions. The sequence on bottom shows the test setup with dense fog. Between the shown images from left to right are 55 frames each.

3.2 Dataset Preparation

As a dataset we used a set of ten videos recorded in the indoor test facility of CARISSMA. Half of the videos were recorded in normal weather conditions, while the other half was recorded with fog. All videos were edited to match the point in time when the EVT starts and stops. From the edited videos, we took 220 frames per video, where the first frame is always the point in time when the vehicle begins to move. In total, we considered 2200 frames, 1100 for normal and foggy conditions each. Each frame was hand labeled with a bounding box enclosing the EVT. The size of each frame was downscaled to a resolution of 800×600 pixels.

3.3 Object Detection

For the evaluation of the object detection algorithms under normal and foggy environmental conditions we chose four object detection algorithms: Faster R-CNN, SSD, YOLOv3 and RetinaNet. These algorithms are all capable of detecting objects in real time and with high accuracy. Each of them uses a pre-trained weight file trained on the COCO dataset. The COCO training split contains 118.000 images for training with 80 different object categories [11].

We have chosen different variants for each algorithm, which differ in training time and training image size. This gives us a better insight into how the algorithms behave and how training images and training time affect performance. For SSD we chose SSD-300 and SSD-512 and for YOLOv3 the variants YOLOv3-416 and YOLOv3-spp. They only differ in training image size. For the algorithms RetinaNet and Faster R-CNN, we have selected two variants that differ in terms of training time marked as 1x and 3x. The 3x variants were trained three times as long as the 1x variants.

Each object detector was executed on each image from the data set and predicted a confidence score, a class and an associated bounding box. The detection threshold was set to 0.1. This means that each result with a predicted confidence score of greater than the value of 0.1 was saved to a file for further processing.

3.4 Evaluation Metrics

In order to evaluate the object detectors against each other we considered several object detection metrics from the PASCAL VOC Challenge [4]. We considered the Intersection over Union (IoU), also known as the Jaccard similarity coefficient. It is defined by

$$IoU = \frac{area(a \cap b)}{area(a \cup b)} \tag{1}$$

where $a \cap b$ denotes the intersection of the predicted box with the ground truth box and $a \cup b$ the union of their bounding boxes. IoU is a measure for the accuracy of an object detector's predicted bounding boxes.

Furthermore we plot a Precision-Recall-Curve for each algorithm. It is a plot of precision and recall for ranked confidence scores. Precision is a measure for the accuracy of an object detector, whereas recall measures the the amount of returned results, also called sensitivity. Precision and Recall are defined by

$$Precision = \frac{True\ Positives}{True\ Positives + False\ Positives} \tag{2}$$

$$Recall = \frac{True\ Positives}{True\ Positives + False\ Negatives} \tag{3}$$

where a True Positive (TP) is defined as a correct detection with $IoU > t$. A False Positive (FP) is either a wrong detection or a detection with $IoU < t$. The IoU threshold value t is defined as the value above which we consider the IoU of a bounding box to be sufficiently correct. A False Negative (FN) is a ground truth that was not detected due to a low confidence score.

Additionally, we calculate the Average Precision (AP) for every object detector which is the estimated area under curve of a Precision-Recall-Curve. It is defined by

$$AP = \sum_{n=0} (r_{n+1} - r_n) p_{interp}(r_{n+1}) \tag{4}$$

The interpolated precision $p_{interp}(r_{n+1})$ is defined by taking the maximum precision at each recall level r, where the corresponding recall value is greater than r_{n+1}. It is defined by

$$p_{interp}(r_{n+1}) = \max_{\tilde{r}:\tilde{r} \geq r_{n+1}} p(\tilde{r}) \tag{5}$$

4   Results and Discussion

In this section we present the results of the object detection algorithms on our recorded dataset. First, we will investigate how increasing distance affects detection results and the predicted bounding boxes. Then we look at precision and recall, plot a Precision-Recall-Curve and calculate the AP for each algorithm. It is to note, that we do not consider inference time in our evaluation.

4.1   Detection over Time

Confidence Score. For the evaluation of the detection capabilities we run each object detector on every frame in our dataset and save the predicted confidence scores, classes and bounding boxes. The evaluation results of all algorithms under normal and foggy environment conditions can be seen in Fig. 2. It shows the confidence scores of the respective algorithms on the left side and the IoU on the right side. For each value in the graph the average of the respective five recordings was taken.

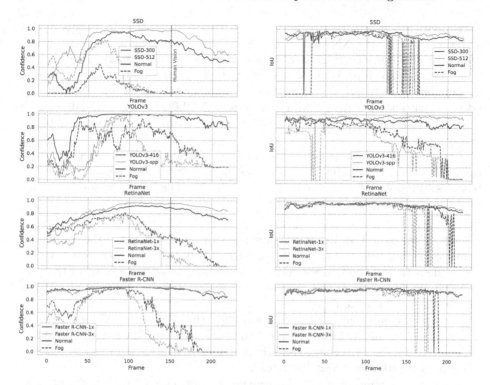

Fig. 2. Evaluation results of object detection for the dynamic scenario. The plots on the left show the confidence score for each frame and algorithm. The plots on the right show the IoU for each frame and algorithm. The values of confidence and IoU are averaged over five recordings each. (Color figure online)

The distance to the EVT increase with the number of frames. It should be noted that the frames do not accurately reflect the actual distance driven, as the unmanned vehicle platform may have minimal inaccuracies in the trajectory and acceleration.

Regarding Fig. 2 it is clearly visible that the object detectors show high performance under normal conditions. For most frames the confidence scores are higher than for the respective scenario with fog. We found that almost all algorithms - except of Faster R-CNN - have problems to detect the EVT within the first 30 frames, when the EVT is not completely visible in the camera's FOV. This is indicated by a low confidence score at the beginning and consequently higher uncertainty about the object class. This effect increases further with the presence of fog and leads to missed detections for the case of SSD-300.

Regarding the object detectors under foggy conditions, it can be seen that the confidence scores start to decrease with increasing distance. The fog particles scatter light and lead to reduced contrast and unsharp contours. This leads to a degradation in the object detector's performance.

However, there are also measureable differences among the algorithms. While YOLOv3, Faster R-CNN and RetinaNet show decreasing confidence scores around frame 100, the SSD algorithm's score decreases already at frame 60. Also the SSD algorithm is unable to detect the EVT at all after frame 120. The rest of the algorithms are still capable of detecting the EVT until frame 190, although with a low confidence score near zero. YOLOv3 managed to detect the car in one video for all frames, therefore it does not drop below a value of 0.2 in the evaluation.

For the authors of this paper the EVT is still clearly visible as a car up to frame 150. From this point on it becomes more difficult to recognize the EVT, but it is still often recognizable until the last frame. The human vision boundary for fog is marked in Fig. 2 as red line.

Intersection over Union. In the previous section we evaluated the confidence scores over time. However, a high confidence value alone is not sufficient for object detection. Therefore we evaluate the quality and correctness of the predicted bounding boxes in this section. The results of the comparison of IoU can be seen in Fig. 2 on the right side.

In normal conditions the IoU for each algorithm is constantly above a value of 0.8. Hence, all algorithms can detect the location of the EVT with high accuracy in normal environmental conditions. We cannot even notice a decrease in performance with increasing distance.

For the fog environment we also see very accurate bounding box predictions. It is to note that an IoU value of 0 was chosen when there is no bounding box predicted for a frame. For SSD, RetinaNet and Faster R-CNN the IoU value stays above a value of 0.8 as long as there exists a prediction. If no detection result is available, this can be recognized by outliers in the curve that drop to a value of 0. We can note, that even in foggy conditions the bounding boxes are highly accurate, even when the size of the EVT becomes small.

For YOLOv3 algorithm we see a steady decrease in IoU starting at frame 100. It seems to have problems to detect the correct boundaries of the EVT when the image contours become blurred and contrast decreases.

4.2   Overall Detection Capabilities

In this section we analyze the overall detection capabilities of each algorithm in normal and foggy environmental conditions. The results of our analysis can be seen in Fig. 3. We calculate precision and recall and plot a Precision-Recall-Curve. As IoU threshold we have chosen a value of 0.5.

All of the object detectors have very high precision and recall in the normal environment. This can be seen from the high curve, which only begins to fall at a high recall value. However, the same object detectors show significant differences when tested on the foggy dataset. All algorithms show a high drop in performance compared to normal weather conditions.

Table 1 shows the AP for each detector under foggy and normal environmental conditions. The highest performing algorithm is RetinaNet-1x. It shows the

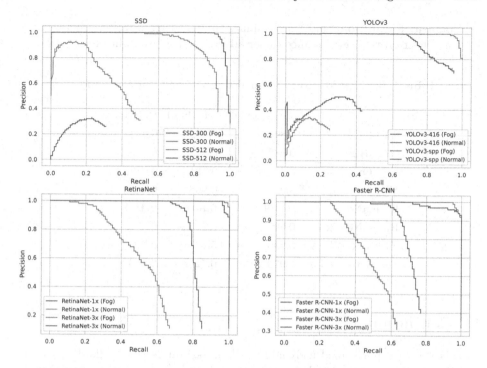

Fig. 3. Precision-Recall-Curves for the dynamic object detection scenario under normal and foggy environmental conditions.

best overall results on our dataset with an AP of 0.807 on the foggy dataset. It is only by a value of 0.192 worse than under normal weather conditions. SSD and YOLOv3 show a decline of more than 0.6 in AP compared to normal environmental conditions.

RetinaNet and Faster R-CNN are the most promising detectors. We also found that the models with less training cycles (1x) show higher AP than the corresponding models with more training cycles. RetinaNet-1x has an AP that is 0.292 higher than RetinaNet-3x. We see a similar behavior for Faster R-CNN. Those models could be less overfit to training data and thus be more unbiased towards environmental conditions.

For SSD we see that the model with larger training image size (SSD-512) performs better than the one with smaller image size (SSD-300). Here, the SSD-300 model seems to underfit as its performance is worse for the normal and the foggy case. YOLOv3 shows a contrary behaviour: The model with larger training image size (YOLOv3-spp) has worse performance than the model with smaller training image size (YOLOv3-416). Further research would be necessary at this point to clarify this behavior.

While we see very high AP for all models under normal conditions, there is still a large gap between the algorithms when exposed to bad visibility conditions. Our evaluation indicates, that different models are suited better to run in foggy environmental conditions and that training time and training parameters also have an effect on the performance under adverse weather conditions.

Table 1. The AP for algorithms under normal and foggy conditions.

	AP (Normal)	AP (Fog)	Difference
SSD-300	0.893	0.080	0.813
SSD-512	0.983	0.361	0.622
YOLOv3-416	0.996	0.181	0.785
YOLOv3-spp	0.907	0.068	0.839
RetinaNet-1x	**0.999**	**0.807**	**0.192**
RetinaNet-3x	0.997	0.515	0.482
Faster R-CNN-1x	0.998	0.728	0.270
Faster R-CNN-3x	0.992	0.526	0.466

5   Conclusion

In this work we performed a dynamic indoor test under controllable environmental conditions. We recorded data with and without fog and evaluated various object detectors on it. The results were first analysed time-based and then examined for their general performance.

We showed that our tested object detection algorithms show high confidence and IoU in the scenario without fog. Even with increasing distance the overall performance is still high. In contrast, the object detectors in fog show strongly reduced performance. The uncertainty about the existence of the EVT raises with increasing distance to it.

However, while we see a general decline in performance, we have noticed that the algorithms also show strong differences among themselves when exposed to fog. We could show that RetinaNet and Faster R-CNN have a generally higher accuracy and sensitivity than the other tested algorithms. In addition, we found better results when the algorithms were trained for less time in the case of RetinaNet and Faster R-CNN. We explain this by the fact that the algorithms are less biased due to less training time and therefore also recognize blurred and low-contrast structures in the image as a vehicle. With these results we contribute towards testing object detection algorithms in adverse weather conditions.

The results of this work are limited in that we consider a very simple scenario with only one object. Furthermore, only the performance in dense fog is considered, other environmental influences like rain or snow are neglected. However, it should be noted that the evaluation method was deliberately kept simple in order to obtain representative results. New, and more complex scenarios can be designed and researched based on the test method and evaluation approach presented in this work.

Future work should adapt the training data to take weather conditions into account. In addition, the algorithms should be made more independent of weather domains. A first approach was already explored in the work of Chen et al., where they proposed a domain adaptive Faster R-CNN which is more robust towards different domains [3].

References

1. Berman, D., Treibitz, T., Avidan, S.: Non-local image dehazing. In: 2016 IEEE Conference on Computer Vision and Pattern Recognition (CVPR), pp. 1674–1682. IEEE, Las Vegas, June 2016

2. Bijelic, M., et al.: Seeing through fog without seeing fog: deep multimodal sensor fusion in unseen adverse weather. arXiv:1902.08913 [cs], February 2020

3. Chen, Y., Li, W., Sakaridis, C., Dai, D., Van Gool, L.: Domain adaptive faster R-CNN for object detection in the wild. In: 2018 IEEE/CVF Conference on Computer Vision and Pattern Recognition, pp. 3339–3348. IEEE, Salt Lake City, June 2018

4. Everingham, M., Van Gool, L., Williams, C.K.I., Winn, J., Zisserman, A.: The Pascal Visual Object Classes (VOC) challenge. Int. J. Comput. Vis. **88**(2), 303–338 (2010)

5. Fattal, R.: Single image dehazing. ACM Trans. Graph. **27**(3), 1–9 (2008)

6. Hasirlioglu, S., Kamann, A., Doric, I., Brandmeier, T.: Test methodology for rain influence on automotive surround sensors. In: 2016 IEEE 19th International Conference on Intelligent Transportation Systems (ITSC), pp. 2242–2247, November 2016

7. Hasirlioglu, S., Reway, F., Klingenberg, T., Riener, A., Huber, W.: Raindrops on the windshield: performance assessment of camera-based object detection. In: 2019 IEEE International Conference on Vehicular Electronics and Safety (ICVES), pp. 1–7, September 2019

8. Hasirlioglu, S., Riener, A.: Challenges in object detection under rainy weather conditions. In: Ferreira, J.C., Martins, A.L., Monteiro, V. (eds.) INTSYS 2018. LNICST, vol. 267, pp. 53–65. Springer, Cham (2019). https://doi.org/10.1007/978-3-030-14757-0_5

9. Hnewa, M., Radha, H.: Object detection under rainy conditions for autonomous vehicles (2020)

10. Lin, T.Y., Goyal, P., Girshick, R., He, K., Dollér, P.: Focal Loss for Dense Object Detection. arXiv:1708.02002 [cs], February 2018

11. Lin, T.Y., et al.: Microsoft COCO: Common Objects in Context. arXiv:1405.0312 [cs], February 2015

12. Liu, W., et al.: SSD: Single Shot MultiBox Detector, vol. 9905, pp. 21–37. arXiv:1512.02325 [cs] (2016)

13. Oakley, J., Satherley, B.: Improving image quality in poor visibility conditions using a physical model for contrast degradation. IEEE Trans. Image Process. **7**(2), 167–179 (1998)

14. Pavlić, M., Belzner, H., Rigoll, G., Ilić, S.: Image based fog detection in vehicles. In: 2012 IEEE Intelligent Vehicles Symposium, pp. 1132–1137, June 2012

15. Pavlic, M., Rigoll, G., Ilic, S.: Classification of images in fog and fog-free scenes for use in vehicles. In: 2013 IEEE Intelligent Vehicles Symposium (IV), pp. 481–486, June 2013

16. Pfeuffer, A., Dietmayer, K.: Optimal Sensor Data Fusion Architecture for Object Detection in Adverse Weather Conditions. arXiv:1807.02323 [cs], July 2018
17. Redmon, J., Farhadi, A.: YOLOv3: An Incremental Improvement. arXiv:1804.02 767 [cs], April 2018
18. Ren, S., He, K., Girshick, R., Sun, J.: Faster R-CNN: Towards Real-Time Object Detection with Region Proposal Networks. arXiv:1506.01497 [cs], January 2016
19. Reway, F., Huber, W., Ribeiro, E.P.: Test methodology for vision-based ADAS algorithms with an automotive camera-in-the-loop. In: 2018 IEEE International Conference on Vehicular Electronics and Safety (ICVES), pp. 1–7. IEEE, Madrid, September 2018
20. Sandner, V.: Development of a test target for AEB systems, p. 7 (2013)
21. Schechner, Y., Narasimhan, S., Nayar, S.: Instant dehazing of images using polarization. In: Proceedings of the 2001 IEEE Computer Society Conference on Computer Vision and Pattern Recognition. CVPR 2001, vol. 1, p. I, December 2001
22. Volk, G., Müller, S., von Bernuth, A., Hospach, D., Bringmann, O.: Towards robust CNN-based object detection through augmentation with synthetic rain variations. In: 2019 IEEE Intelligent Transportation Systems Conference (ITSC), pp. 285–292 (2019)
23. Xu, Z., Liu, X., Chen, X.: Fog removal from video sequences using contrast limited adaptive histogram equalization. In: 2009 International Conference on Computational Intelligence and Software Engineering, pp. 1–4 (2009)

Automotive Radar Signal and Interference Simulation for Testing Autonomous Driving

Alexander Prinz[1]([✉]), Leo-Tassilo Peters[1], Johannes Schwendner[2], Mohamed Ayeb[3], and Ludwig Brabetz[3]

[1] Bayerische Motoren Werke AG, Petuelring 130, Munich, Germany
{alexander.prinz,leo-tassilo.peters}@bmw.de
[2] Expleo Germany GmbH, Munich, Germany
johannes.schwendner@expleogroup.com
[3] Universität Kassel, Wilhelmshöher Allee 73, 34121 Kassel, Germany
{ayeb,brabetz}@uni-kassel.de

Abstract. With the development of automated driving functions, more and more environmental sensors are combined for the vehicle perception. A problem that arises with the extensive use of radar sensing is called interference. It describes the confounding effects from the wave overlay of two or more radar sensors operating in the same frequency-band. At this point, methods for interference avoidance and mitigation come to apply. For a valid design and development of such methods, real sensor measurements were required in the past. This publication instead proposes a novel sensor modelling technique that represents the interference mechanisms within the radar sensor signals. It is based on a full radar time signal simulation coupled with a broad range of influencing factors. The concept is validated by comparing the simulated signal processing steps to the real sensor measurement behavior. As a result, mitigation methods for the sensor fault behavior can be fully assessed within a simulation environment. The opportunity for applying new scenario data and a variable set of radar sensors underlines the importance of this approach in the development of future radar systems.

Keywords: Driver assistance · Automotive radar · Radar interference · Sensor modelling · Sensor model validation · Testing process

1 Introduction

Continuous development of active safety has had a decisive impact on the accident statistics in the past years. In particular the effectiveness of a lane change warning was analyzed by the association of German insurance companies over a time duration of five years. According to their statistics, the deployment of such

A. L. Martins et al. (Eds.): INTSYS 2020, LNICST 364, pp. 223–240, 2021.
https://doi.org/10.1007/978-3-030-71454-3_14

systems has the potential to prevented 3.582 accidents and 5.191 injured traffic participants annually [1]. For that reason, most modern cars are equipped with these systems to fulfill the EuroNCAP test requirements [2]. This trend in active safety also drives the current development for more advanced driving functions. Beside safety reasons, automated driving also creates a new business model for private transportation. Especially in urban areas innovative driver-less mobility solutions can prevent traffic jams and save the space for parking facilities in the city area [3]. This promising innovation requires sophisticated systems that are capable to interact with the traffic environment. For that reason the perception task is one key element of modern assistance systems. Among the variety of automotive sensors, radar is a common technology for environment perception. Radar sensors use an active measurement principle by sending and receiving electromagnetic waves. The reserved frequency band for the automotive application is between 77 GHz and 81 GHz [4]. Compared to other environmental sensors, radar sensing can directly measure the range, azimuth angle, and radial velocity of a target with the help of a single measurement in a short period of time [5]. Furthermore the radar signal processing is very resilient to bad weather conditions [6]. Beside these advantages the application of radar sensors is problematic due to the effect of mutual interference [7]. Radar-Interference summarizes the effects that emerge when two or more radar sensors are operating in the same frequency-band at the same time. Previous trends also promote a higher likelihood for interference because more and more cars are equipped with a rising number of up to ten radar sensors [6]. Interference mitigation methods exist, but their applicability for a variety of scenarios is still unproven [8–10]. This research paper addresses this problem by presenting a novel radar simulation for the application and test of radar interference methods. In contrast to other publications from [11–13] this approach has the main focus on a closely meshed modelling and validation process. The application of this simulation enables a trustworthy evaluation of radar performance metrics for a variety of possible interference scenarios. This supports the development of radar interference mitigation methods for future driver assistance systems.

2   Radar Basics

2.1   Measurement Principle and Signal Processing for FMCW Radar

The most common technique in automotive radars is the generation of Frequency-Modulated Continuous Wave (FMCW) signals. The main idea of this waveform is to send out frequency modulated signals in a short period of time and repeat this several times. These signal portions are also called chirps and will be received after being reflected by a target. As a next step, the time signal at the receiver antennas $x_{rx}(t)$ will be directly mixed with the transmitted signal $x_{tx}(t)$. This results in the signal $x_m(t)$ which can be sampled in a lower frequency band, the so called baseband. For an interpretation of the sampled time signal, it is transformed into the frequency domain. After applying a two-dimensional Fourier Transformation (FT), the signal processing results in a complex matrix [5]. Then, the range-velocity map (RV-map) separates targets in radial distance and velocity. Each cell inside this matrix contains the amplitude and the phase of the corresponding spatial frequency bin. By comparing the amplitude of each cell with the neighbouring cells, targets can be detected on the RV-map [14]. While targets are separated in range- and velocity-domain, the azimuth angle can be estimated based on a single bin in the RV-map. The main idea about the angle estimation is the simultaneous sampling along a horizontally distributed antenna array. The angle of incidence α corresponds to a different pathway over the antenna array. By evaluating the phase change $\delta\theta$ the angle of incidence can be calculated as described in [15].

2.2   Interference on FMCW Radars

At first, Hischke [16] conducted a study on radar interference in automotive applications. From his investigations the exposure time and the signal-power of the received interference signal determines the severity of the effect. Based on these fundamentals, Brooker [8] worked out a distinction for the interfering effects. In case that two chirps have the same slope and both are sent out within a short time delay (~ns), the **synchronous interference** can be observed. In addition, he analyzed interference from different waveforms and their intersection points. This case is summarized in the so called **asynchronous interference** and is more likely to occur because automotive radar systems typically differ in their transmitted waveform. For the time span around the intersection point the mixer signal frequency changes linearly [7]. Furthermore, the slope of the changing frequency portions is depending on the slopes difference of both radar waveforms. Subsequently, the mixer signal will be filtered by a high- and low pass in time domain. This suppresses the out-of band frequencies that cannot be interpreted by the radar sensors signal processing. In the end, the interfering signal portions are spread on all range-frequencies and will raise the noise floor in the subsequent processing steps [8,17]. An increased noise floor has a direct impact on the target detection because radar signal processing uses the Signal-to-Noise Ratio (SNR) to detect targets on the range-velocity map.

Due to the fact that radar interference is a serious problem for object detection, various researchers have worked on this topic. A first group of publications looked at theoretical aspects [12,18]. Others focused on empirical measurements [7,17,19]. Beside that some publications addressed the integration of an interference model in an environment simulation [11,20]. For differentiation, the model approach from [11] is modelling interference in the radar baseband. Whereas [20] simplified approach is only calculating the Signal-to-Interference-Ratio (SIR) to estimate the SNR-drop for the received target hit point. Since both model approaches were not combined with real sensor measurements, their validation is still pending. Based on the existing work, a general radar and interference simulation with good applicability is still missing. This can be traced back to a high effort in the acquisition of measurement data with distinct interference influence. Apart from that, the validation has to be considered on various levels in the signal processing chain. At this point, the paper presents a novel radar time signal simulation with all relevant interfaces for the applied validation strategy. The resulting simulation framework can be used for the test and development of interference mitigation techniques.

3   Automotive Radar Simulation

3.1   Architecture and Interfaces

The architecture of the automotive radar simulation is combining a virtual vehicle environment with a radar time signal simulation and its signal processing. Besides that, the architecture in Fig. 1 has to ensure that the different processing levels are clearly defined. This is particularly relevant for the bidirectional comparison in the validation procedure. The first layer in the simulation handles the scenario which describes the observed vehicles and their interaction in the driving situation. The scenario itself can be derived from the accident statistics in [1]. Based on the scenario data the geometric hit points can be generated from the parametrized sensor resolution on the second level. On the third level, the hit points of each time step in simulation will be converted into time signals. The superposition properties allow us to generate the signals from each hit point independently. Subsequently the sampling layer on the radar front-end accumulates the time-discrete signals. A signal processing model is then applied to compare the scenario input and simulation output hit points directly over the scenario. In the development of interference mitigation techniques, the hit point loss over the scenario time has to be minimized.

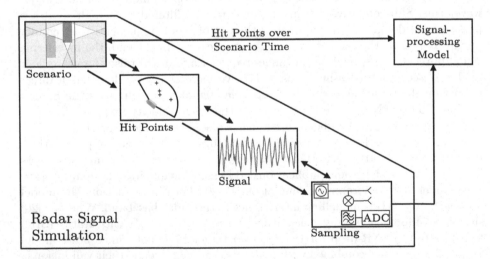

Fig. 1. General architecture and model interfaces: the simulation runs top-down (single arrows) while the validation is also applied bottom-up (double arrow).

3.2   Radar Signal Simulation

The scenario environment is capable of predicting the perception of the sensor based on a concrete driving scenario. For this reason, each traffic participant in the sensors Field-of-View (FoV) corresponds to a number of geometrical hit points. These reflection points can be described in radial distance r, radial velocity $\dot{r}$ and azimuth angle α based on the resolution of the sensor [21].

As a next step, the simulated geometrical hit points will be transferred into the *Hit Point Time Signal* block (see Fig. 2) which generates the echo time signal. For each antenna the target is interpreted as a sum of independent echos.

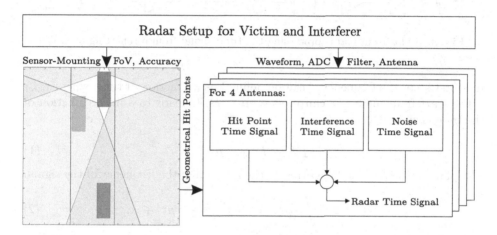

Fig. 2. Radar time signal calculation based on simulated hit points and interference. (Color figure online)

The *Interference Time Signal* block generates the received radar signal from an interferer. As part of the *Noise Time Signal* block, the noise in the radar front-end is synthetically generated. In the end, all three components get superimposed. The time signal equations will be analytically derived in the following.

Hit Point Time Signal. The Hit Point Time Signal is based on the general principle of the radar front-end illustrated in Fig. 3. First, the local oscillator (LO) is generating frequency modulated chirps in the radar band. Then, phase modulation (PSM) and power amplifier (PA) is applied and the Tx-antenna is emitting the radar transmit signal $x_{\text{tx}}(t)$. After being reflected by the object, the received echo signal $x_{\text{rx}}(t)$ is amplified by the low noise amplifier (LNA) and transferred into the baseband $x_{\text{m}}(t)$. After that, the signal is filtered with a high-pass filter (HPF) and a variable gain amplifier (VGA) can be adjusted to prevent saturation. Finally, the low-pass filtered signal is sampled by an analog-to-digital converter (ADC) and is ready for further digital signal processing.

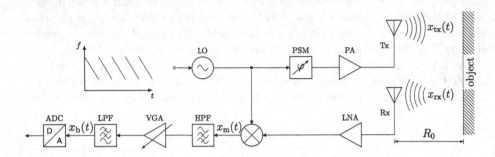

Fig. 3. Radar front-end is processing the time signal from a reflecting object.

In a first step, the frequency f can be defined as a function of time, where $f_{s,ref}$ is the start frequency. The chirp's slope $\mu = B/T_c$ leads to a linear function of the frequency over time.

$$f(t) = f_{s,ref} + \mu \cdot t \tag{1}$$

The phase over time can be written as the integral of the frequency of the signal.

$$\phi(t) = 2\pi \cdot \int f(t)dt = 2\pi f_{s,ref}t + \pi\mu t^2 + \phi_0 \tag{2}$$

This expression can be used to describe the transmitted signal amplitude $x_{tx}(t)$ by a trigonometric function.

$$x_{tx}(t) = A_{tx}cos(2\pi f_{s,ref}t + \pi\mu t^2 + \phi_0) \tag{3}$$

For the received signal amplitude $x_{rx}(t)$ the time variable t is substituted by $(t - \tau)$ where τ is the time delay between sending and receiving the signal. A_{tx} and A_{rx} describe the signal's amplitude and are linked to the receiver gain, pathloss and transmission power.

$$x_{rx}(t) = A_{rx}cos\big(2\pi f_{s,ref}(t - \tau) + \pi\mu(t - \tau)^2 + \phi_0\big) \tag{4}$$

The time signal of the mixer in Fig. 3 is derived by these two time signals

$$x_m(t) = x_{rx}(t) \cdot x_{tx}(t). \tag{5}$$

With the help of Euler's formula the signals can be transformed and the mixed signal $x_m(t)$ can be written as a function of sum and difference phase.

$$x_m(t) = \frac{A_{tx} \cdot A_{rx}}{2}\big(cos(\phi_{dif}(t)) + cos(\phi_{sum}(t))\big) \tag{6}$$

According to [22] the phase portions from $\phi_{\text{sum}}(t)$ result in an oscillation with a frequency greater than that originally sent. The latter will be eliminated by the low-pass-filter in Fig. 3 so only the $\phi_{\text{dif}}(t)$ has to be considered for the beat signal $x_{\text{b,tar}}(t)$ in Eq. 7.

$$x_{\text{b,tar}}(t) = \frac{A_{\text{tx}} \cdot A_{\text{rx}}}{2}\left(cos(2\pi f_{\text{s,ref}}\tau + 2\pi\mu\tau t - \pi\mu\tau^2)\right) \tag{7}$$

The trip time τ is related to the radial distance R_0 at the beginning t_0 of the chirp. The radial velocity v_r of the reflecting object is assumed to be constant during the chirp-duration T_c.

$$\tau(t) = 2 \cdot \frac{R_0 + v_r(t - t_0)}{c_0} \quad \text{with} \quad t \in [t_0, t_0 + T_c] \tag{8}$$

With the given trip time τ the beat signal can be derived by the hit point state variables in Eq. 9. Beside that, the quadratic τ-terms were neglected because they have no quantifiable impact on the beat signal $x_{\text{b,tar}}(t)$.

$$x_{\text{b,tar}}(t) = \frac{A_{\text{tx}} \cdot A_{\text{rx}}}{2} cos\left(2\pi\left(2f_{\text{s,ref}}\frac{R_0}{c_0} + \underbrace{2f_{\text{s,ref}}\frac{v_r}{c_0}t}_{\text{Doppler}} + \underbrace{2R_0\frac{\mu}{c_0}t}_{\text{Range}}\right)\right) \tag{9}$$

When analyzing Eq. 9, the Doppler frequency can be identified. In the simulation architecture from Fig. 1, the Eq. 9 is computed for every geometric hit point simulated in the environment simulation for all antenna positions. Then, the time signal of an extended object can be described by adding up the beat signals from the simulated point targets.

Interference Time Signal. Apart from the reflecting targets the simulated time signal also consists of mixing products from an interfering radar. The task of this simulation part is the analysis of the time signal of both radar waveforms. The following figure gives a better idea about the chirp superposition in frequency domain.

As shown in Fig. 4, a mixer signal is only present while both radars are transmitting. The current frequency-difference between reference- and interference-signal is changing over the time. The reason for this is the difference in chirp-slope of both radars. Beside the frequency-difference also the chirp time delay β for the interfering radar waveform has to be considered. Next, the simulation has to estimate the point in time $t_{\text{int,i}}$ where the interfering chirp i and the observed reference chirp have the same frequency according to Eq. 10.

$$t_{\text{int,i}} \cdot \mu_1 + f_{s,\text{ref}} = (t_{\text{int,i}} - \beta) \cdot \mu_2 + f_{s,\text{int}} \quad \text{for} \quad t_{\text{int,i}} \in [t_{s,i}; t_{e,i}] \tag{10}$$

Based on this point in time, a time duration can be calculated for each of N_{int} interfering chirps. From Fig. 4 the chirp slope difference determines the derivative of the frequency deviation δf. For the considered application we recommend δf to be ten times higher than the low-pass frequency f_{LP}. With this given frequency

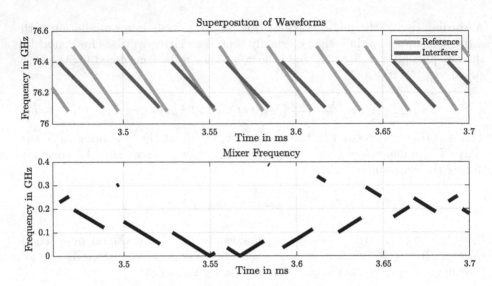

Fig. 4. The top plot visualizes the frequency over time of two radars operating in the same frequency band. In the lower plot the idealized mixer frequency is presented.

deviation δf, the interference time duration results in the time interval $[t_{s,i}; t_{e,i}]$ for each chirp number i. Then, the time bounded subsets can be unified to a superset M of all interfering time intervals.

$$M = \{t \mid t_{s,i} < t < t_{e,i}, i \in \{1, \dots N_{\text{int}}\}\} \tag{11}$$

After resolving the interference time interval M, the phase equations for both waveforms can similarly be formulated with reference to Eq. 2.

$$\phi_{\text{ref}}(t) = 2\pi \cdot \int f_{\text{ref}}(t) dt = 2\pi f_{s,\text{ref}} \cdot t + \pi\mu t^2 + \phi_{0,r} \tag{12}$$

$$\phi_{\text{int}}(t) = 2\pi \cdot \int f_{\text{int}}(t - \beta) dt = 2\pi f_{s,\text{int}} \cdot (t - \beta) + \pi\mu(t - \beta)^2 + \phi_{0,i} \tag{13}$$

As the transmit time signal in Eq. 3 persists, the corresponding receiver time signal can be estimated equally from the phase in Eq. 13. After applying the mixer from Eq. 5 and the Euler's formula in Eq. 6, the beat-signal from the interfering signal can be described as

$$x_{\text{b,int}}(t) = \frac{A_{\text{tx,ref}} A_{\text{tx,int}}}{2} \cdot \left(cos(\phi_{\text{dif,int}}(t))\right) \tag{14}$$

with

$$\phi_{\text{dif,int}}(t) = 2\pi\left(t^2\left(\frac{\mu_1 - \mu_2}{2}\right) + t\left(f_{s,\text{ref}} - f_{s,\text{int}} + \mu_2\beta\right)\dots\right.$$

$$\left.\dots - 0.5\mu_2\beta^2 + f_{\text{int},0}\beta\right) + \phi_{0,r} - \phi_{0,i} \tag{15}$$

Now, the time portions from the interference time interval M can be inserted in Eq. 14 to finally get the active interference beat signal $x_{b,int}(t)$. Due to the fact that the beat signal from a reflecting target is independent from the beat signal from an interfering radar the two signals can be added.

$$x_b(t) = x_{b,tar}(t) + x_{b,int}(t) \tag{16}$$

3.3 Signal Processing Model

As already described in the general architecture in Fig. 1 the synthetic signals from the Radar Signal Simulation have to be interpreted. For this task we developed a model-based signal processing chain similar to a regular automotive FMCW signal processing. In Fig. 5 the consecutive components are visualized. Within the model based signal processing each layer can directly be accessed. This is particularly helpful for the validation task. Beside the application in the simulation environment, the signal processing can also be used with real sensor measurements from the reference sensor. Based on the generic approach presented by [11], we developed an application specific variation for our model based signal processing in Fig. 5. First, the processing chain receives the down-converted antenna time signals. On that basis, modules for filtering and windowing are applied to provide the Fourier transformation (FT), similar to [11].

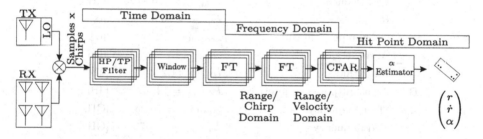

Fig. 5. Block diagram of the signal processing for simulated and measured radar echos.

After resolving in range-velocity domain, a Constant False Alarm Rate (CFAR) algorithm is applied, which is capable to detect targets as hit points in noisy environments [14]. For each detected cell in the RV-map, the phase differences over four receiving antennas will be used to estimate the azimuth angle, as described in [15]. Each hit point then consists of range r, velocity $\dot{r}$ and azimuth angle α.

4 Parametrization and Validation

For the validation of the radar and interference simulation we compared the model response with the real measurement behaviour on different processing

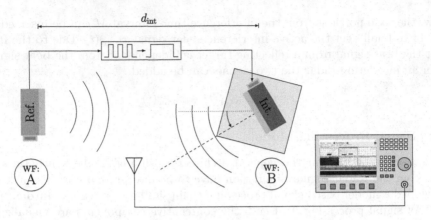

Fig. 6. General radar setup: modifications on the setup will be described in more detail.

Table 1. Parameters used for the measurement setup under asynchronous interference.

WF	Physical quantity	Symbol and unit	SI
A	Transmit power of vict. radar	$P_{\mathrm{Tx,vict}} = 7$	[dBm]
	Start frequency	$f_{\mathrm{start,vict}} = 76.2875$	[GHz]
	End frequency	$f_{\mathrm{end,vict}} = 76.7125$	[GHz]
	Ramp duration	$T_{\mathrm{c,vict}} = 25.6$	[µs]
	Chirp repetition time	$T_{\mathrm{cc,vict}} = 42$	[µs]
	Antenna gain	$G_{\mathrm{ant}} = 13$	[dBi]
	Rx pathloss	$L_{\mathrm{Rx}} = 11.2$	[dB]
B	Transmit power of interferer	$P_{\mathrm{Tx,int}} = 12$	[dBm]
	Start frequency	$f_{\mathrm{start,int}} = 76.25$	[GHz]
	End frequency	$f_{\mathrm{end,int}} = 76.675$	[GHz]
	Ramp duration	$T_{\mathrm{c,int}} = 22.5$	[µs]
	Chirp repetition time	$T_{\mathrm{cc,int}} = 38.8$	[µs]
	Antenna gain	$G_{\mathrm{ant}} = 28.5$	[dBi]

layers. Based on the results, the model gets adapted and parametrized. The measurements were realized on the basis of a general radar setup illustrated in Fig. 6. It consists of two radar sensors with adaptable waveforms. The reference sensor is triggering the interference radar by the first chirp in a sequence. This guarantees a deterministic and reproducible interference impact for the measurements. The sensors are aligned straight to each other and the interferer is mounted on a rotating module. For interference verification a spectrum analyzer is triggered by the same signal to capture the wave superposition. The waveforms of both sensors (**WF:A** and **WF:B**) are described in the following Table 1.

Table 1 contains the chirp-frequencies, the transmit time and the power of both radars. The waveforms were applied with similar chirp slopes. This results in a low mixer frequency-deviation and yields in a good observability of the interfering effects. With the given setup the validation will be performed in the following. The main focus here is the correct estimation of the signal-powers in the RV-map which is crucial for detecting targets with and without interference.

4.1   Sampling Layer

On the sampling layer the filters get validated because they affect the Signal-to-Noise Ratio (SNR) of a reflecting target. The high- and low-pass filters in the radar front-end from Fig. 3 are implemented with the specified parameters from the datasheet. As the spectral components filtered by the high-pass filter correspond to very close objects, that do not occur in automotive scenarios, its performance is not validated as part of this work. Whereas for the low-pass filter we validate our assumptions as follows. The model is parametrized with a 7.5 MHz Butterworth low-pass-filter of order three and a Chebychev decimation filter. The latter is used to reduce the amount of data to be processed, as the ADC operates at 40 MSa/s while the information on frequencies above 20 MHz is not relevant for the sensor. For a better comparability during the validation, we approximate the interference signal's envelope with a clipped Gaussian. This method also features a technical analogy with the filter characteristics, as it approximates the frequency response of the filter. Knowing that the analyzed signal is a frequency sweep, it's envelope can be understood as it's frequency response. Figure 7 shows, that the envelopes of the simulated and measured signals match. We can expect that the simulated signal-power behind the filter induced by an interferer can be simulated sufficiently accurate.

Beside the filter-characteristic the noise also has an influence on the SNR of targets and therefore on their detectability. Typically radar front-ends, like the one depicted in Fig. 3, are System-on-Chip (SoC) solutions in which we expect to find active and passive components. In the literature, the noise of such devices

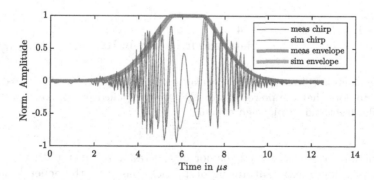

Fig. 7. Validating the low-pass filter by comparing the measured and simulated amplitude response and their envelope from an asynchronous-interfered receive signal.

are mainly described by thermal-noise, which has a constant spectral energy distribution [25]. Beside that, the 1/f-noise decreases with rising frequency. For the detection of targets in the spectrum, we know from Eq. 9 that the frequency is related to the distance of a target. Consequently, the frequency dependence of the noise can be interpreted as range dependent noise. In order to accommodate this effect in the simulation, the spectral density of the noise was measured with the reference sensor. Therefore, the initial measurement setup from Fig. 6 is modified, such that no power is being transmitted by both radar sensors. As the receivers are still operational, it is possible to capture the noise sources mentioned above. The measured spectral distribution (see red graph in Fig. 2) already contains the high- and low pass transfer functions. During simulation the generated noise is added to the signal before the radar front-end with its filters. Therefore it is necessary to undo the effect of the filters on the measurement (see blue graph in Fig. 8). In the simulation the noise is generated according to this data. This is done by generating complex white Gaussian noise in the frequency domain and multiplying it with the depicted transfer characteristic. A transformation into the time domain yields Gaussian noise, that is now correlated according to the sensors noise. This noise characteristic will be applied in the *Noise Time Signal* block from the model architecture in Fig. 2.

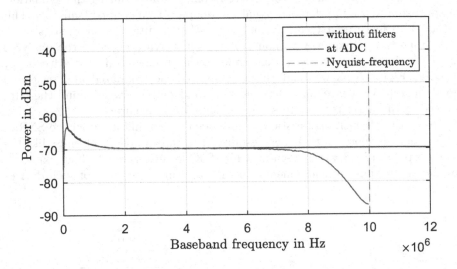

Fig. 8. Noise floor (blue) leads to spectral power density at the ADC (red). It is important to note that the power at the ADC was amplified by 45 dB as part of the analog radar front-end. (Color figure online)

Additionally the nonlinear behavior of the radar receiver path in Fig. 3 is modelled as a device with saturating properties. Based on the general measurement setup depicted in Fig. 6, we rotate the victim radar towards the interferer, which is configured to generate synchronous interference. During this rotation the received signal level changes with the directivity of the antenna. With the given antenna pattern we calculate an expected signal-power for the case of a completely linear receiver. By comparing the measured saturating signal with the expected signal, we extract the saturation curve as depicted in Fig. 9. As radar sensors differ greatly in their operation under the exposure of high signal-powers, we ensure that the operating point of the simulated radar sensor lies within the linear region for all subsequent simulation and measurement sets.

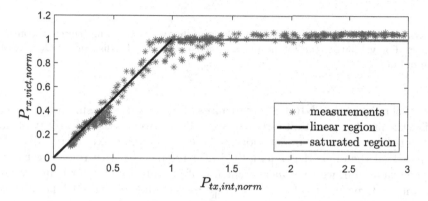

Fig. 9. Measurement analysis and linearization of the receiver path in the victim radar.

4.2   Signal Layer

On the signal-level, we validate the model's ability to reproduce the received signal-power. As a first step, the model was parametrized with the receiver ampli-fier gains according to the datasheet. As a validation step, we conducted a series of measurements and simulations of that same set-up. Finally, we compared the reflected signal-powers in the simulation and measurements. The target of inter-est is a corner reflector with the side-length of 12 cm. According to [23] these dimensions translate into an radar cross section (RCS) of 17.5 dBm^2. While this value was confirmed with a calibrated setup our non-calibrated reference sensor outputs 1.3 dBm^2. The deviation of 16.2 dB originates from PCB losses and the sensor specific gain. Based on additional measurements by the manufacturer, we decreased the transmitted signal-power by 5 dB to accommodate the PCB losses in the transmitter path. In the receiver path we reduced the amplification gain by 11.2 dB.

4.3   Hit Point Layer

Whether a hit point gets detected as such depends on the Signal-to-Noise Ratio (SNR). The signal level is unaffected by interference, while the inter-ference components can often be interpreted as noise. Therefore, the increased

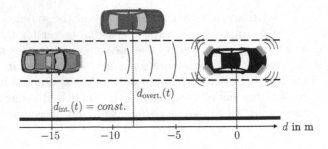

Fig. 10. The scenario describes an overtaking maneuver with an interferer in constant distance. For validation the hit points are measured over the distance $d_{\text{overt.}}$. (Color figure online)

noise level reduces the SNR, leading to a loss of hit points. The simulation should predict the number of lost hit points on extended objects. The reflectivity of each hit point depends on the orientation of the corresponding extended object. We parametrized the angle dependent RCS of a regular car with reference to [26]. For the evaluation, we took measurements of an approaching car (blue) with a constant relative velocity of $v_{\text{overt.}} = 10\ \frac{\text{km}}{\text{h}}$ as described in Fig. 10. The observed sensor (light blue) inside the ego vehicle (black) gets interfered by the front radar (red) mounted on the follower car (grey). In the simulation, we positioned a car at the same distance $d_{\text{overt.}}(t = 0)$ and recreated the trajectory relative to the ego vehicle. The post-processing was conducted on both datasets. An analysis of the hit points over the scenario yields a similar accumulation of the received signal-power. In Fig. 11 the power distributions for two exemplary $d_{\text{overt.}}$ are depicted. Especially for the low powered hit points which might be affected by interference, the distribution fits very well. The remaining deviation in the distribution of the received signal-power can be attributed to the fact that the RCS is parametrized for a different car. Beside that, the geometric scenario simulation has a lack of modelling details. For example, the rotating wheels and the car's

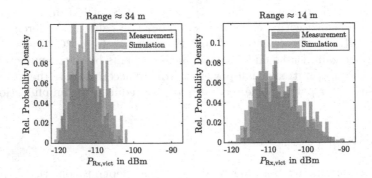

Fig. 11. Energy distribution from the hit points of a radially approaching car.

shape are not taken into account. At the same time, the distribution fits well enough to simulate the number of hit points getting lost at a varying noise level.

4.4 Scenario Layer

On the scenario layer the estimation of the overtakers' state (position and radial velocity along with other parameters) is particularly important. In the automotive application the objects' state is estimated with tracking algorithms, which consider information from the past. Instead of using tracking algorithms, which introduce complexity while obscuring the causality, we use a different measure. As all trackers rely on the availability of hit points, we compare the number of observed hit points along the scenario. The comparison in Fig. 12 shows the measurement and simulation results with and without the influence of interference.

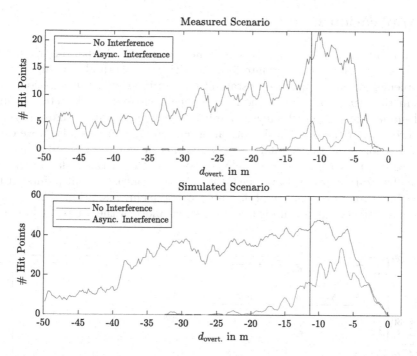

Fig. 12. Hit points from the overtaking car over $d_{overt.}$ in the simulation and the measurement. For a better comparability, the number of hit points were averaged over five time-steps. The vertical line indicates the boundary after which the data behind the vehicles RCS is no longer applicable in the simulation.

The graphs indicate that the number of hit points drop significantly with the activated interferer as expected. This result can be observed based on the measurement and simulation.

The quantitative analysis shows, that the simulation yields between up to four times as many hit points. This can be traced down to the fact, that the assumed hit points along the vehicle's contour do not accurately describe the surface details of a car. However the trend appears trustworthy, as well as the ratio of hit points with and without interference. Both, measurement and simulation indicate, that the overtaker can be reliably detected from a distance $|d_{\text{overt.}}|$ of greater than 50 m in the non-interfered case. Both methods similarly indicate that the distance of a reliable detection drops down to 20 m under the influence of the interferer.

The vertical line in Fig. 12 indicate the minimum distance at which the simulation follows the trend of the measurement. The derivation beyond this line can be explained by the assumption concerning the target illumination. The vehicle's RCS from [26] assumes planar waves, which is not valid in close distances.

5   Application Example

Based on the validation with real sensor measurements, the parametrized simulation can be used for testing interference mitigation methods. As an example we implemented and applied one state-of-the-art interference mitigation technique in the framework. First, the interference occurrence is detected by high signal amplitudes. Then, the method substitutes the interfered signal portions with zero [8]. For the test of this mitigation method in the simulation, we chose the overtaking scenario. Similar to previous measurements, the simulated car was approaching with a constant velocity towards the victim radar in the ego vehicle. The following Fig. 13 presents the number of measured hit points for the approaching car over a portion of discrete time steps in simulation. The analysis shows that the zero-algorithm is able to prevent most of the hit point loss from

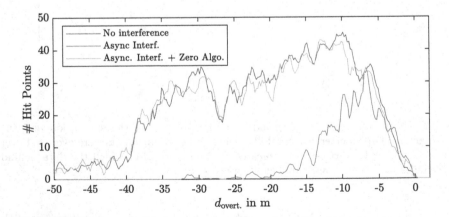

Fig. 13. Evaluation of the zero-algorithm based on the simulated hit points over $d_{\text{overt.}}$..

the target. Nevertheless, a main drawback of this mitigation method is the loss of the former time signal as stated in [9]. As a consequence, this might result in measurement inaccuracies on hit point data level. The simulation framework supports all investigations ranging from the development of such methods to the evaluation with scenario-based metrics.

6   Conclusion

In this research paper, we proposed a Radar Time Signal and Interference simulation for the development and test of interference mitigation techniques. We analyzed and validated all relevant artifacts, that are combined in the interfered target echo signal. We also considered the transmitter and receiver path of the radar front-end and their frequency response. The model was adapted in order to match the analyzed test setup. After model completion, we used our model to generate typical signal energy levels for the observed target and interference sources of a particular scenario. On the underlying sampling and signal layer we ensured that model inaccuracies can be quantified and related to their origin. Especially the power from the simulated hit points with and without interference was proven to be similarly distributed as measured. In the application, we used our simulation to a test state-of-the-art mitigation technique under particular interference scenarios. The resulting radar performance showed that the mitigation technique requires further examination and that the simulation is helpful for that purpose. Our future research will focus on a larger variety of testing scenarios and interference evaluation metrics. With the help of this, mitigation methods can be fully compared in the simulation framework.

References

1. Hummel, T., Kühn, M., Bende, J., Lang A.: Fahrerassistenzsysteme - Ermittlung des Sicherheitspotenzials auf Basis des Schadengeschehes der Deutschen Versicherer. GDV Forschungsbericht FS 03, (2011)
2. European New Car Assessment Programme: Test protocol - AEB VRU systems - Version 2.0.2. EuroNCAP (November 2017)
3. German Association of the Automotive Industry (VDA): Automation - from driver assistance systems to automated driving (2015)
4. ETSI EN 302 264: European Standard. https://www.etsi.org. Accessed 8 May 2020
5. Patole, S.M., Torlak, M., Wang, D., Ali, M.: Automotive radars: a review of signal processing techniques. IEEE Signal Process. Mag. **34**, 22–35 (2017)
6. Bordoux, A., Parashar, K., Bauduin, M.: Phenomenology of mutual interference of FMCW and PMCW automotive radars. In: 2017 IEEE Radar Conference (RadarConf), pp. 1709–1714 (2017)
7. Prinz, A., Roth, J., Schwendner, J., Ayeb, M., Brabetz, L.: Validation strategy for radar-based assistance systems under the influence of interference. In: 2020 German Microwave Conference (GeMiC), pp. 252–255 (2020)
8. Brooker, G.M.: Mutual interference of millimeter-wave radar systems. IEEE Trans. Electromagn. Compat. **49**, 170–181 (2007)

9. Bechter, J., Waldschmidt, C.: Automotive radar interference mitigation by reconstruction and cancellation of interference component. In: 2015 IEEE MTT-S International Conference on Microwaves for Intelligent Mobility (ICMIM) (2015)
10. Bechter, J., Roos, F., Rahman, M., Waldschmidt, C.: Automotive radar interference mitigation using a sparse sampling approach. In: 2017 European Radar Conference (EURAD) (2017)
11. Schipper, T., Schlichenmaier, J., Ahbe, D., Mahler, T., Kowalewski, J., Zwick, T.: A simulator for multi-user automotive radar scenarios. In: IEEE MTT-S International Conference on Microwaves for Intelligent Mobility (ICMIM) (2015)
12. Beise, H., Stifter, T., Schröder, U.: Virtual interference study for FMCW and PMCW radar. In: 2018 German Microwave Conference (GeMiC) (2018)
13. Holder, M., Linnhoff, C., Rosenberger, P., Winner, H.: The Fourier tracing approach for modeling automotive radar sensors. In: 20th International Radar Symposium (IRS) (2019)
14. Kronauge, M., Rohling, H.: Fast two-dimensional CFAR procedure. IEEE Trans. Aerosp. Electron. Syst. **49**, 1817–1823 (2013)
15. Iovescu, C., Rao, S.: The fundamentals of millimeter wave sensors. Texas Instrum. **SPYY005**, 1–8 (2017)
16. Hischke, M.: Collision warning radar interference. In: Proceedings of the Intelligent Vehicles 1995 Symposium (1995)
17. Goppelt, M., Bloecher, H.-L.: Automotive radar-investigation of mutual interference mechanism. In: Advances in Radio Science, pp. 55–60 (2010)
18. Kim, J., Lee, S., Kim, S.: Modulation type classification of interference signals in automotive radar systems. IET Radar Sonar Navig. **13**, 944–952 (2019)
19. Goppelt, M., Blöcher, H.-L., Menzel, W.: Analytical investigation of mutual interference between automotive FMCW radar sensors. In: 2011 German Microwave Conference (GeMiC) (2011)
20. Khoury, J., Ramanathan, R., McCloskey, D., Smith R., Campbell, T.: RadarMAC: mitigating radar interference in self-driving cars. In: 13th Annual IEEE International Conference on Sensing, Communication, and Networking (SECON) (2016)
21. Eder, T., Prinz, A., Brabetz, L., Biebl, E.: Szenarienbasierte Validierung eines hybriden Radarmodells für Test und Absicherung automatisierter Fahrfunktionen. In: Tille, T. (ed.) Automobil-Sensorik 3, pp. 21–43. Springer, Heidelberg (2020). https://doi.org/10.1007/978-3-662-61260-6_1
22. Gardill, M., Schwendner, J., Fuchs, J.: In-situ time-frequency analysis of the 77GHz bands using a commercial chirp-sequence automotive FMCW radar sensor. In: IMS - Recent Advances in Radar Systems Applications (2019)
23. Klausing, H., Holpp, W.: Radar mit realer und synthetischer Apertur - Konzeption und Realisierung. De Gruyter, Berlin (1999)
24. Skolnik, M.I.: Radar Handbook, 2nd edn. McGraw-Hill Inc., New York (1990)
25. Müller, R.: Halbleiter-Elektronik 15. Rauschen, 2nd edn. Springer, Heidelberg (1990). https://doi.org/10.1007/978-3-642-96960-7
26. Kamel, E.B., Peden, A., Pajusco, P.: RCS modeling and measurements for automotive radar applications in the W band. In: 11th European Conference on Antennas and Propagation (EUCAP) (2017)

EMD-SVR: A Hybrid Machine Learning Method to Improve the Forecasting Accuracy of Highway Tollgates Traveling Time to Improve the Road Safety

Atilla Altıntaş$^{(\boxtimes)}$ ⓘ and Lars Davidson ⓘ

Division of Fluid Dynamics, Department of Mechanics and Maritime Sciences,
Chalmers University of Technology, 412 96 Gothenburg, Sweden
altintas@chalmers.se

Abstract. Tollgates are known as the bottleneck of the highways, which cause long waiting queues in rush-hour times of the day. This brings many undesirable consequences such as higher carbon emission and road safety issues. To avoid this scenario, traffic control authorities need accurate travel time forecasts at tollgates to take effective action to monitor potential traffic load and improve traffic safety. Accurate forecasting of the traffic travel time will help traffic regulators to prevent arising problems by taking action. The main objective of this study is to improve the short-term forecasting (minutes) of the traffic flow on highway tollgates by improving a novel hybrid forecasting method that combines Empirical Mode Decomposition with Support Vector Regression (EMD-SVR). Results claim that compared with SVR, the new proposed hybrid prediction model, EMD-SVR, can effectively improve prediction accuracy. Better forecasting of the traffic load will provide safer roads but will also lower the carbon emissions caused by longer traveling times.

Keywords: Empirical Mode Decomposition · SVR · Machine learning · Forecasting

1 Introduction

A number of methodologies have recently been developed for forecasting purposes which can be divided into traditional mathematical statistics and machine learning methods. Regression analysis [2] and time series analysis [8] are some of the examples of traditional mathematical statistics methods. References [10,14] are examples of machine learning algorithm applications to predict traffic load. A review and comparison of the methods are given in Ref. [20].

Recently, Empirical Mode Decomposition (EMD) [12] has become a useful tool to improve forecasting methodologies in many areas from solar and

This work is supported by the Chalmers University, Transport Area of Advance.

A. L. Martins et al. (Eds.): INTSYS 2020, LNICST 364, pp. 241–251, 2021.
https://doi.org/10.1007/978-3-030-71454-3_15

wind energy to financial time series ([3–5,15–17,19]). EMD is a method which decomposes a complex time-series data into its frequency components i.e. so-called intrinsic mode functions (IMFs) ([3,5,12]). EMD divides data into its IMFs, which are a number of high to low-frequency components, where the high-frequency component corresponds to the short term changes, and the low-frequency component corresponds to the long term changes. By using different combination of the frequency components of the data enable us to predict short or long term predictions much more accurately compared to using original (i.e. raw) data. EMD separates data into its components (IMFs) and in this way reduces the complexity of the data and separate trends into different scales which results in a higher accuracy forecasting.

The general approach to EMD-based hybrid prediction methods is to individually predict each IMF and then sum these predicted values to obtain a final prediction. However, the time series of separate IMFs can be categorized in different characteristics and thereby achieve advancement in the time series analysis techniques.

While hybrid methods with EMD come forward as a more effective approach with its higher prediction accuracy, yet there is not a consensus in the literature on which IMFs should be included in the forecasting process.

It is reported that for varying combinations of IMFs a varying prediction accuracy is obtained [6,7,9,11,13,21,22,24]. It is suggested that IMFs that has lower frequency carries the characteristics of the original data, regarded as representing the mean tendency trend [7,9,11,22,24]. The authors associated the higher frequency IMFs with a large amount of noise, which results in a lack of accuracy on the prediction of the wind data. References [9,11,21,24] claimed that the elimination of the IMFs which have high frequency resulted in improved predictive accuracy. References [9,11] carried on an analysis by eliminating the first IMF. Quite the opposite, Ref. [13] excluded the residue from the prediction and reported that omitting the residue is not showing a significant effect on prediction results. As a different approach, instead of removing the high-frequency IMFs from the calculation Refs. [7,22,23] decomposed them separately and reconstructed them. A detailed review could be found in Ref. [6].

Lin et al. [14] have studied travel time and volume predictions with SVR by including scaling methods and they achieved accurate forecasting for the rush hours [4]. In a previous study by Altıntaş et al. [3], it has been shown that the EMD method is superior to conventional filter-based mode decomposition methods. In this study we improve the tollgate traffic travel time predictions by using the EMD-SVR method. We have obtained higher prediction by using selected IMFs as input for the SVR regression model.

The paper is organized as follows. First, the theory and method is given followed by the application of the method to traffic travel time data. The results are summarized and addressed in the following section, and some concluding remarks are given in the final section.

2   Theory and Method

2.1   Scale Decomposition by Empirical Mode Decomposition

EMD is constructed on the premise that any data signal consists of various simple intrinsic modes of oscillations, the original signal being a superposition of these oscillations. Each mode is referred to as an IMF [12] that satisfies the subsequent two conditions: (i) the local extrema and zero-crossing numbers must be equal or differ by one at the most; (ii) the mean of the curve that is constructed by connecting the maxima and minima should be zero.

EMD Algorithm. For a continuous times series $X(t)$, an algorithm could be written as follows to apply the EMD. Fluctuations will be obtained by subtracting the data from its time averaging (therefore the time history data will oscillate around zero).

i. All the maxima and minima will be obtained, see Fig. 1(a).

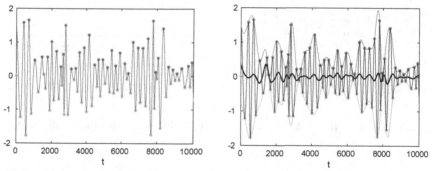

(a) All local maxima (red points), and local minima (green points).

(b) Construction of the mean curve by applying a cubic spline.

Fig. 1. Finding maxima, minima, and constructing a curve. (Color figure online)

ii. An envelope will be constructed for both maxima and minima and a mean curve of these two envelope curves, i.e. $m_{11}(t)$, see Fig. 1(b).

iii. First IMF will be constructed from the original data, i.e. $h_{10} = X(t)$. The first index in h_{ij} represents the number of the IMF in construction, the second represents the number of the iteration. As an example, the first iteration to find the IMF 1 represented as, $h_{11}(t) = h_{10}(t) - m_{11}(t)$.

iv. The steps (i), (ii), (iii) will be done recursively, $h_{1k}(t) = h_{1(k-1)}(t) - m_{1k}(t)$. The stopping criteria is: for $0 \leq t \leq T$

$$sd_n = \sum_{t=0}^{T} \left(\frac{\left| h_{n(k-1)}(t) - h_{nk}(t) \right|^2}{h_{n(k-1)}^2(t)} \right)$$

Empirically a number $sd_n < \epsilon$ is defined as a stopping criterion where ϵ is a number between 0.1 and 0.3.

v. When the first IMF, i.e. $h_{1k}(t)$ is found, it is subtracted from $h_{10}(t)$ to obtain $h_{20}(t)$. The process then restarts from (i) to find the second IMF.

vi. Set $c_i(t) = h_{ik}(t)$, where $c_i(t)$ is the ith. IMF. All the IMFs has been obtained when subtraction at step (v) gives a monotonic or constant data (residue).

As a result, a set of IMFs are obtained. As an example, for the signal $X(t)$ given as in (Fig. 2):

$$X(t) = 4cos(10t) + 2cos(t) + 3.$$

The resulting IMFs of the EMD process will be the frequency components of the raw signal $X(t)$. The highest frequency component, $4cos(t)$, is the first IMF, the second IMF is, $2cos(t)$, finally the residual is 3 (Fig. 3).

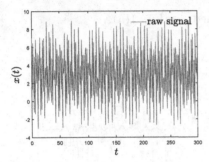

Fig. 2. $x(t) = 4cos(10t) + 2cos(t) + 3$.   **Fig. 3.** IMF1 $= 4cos(10t)$, IMF2 $= 2cos(t)$, residual $= 3$.

2.2 SVR Method

The Support Vector Regression (SVR) is an algorithm for machine learning, which is a variant of Support Vector Machine (SVM). ([18]). SVR has widely been applied to forecasting problems. For a time-series data,

$$D = (X_i, y_i), 1 \le i \le N,$$

where X_i represents the ith element and y_i corresponds the target output data. The SVR function, f, is a linear function which is issued to formulate the nonlinear relation between input and output data as: $f(X_i) = \omega^T \phi(X_i) + b$, where ω, b and $\phi(X_i)$ are the weight vector, bias and function that maps the input vector X into a higher dimensional feature space, respectively. ω and b are obtained by solving the optimization problem:

$$min\frac{1}{2}\|\omega\|^2 + C\sum_{i=1}^{N}(\xi_i + \xi_i^*) \tag{1}$$

subject to:

$$y_i - \omega^T(\psi(x)) - b \leq \epsilon + \xi_i$$
$$\omega^T(\psi(x)) + b - y_i \leq \epsilon + \xi_i \qquad (2)$$
$$\xi_i, \xi_i^* \geq 0.$$

The first term of Eq. 1 measures the flatness of the function. The parameter C balances the trade-off between the complexity of the model and its generalization ability. The cost of error is measured by the variables, ξ_i and ξ_i^*.

The final SVR function is obtained as:

$$y_i = f(X_i) = \sum_{i=1}^{N}((\alpha_i - \alpha_i^*)K(X_i, X_j)) + b \qquad (3)$$

where $K(X_i, X_j)$ is the Kernel function [18] and α_i and α_i^* are the Lagrange multipliers.

2.3 Application to Traffic Travel Time Data

The data are provided by the Knowledge Discovery and Data Mining (KDD) 2017 web site [1]. The data consist of the travel time of vehicles for the period of 19th June to 24th October 2016 for six routes. These are from intersection A to tollgates 1 and 2, and from intersection B and C to tollgates 1 and 3 (Fig. 4).

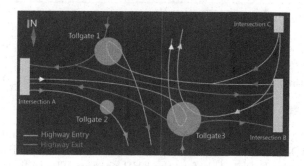

Fig. 4. Road map. [1]

The data consist of a list of records of actual vehicles including intersection ID, tollgate ID, vehicle ID, the time point when the vehicle enters the road, trajectory and travel time which is the total time taken from intersection to the tollgate (Table 1). The travel time data of the vehicles are averaged over 20 min of time-windows (Table 2). There are missing records which means that the time-window has no vehicle recorded, taken as zero average.

The prediction is performed for route B-3 (see Fig. 4) for the morning rush hours (08:00–10:00). The prediction is for every 20 min time-window between 08:00–10:00 and therefore there are six time-windows to forecast. The previous

20 min time-window has been used as the feature to forecast the next 20 min time-window, i.e., time-window 07:40–08:00 enters the process to forecast the next time-window, 08:00–08:20. The data that have been used in the predictions are given in Fig. 5. The data set is split into two data sets as training for the period of 19-07-2016 to 18-10-2016 (first 13 weeks) and test for the period of 18-10-2016 to 24-10-2016 (last 1 week), respectively.

Table 1. Original data from 19th June to 24th October 2016 for six routes.

Field	Type	Description
intersection_id	string	intersection ID
tollgate_id	string	tollgate ID
vehicle_id	string	vehicle ID
starting_time	datetime	minute the vehicle enters the route
travel_seq	string	trajectory of the link traces
travel_time	float	total travel time (in seconds).

Table 2. The data used in this study is given in the table below. The travel time data is averaged over 20 minutes of time-windows.

Field	Type	Description
intersection_id	string	intersection ID
tollgate_id	string	tollgate ID
time_window	string	20-minute time-window, e.g., [2016-19-07 07:40:00, 2016-19-07 08:00:00]
average_travel_time	float	the average travel time of vehicles in the time-window

In this study, we use SVR method as the baseline method and we compare it with the EMD-SVR hybrid method. The data are scaled by Min-Max scaling method to an interval of [-1, 1] before the SVR process. The radial basis function (RBF) is chosen as the kernel function, then Kernel function written as:

$$K(X_i, X_j) = exp(-\gamma \|X_i - X_j\|^2), \tag{4}$$

where the parameter γ, intuitively defines the degree to which the effect of a single example of training reaches. In this study parameters are set to $\gamma = 0.96$, $C = 1.0$, $\epsilon = 0.1$ and are used for all the predictions.

In this text, original data represents the data used in SVR method (first 13 weeks of the data). Original data prediction is the prediction made with SVR. Real data is the test data that never entered any prediction method, traffic travel time data of the last 7 days (last week).

In the EMD-SVR hybrid method, EMD used as a preprocessor to SVR. EMD splits data into IMFs and each IMF is a feature (input) for SVR. IMFs are frequency modes that are obtained by applying EMD to the original data. The sum of all IMFs is equal to the original data. In Fig. 6, the original data of average travel time 07:40–08:00 and its IMFs' obtained by EMD are given. The data set has been split into its IMFs. The number of IMFs has been limited to four, the fourth IMF is including the residual. Each four IMF has been an input for SVR. The combinations of the outputs are the predictions. That process is repeated for all six time-window predictions in the EMD-SVR hybrid method. A process of EMD combined with SVR is given in Fig. 7.

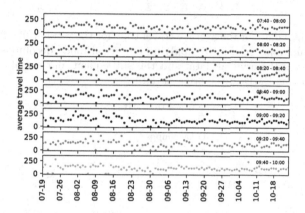

Fig. 5. The rush-hour average travel time data for the route B-3 for the dates 19-07-2016 to 24-10-2016. The data for the time-window 07:40–8:00 are also added since they were used to predict the first rush-hour window, 08:00–8:20.

3   Results and Discussion

The predictions for the test data which is the last week of 14 weeks data is obtained for both the SVR and the EMD-SVR method. We would like to clarify that all the parameters in both SVR and EMD are kept the same for all predictions. SVR is performed by using the original data as the feature. In EMD-SVR, EMD used as a preprocessor to SVR that splits original data into its IMFs. In EMD-SVR, each IMF is a feature for SVR instead the original data.

A total of six 20-min time-window predictions for the rush hours, 08:00–0:00, for the dates between 18-10-2016 and 24-10-2016 are given in Figs. 8(a) to 8(f). Mean square (MSE) and root mean square error (RMSE) are given in Table 3, where the best approximation is given in a separate column and also highlighted in red.

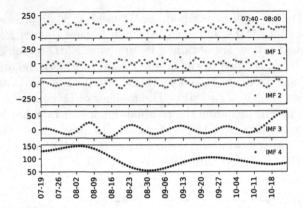

Fig. 6. The original data for the average travel time for the window 07:40–8:00 and the intrinsic mode functions (IMFs) by applying empirical mode decomposition (EMD). The upper signal is the original data, and the subsequent four signals are the IMFs obtained by applying EMD to the original data.

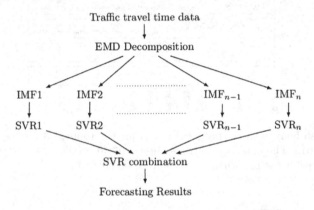

Fig. 7. Process schema of EMD-SVR method.

For the travel time windows 08:00–8:20, 08:20–8:40 and 09:20–9:40, IMF 1 gives a better approximation compared to the original data and all the other combinations of IMFs (see Figs. 8(a), 8(b), 8(e), respectively and Table 3). For the time windows 08:40–9:00 and 09:00–9:20, a combination of IMF 3 + IMF 4 and IMF2 + IMF 3, respectively, agree better with real data than all the other IMF combinations and original data (see Fig. 8(c), Fig. 8(d), respectively and Table 3). For the time-window 09:40–0:00, the original data approximate the real data better than all the other IMFs and their combinations. However, IMF 1 approximates the real data with less than an MSE error of 1% difference compared to the original data prediction.

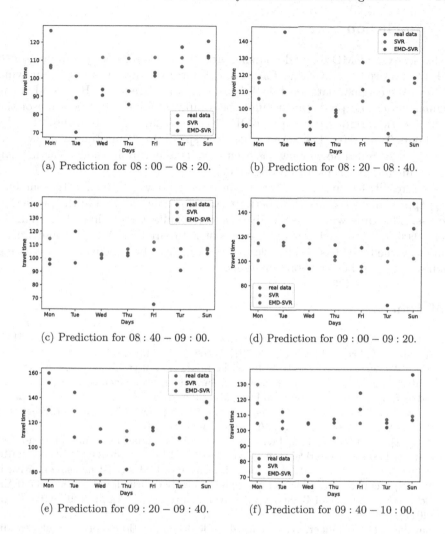

Fig. 8. Traffic travel time predictions for the rush hours, 8:00–0:00, for the 20 minutes time interval. The data is the date between 18-10-2016 to 24-10-2016 (Monday to Sunday).

Table 3. The travel time predictions errors for the rush hours, 08:00–0:00, for 20 min time-window (see Figs. 8(a) - 8(f)). MSE = mean square error, RMSE = root mean square error.

	Original data		IMF 1		IMF 2		IMF 3		IMF 4		IMF 3 + IMF 4		IMF 2 + IMF 3		Best Approximation
	MSE	RMSE	MSE	RMSE	MSE	RMSE	MSE	RMSE	MSE	RMSE	MSE	RMSE	MSE	RMSE	
08.00-08:20	0.2000	0.4472	0.0783	0.2796	0.2749	0.5243	0.9813	0.9906	0.1853	0.4304					IMF 1
08.20-08:40	0.2346	0.4844	0.2108	0.4592	0.2190	0.4679	0.7614	0.8726	0.2655	0.5153					IMF 1
08.40-09:00	0.2014	0.4488	0.2419	0.4919	0.2591	0.5091	0.2093	0.4575	0.2022	0.4497	0.1690	0.4112			IMF 3 + IMF 4
09.00-09:20	0.1787	0.4228	0.3306	0.5749	0.2405	0.4904	0.5427	0.7367	0.9815	0.9907			0.1542	0.3927	IMF 2 + IMF 3
09.20-09:40	0.1912	0.4373	0.1676	0.4094	0.8584	0.9265	0.8328	0.9126	0.3163	0.5624					IMF 1
09.40-10:00	0.1836	0.4285	0.1850	0.4301	0.3050	0.5523	0.2112	0.4595	0.3367	0.5803					Original data

4 Conclusion

In this study, an EMD-based decoupling procedure is applied as a preprocessor to SVR to improve the travel time forecasting. First, IMFs are obtained by applying EMD to the original data, each IMF is used as a feature for SVR instead of the original data. The prediction results are compared for the combination of the IMFs and the original data. The KDD Cup 2017 data have been used for the rush hours 08:00–0:00. The data set has been split into 20 min time windows and a previous 20 min time-window has been used as a feature in the forecasting. All the parameters are kept for all predictions.

As a result, for five out of six 20 min time-windows, IMF or IMF combinations approximate the real data better than using original data in the prediction process. The time-window that gives better results for original data, namely 09:40–0:00, only gives 1% better agreement compared to IMF 1. Therefore we claim that the EMD based signal decomposition could be beneficial in forecasting studies to obtain better approximations.

References

1. Kdd2017. https://tianchi.aliyun.com/competition/information.htm?spm=5176. 100067.5678.2.ru0ea4&raceId=231597. Accessed 15 Mar 2017
2. Alam, I., Farid, D., Rossetti, R.J.F.: The prediction of traffic flow with regression analysis. In: Abraham, A., Dutta, P., Mandal, J., Bhattacharya, A., Dutta, S. (eds.) Emerging Technologies in Data Mining and Information Security. Advances in Intelligent Systems and Computing, vol. 813, pp. 661–671. Springer, Singapore (2019). https://doi.org/10.1007/978-981-13-1498-8_58
3. Altıntaş, A., Davidson, L., Peng, S.: A new approximation to modulation-effect analysis based on empirical mode decomposition. Phys. Fluids **31**(2), 025117 (2019)
4. Andersson, L.E., Aftab, M.F., Scibilia, F., Imsland, L.: Forecasting using multivariate empirical mode decomposition-applied to iceberg drift forecast. In: 2017 IEEE Conference on Control Technology and Applications (CCTA), pp. 1097–1103. IEEE (2017)
5. Barnhart, B., Eichinger, W.: Empirical mode decomposition applied to solar irradiance, global temperature, sunspot number, and $CO2$ concentration data. J. Atmos. Solar Terr. Phys. **73**(13), 1771–1779 (2011)
6. Bokde, N., Feijóo, A., Villanueva, D., Kulat, K.: A review on hybrid empirical mode decomposition models for wind speed and wind power prediction. Energies **12**(2), 254 (2019)
7. Dejun, L., Hui, L., Zhonghua, M.: One hour ahead prediction of wind speed based on data mining. In: 2010 2nd International Conference on Advanced Computer Control, vol. 5, pp. 199–203. IEEE (2010)
8. Ghosh, B., Basu, B., O'Mahony, M.: Multivariate short-term traffic flow forecasting using time-series analysis. IEEE Trans. Intell. Transp. Syst. **10**(2), 246–254 (2009)
9. Guo, Z., Zhao, W., Lu, H., Wang, J.: Multi-step forecasting for wind speed using a modified EMD-based artificial neural network model. Renew. Energy **37**(1), 241–249 (2012)
10. Hong, W.C., Dong, Y., Zheng, F., Lai, C.Y.: Forecasting urban traffic flow by SVR with continuous ACO. Appl. Math. Model. **35**(3), 1282–1291 (2011)

11. Hu, J., Wang, J., Zeng, G.: A hybrid forecasting approach applied to wind speed time series. Renew. Energy **60**, 185–194 (2013)
12. Huang, N.E., et al.: The empirical mode decomposition and the Hilbert spectrum for nonlinear and non-stationary time series analysis. In: Proceedings of the Royal Society of London A: Mathematical, Physical and Engineering Sciences, vol. 454, pp. 903–995. The Royal Society (1998)
13. Liang, Z., Liang, J., Zhang, L., Wang, C., Yun, Z., Zhang, X.: Analysis of multi-scale chaotic characteristics of wind power based on Hilbert-Huang transform and Hurst analysis. Appl. Energy **159**, 51–61 (2015)
14. Lin, A.Y., Zhang, M., Selpi: Using scaling methods to improve support vector regression's performance for travel time and traffic volume predictions. In: Rojas, I., Pomares, H., Valenzuela, O. (eds.) ITISE 2017. Contributions to Statistics, pp. 115–127. Springer, Cham (2018). https://doi.org/10.1007/978-3-319-96944-2_8
15. Monjoly, S., André, M., Calif, R., Soubdhan, T.: Hourly forecasting of global solar radiation based on multiscale decomposition methods: a hybrid approach. Energy **119**, 288–298 (2017)
16. Nava, N., Di Matteo, T., Aste, T.: Financial time series forecasting using empirical mode decomposition and support vector regression. Risks **6**(1), 7 (2018)
17. Premanode, B., Vongprasert, J., Toumazou, C.: Noise reduction for nonlinear non-stationary time series data using averaging intrinsic mode function. Algorithms **6**(3), 407–429 (2013)
18. Qiu, X., Suganthan, P.N., Amaratunga, G.A.: Short-term electricity price forecasting with empirical mode decomposition based ensemble kernel machines. Procedia Comput. Sci. **108**, 1308–1317 (2017)
19. Ren, Y., Suganthan, P., Srikanth, N.: Ensemble methods for wind and solar power forecasting-a state-of-the-art review. Renew. Sustain. Energy Rev. **50**, 82–91 (2015)
20. Salotti, J., Fenet, S., Billot, R., El Faouzi, N.E., Solnon, C.: Comparison of traffic forecasting methods in urban and suburban context. In: 2018 IEEE 30th International Conference on Tools with Artificial Intelligence (ICTAI), pp. 846–853. IEEE (2018)
21. Sivanagaraja, T., Veluvolu, K.: A hybrid approach for short-term forecasting of wind speed. Sci. World J. **2013**, 548370 (2013). https://doi.org/10.1155/2013/548370
22. Sun, C., Yuan, Y., Li, Q.: A new method for wind speed forecasting based on empirical mode decomposition and improved persistence approach. In: 2012 10th International Power & Energy Conference (IPEC), pp. 659–664. IEEE (2012)
23. Yu, C., Li, Y., Zhang, M.: Comparative study on three new hybrid models using Elman Neural Network and Empirical Mode Decomposition based technologies improved by Singular Spectrum Analysis for hour-ahead wind speed forecasting. Energy Convers. Manag. **147**, 75–85 (2017)
24. Zhang, K., Qu, Z., Wang, J., Zhang, W., Yang, F.: A novel hybrid approach based on cuckoo search optimization algorithm for short-term wind speed forecasting. Environ. Progress Sustain. Energy **36**(3), 943–952 (2017)

Smart Surveillance of Runway Conditions

Gabriel Pestana[1](✉) ⓘ, Pedro Reis[2], and Tiago Rocha da Silva[1]

[1] INOV Inesc Inovação, Lisbon, Portugal
{gabriel.pestana, tiago.r.silva}@inov.pt
[2] Ana Aeroportos - Vinci, Lisbon, Portugal
pereis@ana.pt

Abstract. Runway safety-related accidents represent the most significant source of aviation accidents worldwide. Runway contaminants are typically associated with extreme weather conditions but can also include other safety-issues such as foreign object debris, cracks, and pavement deformation. Although airports are required to perform periodic runway inspections, it is clear that manual inspections alone are not sufficient to mitigate this type of threat. The paper outlines the need to implement automated procedures for runway inspections, seeking to improve runway safety.

The paper presents a project with an innovative approach for automated runway inspections using laser scanning equipment. The compliance with airport regulation, standards, and business logic has driven the architectural solution, co-designed with end-users to increase understandability, and to create a product that provides the best possible user experience, addressing relevant concerns and information needs. The project solution provides a set of data analysis services addressing the Analytics-as-a-Service (AaaS) paradigm, where the concepts of information visualization and context-awareness are essential in supporting the surveillance of the runway status, in particular, for events which may lead to aquaplaning phenomena. Monitoring such water-events enables the detection of drainage problems as well as the identification of areas that might compromise runway safety.

Keywords: Spectral analysis · Runway contamination · Context-awareness · Information visualization · Terrestrial Laser Scanning

1 Introduction to Airport Runway Safety

The international civil aviation network carries over 4 billion passengers around the world annually [1], corresponding to a significant number of runway movements (i.e., aircrafts' landing and take-off). Assessing and reporting runway surface conditions is, therefore, a critical task when analyzing the runway functional and operational conditions for improved safety.

Runway safety-related accidents represent the most significant source of aviation accidents worldwide and remain aviation number one safety risk category [2]. Over the past eight years, most of the aviation accidents reported to ICAO[1] was Runway safety-

---

[1] ICAO - International Civil Aviation Organization (www.icao.int).

A. L. Martins et al. (Eds.): INTSYS 2020, LNICST 364, pp. 252–270, 2021.
https://doi.org/10.1007/978-3-030-71454-3_16

related. Of those runway-related accidents, 35% were the result of a runway excursion, which occurs when an aircraft veers off or overruns the runway.

A runway excursion occurs when "An aircraft veers off or overruns the runway surface during either take-off or landing" [3]. One of the contributing factors involves adverse weather conditions that result in the runway surface being contaminated. Runway contaminants are typically associated with extreme weather conditions (e.g., snow, ice, mud, frost, and water) but can also include other safety-issues, namely extreme hot weather. Such weather conditions may cause the pavement to blow up and buckle. A deteriorating runway may also pose a foreign object debris (FOD) threat.

The runway is constantly suffering damage, such as potholes due to wear and tear of aircraft or other vehicles using the pavement. Sometimes debris or foreign objects may appear on the runway, which may be caused by jet explosions, aircraft take-offs, and landings, natural causes, etc. On active runways involving aircraft movement, the existence of FOD may cause air disasters and subsequent loss of life, causing significant losses to airlines. Therefore, different methods are used to conduct runway inspections and surveillance. By convention, inspectors will move around the runway for visual and manual inspections periodically (i.e., multiple times a day). However, such type of inspections is slow and labor-intensive. Furthermore, manual visual inspection is unreliable as it is subjected to human errors and conditions surrounding the runway. Accordingly, there is a need to implement automated procedures for runway inspections, seeking to improve Runway safety.

In this paper, we present a research project, named *Monitorização Persistente de Pista* – MPP, (ref. ANI 31/SI/2017 ID: 39876), that is funded by the Portugal 2020 program. The Portugal 2020 is a partnership agreement between Portugal and the European Commission. It applies to the principles of the European Strategy 2020[2] and focuses on the economic, social, environmental and territorial development policy aspects that may stimulate Portugal's growth and job creation.

Within the Portugal 2020 program, the main goals of MPP are to strengthening research, promote technological development and innovation. As such, MPP addresses the following thematic objectives: transfer of knowledge from the scientific community to the market (airport sector), promoting sustainable transport, and eliminating bottlenecks in major infrastructures, as it is the case of an airport and, in particular, actions to improve the awareness of safety issues at the runway.

MPP will implement a non-intrusive solution, based in LIDAR technology (TLS - Terrestrial Laser Scanning) to perform inspections in an automated way and to report measurements on the conditions of the runway, including data related to the risk of runway contamination, deformations in the pavement and FOD, while simultaneously allowing the visualization of a high precision 3D representation of the runway status. In terms of innovation, the proposed process includes mechanisms for information awareness and visualization. The objective is to provide information semantically aligned with the stakeholder's information needs, allowing quick navigation through the information structure for rapid identification of situations related to a safety risk, triggering notification regarding the severity level associated with each type of

---

[2] EUROPE 2020: A strategy for smart, sustainable and inclusive growth.

occurrence. MPP is a web-based platform designed to provides a set of data analysis services addressing the Analytics-as-a-Service (AaaS) paradigm.

The remainder of the paper is structured as follows. Section 2 presents an overview of the classification of runway events; in particular, events relate to FOD, deformation, and runway contamination. Section 3 provides a short introduction to the scope of the MPP project, with an overview of the Terrestrial Laser Scanning equipment. The section explains how the proposed solution uses spectral analysis to analyze the runway pavement based on the current environment/context conditions. Section 4 describes how the proposed technology is being tested at Lisbon airport, presenting a business scenario related to inspections and the report of measurements on the conditions of the runway, namely for identifying risks of Runway contamination. Finally, In Sect. 5, the paper presents the achievements accomplished up to now and future work for the MPP project.

2   Classification of Events Related to Runway Conditions

The aviation industry has recognized the need to develop appropriate procedures and guidelines for operations on contaminated runways. In response, ICAO is committed to formulating a unified global reporting format (GRF) for timely and more accurate assessment and reporting of runway surface conditions [4]. The GRF comprises a standardized runway condition matrix - Runway Condition Code (RWYCC), covering conditions found in all climates. The goal is to enable airport operators to quickly and correctly assess the state of the runway surface regardless of whether it is in wet runway conditions, snow, mud, ice or frost.

The results of the RWYCC assessment are forwarded to air traffic services and aviation information services for dissemination to pilots. This helps the pilot to correctly perform landing and take-off performance calculations for wet or contaminated runways. Another essential element of GRF is the process of enabling pilots to report their observations of runway conditions, thereby confirming RWYCC or alerting to changes in conditions [5]. GRF proposes a method that is easy to understand and implement on a global scale. This is an important means to reduce the risk of runway excursion risk and improve the safety of runway operations. According to [4], in November 2020, all airports will have to report runway conditions according to the GRF format.

2.1   Pavement Cracks and Deformations

The structure of the runway pavement can provide sufficient support for the loads applied by the aircraft, and produce a firm, stable, smooth, all-weather surface, free of debris or other particles that may be blown or picked up by propeller wash or jet blast. In order to meet these requirements, the pavement must have a certain quality and thickness so that it will not fail under the applied load. In addition, it must have sufficient inherent stability to withstand and not be affected by damaging traffic erosion, adverse weather conditions, and other deterioration influences [6].

However, runway pavement deteriorates during service due to traffic and climate effects; therefore, systematic monitoring is required to assess their structural and functional condition. It is vital to identify the different surface defects and link them to a cause. Gradual deformations are typically the result of drainage and geotechnical characteristics. The majority of runway inspections tries to identify the following situations: surface defects, surface deformation, cracks, and patches, which may represent safety hazards. Therefore, the key to a useful pavement evaluation is identifying different types of pavement distress and types of pavement distress and linking them to a cause [7]. Understanding the cause of the pavement condition along with the historic deterioration rate, assist in making appropriate maintenance and rehabilitation plans.

Some airports use radar-based automated systems to detect damage, debris, and other hazards in the runway and its adjacent areas. However, the use of any radar system for runway surveillance has its limitations. Although radar is an excellent method for detecting metallic objects, it is not as sensitive in detecting non-metallic objects such as rubber. Alternatively, some airports use infrared or thermal imaging systems to detect objects and cracks voids. However, systems that use infrared or thermal imaging systems can only sense infrared radiation (radiation emitted by objects), which is outside the thermal balance of the surrounding environment. Such infrared or thermal imaging systems can only detect objects (e.g., in a warm metal fragment on the runway) that have sufficient thermal contrast. Small objects with poor thermal contrast can pose significant challenges to infrared/thermal imaging systems. Besides, under adverse weather conditions (such as cold weather), the performance of these systems is unpredictable.

Other tools [8] provide information about runway deformation using heatmaps, which is an efficient way to show an overall picture of the situation. The outcome (e.g., deformation data) feeds directly into the maintenance planning in the form of increased runway pavement periods, premature infrastructure life cycle shortening, or as a response to geohazards from flooding and seismic activity. Such systems typically provide static dashboards (with pre-processed images) for airport officers to get access to the information relevant for their decision-making process.

2.2 Detection of Foreign Object Debris

Foreign body debris (FOD) materials may cause hazards to aircraft operations. Every year, more than 66% of airport emergencies are related to FOD, causing nearly 4 billion U.S. dollars in financial losses in the global aviation industry every year [9]. All aircraft occasionally lose small metal or carbon parts during take-off and landing. These parts remain on the runway and may damage the tires of other aircraft, hit the fuselage or windshield, or get sucked up into an engine. Other examples of FOD include tire parts, asphalt blocks, screws, inset lights, and anything that may appear on the runway but is not part of the runway. During take-off and landing operations, the presence of these objects may become extremely dangerous. FOD also brings operational difficulties to the airport. It takes approximately 30 min to collect debris, during which time the runway remains closed for aircraft operations.

Even if the airport is required to conduct manual inspections of the entire runway surface multiple times a day, it is clear that manual inspections alone are not enough to mitigate FOD threats [9]. It is foreseeable that an automated method for detecting FOD or damage on the runway can reduce the cost and human error, acting in a complementary way to manual inspections. Continuous inspections using an automated surveillance system facilitate FOD detection 24/7 in all weather conditions. The advantages of such a system over conventional vehicle inspections are:

- Continuous monitoring, including night and low visibility conditions.
- Detect FOD faster and more reliable.
- More efficient traffic flow (e.g., uninterrupted by inspection vehicles).
- Reduce the risk of inspection vehicles entering the runway (e.g., runway incursions due to a controller error).
- Reduced risk of birdstrikes (e.g., optical sensors to identify birds).

Current solutions use a combination of radar and photoelectric sensors. Other (more reliable for runway FOD) solutions include installing cameras to capture images of the runway under ambient light conditions during day and night without the need for auxiliary lightings such as infrared or laser illuminator. Although image processing systems can apply image enhancement methods to enhance images captured by cameras, such systems have some limitations in FOD detection. It depends on ambient lighting conditions and is not suitable for low lighting conditions, which can cause major problems in pixel characterization. Cameras used in existing surveillance systems require additional auxiliary lightings, such as lasers or infrared light for night surveillance. In turn, this requires a large amount of infrastructure in the airport using this system, which increases the cost.

2.3 Runway Contamination

According to ICAO [1], runway contaminants are associated with extreme weather conditions (e.g., snow, ice, slush, frost, or water). Such adverse weather, resulting in the runway surface being contaminated, is responsible for 35% runway-landing incidents/accidents [5]. These overruns have occurred on grooved and smooth runways during periods of moderate to heavy rain. The analysis of these events shows that the braking friction coefficient in each case is significantly lower than expected, and if the runway changes from a wet state to a contaminated state based on rainfall intensity or reported data, it may take 30% to 40% % extra stopping distance. The water contaminated value is within the threshold shown in Table 1.

When 25% of the runway surface area (regardless of whether it is in an isolated area) is covered by standing water with a depth of more than 3 mm or an equivalent amount of snow or loose snow, the runway is considered to be contaminated. As mentioned in Sect. 1, when the average friction value of any 152-m section of the runway is below the recommended minimum friction level, the runway is also considered to have been contaminated with rubber deposits or other materials that degrade friction.

Table 1. Parameter considered by ICAO for Runway Contamination.

Standing water	Slush (Mud)	Loose wet snow	Loose dry snow
3.2–6.4 mm	3.8–7.6 mm	7.6–15.2 mm	15.2–30.5 mm

The type of runway contamination covered by the MPP project is focused on detecting water-sheets, which are generally associated with the risk of aquaplaning. The thickness of the water sheet can affect the operating conditions of the runway, which may lead to aquaplaning phenomena, leading to loss of control of the aircraft in the ground, with the risk of excursion. Monitoring such water-events is essential not only for the detection of drainage problems but also to identify areas at higher risk of occurrence on the runway.

Several types of descriptive terms can be used to report runway surface conditions, such as the type and depth of pollution, readings from runway friction measurement equipment, and aircraft braking action reports. The investigation of reported runway safety incidents found that the accuracy and timeliness of the runway surface condition report were insufficient, which contributed to many runway deviations. Such short-comings include the lack of standardization in the aggregation and reporting of runway surface conditions to end-users (e.g., airport operators and crew), especially the use of different terminology, formats, and timeliness of reporting.

In order to overcome the lack of standards for reporting runway pollution, ICAO has developed the Global Runway Condition Assessment and Reporting Format (GRF). As shown in Table 2, the method includes the evaluation of the runway and the allocation of RWYCC, ranging from 0 for a very slippery surface to 6 for a dry surface. The code is supplemented on the basis of a description of surface contaminants based on their type, depth and coverage, for every third of the runway.

The runway condition assessment matrix provides a common standardized termi-nology for runway surface condition description. An agreed set of criteria used, in a consistent manner, for runway surface condition assessment [5, 10]. Within the scope of the MPP project, we particularly want to monitor conditions related to water events (i.e., situations where stagnant water may encourage water skiing). The presence of water reduces the braking coefficient to that of an icy or "slippery" runway [11]. In this case, due to the formation of a water wedge between the runway and the tires, the tires can no longer provide directional control or effective braking, causing the aircraft to be completely water-borne. There are three types of aquaplaning:

- **Dynamic aquaplaning** (also called hydroplaning) is related to speed and tire pressure. High speed and low tire pressure are the worst combinations, with the lowest aquaplaning speeds. When dynamic aquaplaning occurs, the tiers of the aircraft rise from the water and ride on the water wedges like water skis.
- **Viscous aquaplaning** occurs on all wet runways and describes the abnormal slipperiness or lubricating action of the water. Typically, it corresponds to a small amount of water mix with surface contaminants. Compared with dynamic aqua-planing, a much thinner layer of a contaminant is required in the event of viscous aquaplaning. It appears in the same way as dynamic aquaplaning but on abnormally

smooth surfaces such as touchdown zones contaminated with excessive rubber deposits, which may start and continue at any ground speed.

- **Reverted rubber aquaplaning** occurs when the water is thin, and the surface of the runway is smooth. Dynamic or viscous aquaplaning is usually done with the wheels locked. The locked wheels generate enough heat to vaporize the water film underneath, thereby forming a steam cushion, which eliminates contact between the tire and the surface and begins to restore part of the rubber on the tire to an uncured state. This is the only type of aquaplaning which leaves physical evidence on the runway surface. Before anti-skid devices were widely used, this situation was much more common, and usually only happened on aircraft with such emergency brakes.

Table 2. The runway condition assessment matrix, source [4].

Assessment criteria		Downgrade assessment criteria	
RWY Code	Runway (RWY) surface description	Aeroplan deceleration or directional control observation	Pilot report RWY braking action
6	- Dry	---	---
5	- FROST - WET (the runway surface is covered by any visible dampness or water up to and including 3 mm depth) Up to an including 3 mm depth: - SLUSH - DRY SNOW - WET SNOW	Breaking deceleration is normal for the wheel braking effort applied AND directional control is normal.	GOOD
4	- 15º C and Lower outside air temperature: - COMPACTED SNOW	Breaking deceleration OR directional control is between Good and Medium.	GOOD to MEDIUM
3	- WET ("slipper wet" runway) - DRY SNOW or WET SNOW (any depth) on top of COMPACTED SNOW More than 3 mm depth: - DRY SNOW - WET SNOW Higher the -15º C outside air temperature: - COMPACTED SNOW	Breaking deceleration is noticeably reduced for the wheel braking effort applied OR directional control is noticeably reduced.	MEDIUM
2	More than 3 mm depth of water slush: - STANDING WATER - SLUSH	Breaking deceleration OR directional control is between Medium and Poor.	MEDIUM to POOR
1	- ICE	Breaking deceleration is significantly reduced for the wheel braking effort applied OR directional control is significantly reduced.	POOR
0	- WET ICE - WATER ON TOP OF COMPACTED SNOW - DRY SNOW or WET SNOW ON TOP OF ICE	Breaking deceleration is minimal to non-existent for the wheel braking effort applied OR directional control is uncertain.	LESS THAN POOR

The LIDAR solution proposed by MPP (TLS-Ground Laser Scanning) constitutes an innovative method that overcomes the challenge of automatic runway contamination inspection and provides indicators about the target runway condition (i.e., deformation, foreign bodies, and contamination) while allowing the visualization of a high-precision 3D representation. In this domain, information visualization combined with visual analytics provides an interdisciplinary field that seeks to combine the advantages of human perception and the processing power of computers in establishing the extent of information governance. This means that information governance encompasses more than traditional records management. It incorporates information security and protection, compliance, risk management, data security, knowledge management, and business operations.

3   Project Context – Automated Runway Inspections

MPP will implement a non-intrusive web-based solution, based in LIDAR technology (TLS - Terrestrial Laser Scanning) to perform inspections and to report measurements on the conditions of the runway, namely the identification of risks related to aquaplaning (caused by water sheet thickness), deformations in the pavement and detection of foreign objects. MPP addresses an automatic runway surface condition assessment and reporting of runway contaminants for improved safety and operational efficiency. The goal is to streamline the visualization of events according to three criteria:

- Foreign Object Debris (FOD)
- Cracks & Deformation (CD)
- Runway Contamination (RC)

MPP follows a user-centric design approach, covering the entire process of acquiring sensoring data, processing those (raw) data at the service layer to enhance the information by integrating the collected data with additional operational data provided by existing systems within the airport. In the end, an interactive dashboard provides decision-makers with accurate and real-time information about runway safety conditions. The goal is to increase understandability and to create a product that provides the best possible user experience. During the project execution, informational artifacts will be specified in close collaboration with the end-user group and compliance with existing standards, namely:

- ISO/IEC/IEEE 42010:2011: Systems and software engineering, this standard addresses the creation, analysis, and sustainment of architectures of systems through the use of architecture descriptions. A conceptual model of the architecture description is established.
- ISO9241–210:2019: Ergonomics of human-system interaction, this standard provides requirements and recommendations for human-centred design principles and activities throughout the life cycle of computer-based interactive systems. It also improves ergonomics and enhances the conceptualization of interactive dashboards co-designed with end-users to address relevant concerns and information needs.

The project consortium strengthened cooperation in research and innovation, establishing productive partnerships with airport stakeholders to co-design a smart solution for the surveillance of the runway conditions in Lisbon airport.

MPP architectural challenges address the need to support increased scalability – because of real-time and web-scale demands introduced by the LIDAR sensor for surveillance of the runway active segments –, tighter safety events and increased usage of ICAO standards [12]. It embraces and supports a strong API-based philosophy, providing the means to drive decoupling communication between the system software components. With decoupling and segmentation, we can engage effectively with the ideas expressed by the concept of shearing layers, integrating an event-driven architecture with microservices using event sourcing and CQRS[3]. The advantages of CQRS integrated with event sourcing, and microservices are:

- Leveraging microservices for modularity with separate databases. Having separate models and services for read and insert operations.
- Leveraging event sourcing for handling atomic operations. Read operations can be faster as the load is distributed between read and insert services.
- Maintain historical/audit data for analytics with the implementation of event sourcing.

The MPP presentation layer (i.e., client-DAS[4]) was designed to support workflows providing spatio-temporal context awareness, combined with advanced data analytic capabilities. Data governance and collaboration diagrams describing coherent and compliant messages flow between the stakeholders are specified according to ICAO requirements using BPMN[5]. This strategy paves the path to a system prototype for operation in a relevant environment - such as the Lisbon airport. Apart from listing technological challenges, the implementation of tiny cycles of participatory reflection and co-create usage scenarios, discussing factors that facilitate or impair the acceptance and use, according to the user's perspective and user requirements elicitation, will be critical to ensure acceptance.

3.1   Project Context Diagram

Figure 1 presents a high-level view of the system being modeled, establishing the boundaries of the system and its environment. It shows the entities (stakeholders) that interact with the system. By defining and clarifying the boundaries of the system, we can identify flows of information between the system and the external entities. The entire system is shown as a single process.

---

[3] Command and Query Responsibility Segregation (CQRS) pattern maximizes performance, scalability, and security. The flexibility created by CQRS allows a system to better evolve over time and prevents update commands from causing merge conflicts at the domain level.

[4] Data Analysis & Surveillance (DAS), this is a client interface designed to act as a command centre where a set of functionalities to keep decision-makers well informed about the runway condition, enabling them to act when an event requiring their intervention is triggered.

[5] BPMN - Business Process Model and Notation (https://www.omg.org/spec/BPMN).

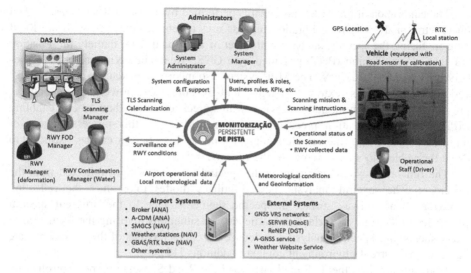

Fig. 1. MPP context diagram.

Although the TLS equipment is responsible for collecting data about the runway status (i.e., runway automatic inspection), for adequately assessing the runway operational condition the MPP system has to interact with multiple airport systems, each one with a specific role in providing information used by the MPP system to analyze the runway status according to airport regulations, the number of movements, weather conditions and the airport operational status (e.g., NVO/LVO[6], maintenance work or any other aspects that might influence airport movements). The MPP system has, therefore, to interact with external systems when assessing the runway status, namely:

- The Airport Collaborative Decision Making (A-CDM), providing (just-in-time) information about aircraft movements.
- The Broker [16], providing information regarding the flight scheduling system (SCORE).
- Local weather stations installed at the airport, providing information useful to improve the TLS scanning context, namely with parameters such as precipitation/ rainfall, temperature, humidity, dew/frost point, air pressure, wind speed and direction, and visibility conditions (compliance with ICAO weather parameters requirements).
- Weather web service, providing global meteorological information and forecast services to be used as additional weather-context to enhance the accuracy of the runway inspection report performed by the TLS equipment.

---

[6] NVO/LVO, these two acronyms define the level of service of the airport, meaning Normal/Low Visibility Operations. LVO are usually defined as a set of procedures established at an airport when either surface visibility is sufficiently low to prejudice safe ground movement without additional procedural controls or the prevailing cloudbase is sufficiently low to preclude pilots obtaining the required visual reference for a safe landing.

The calibration of the TLS equipment is performed by a mobile Road Sensor based on spectral analysis. This calibration process uses a vehicle equipped with the Road Sensor, fusing the spectral analysis with a set of additional data, namely the Position Navigation and Timing (PNT) provided by a GNSS Real-Time Kinematic (RTK) receiver for location accuracy. The MPP system also incorporates data from the ReNEP and SERVIR systems, external systems held by Portuguese governmental entities, providing geo-positioning public services with a precision lower than 10 cm, enabling MPP to improve location precision to a larger scale. In this process (whenever required), the Driver of the vehicle equipped with the Road Sensor can be instructed to drive the vehicle to specific areas of the runway.

The runway diagnosis is based on the spectral analysis of light reflected from the pavement. The spectral analysis method utilizes diodes to capture the reflecting behavior of the runway surface at specific segments. Due to the different spectral properties of the runway surface (in particular, for situations favoring the formation of water sheets), the spectral analysis can deduce the characteristics of the pavement state based on the current environment/context conditions [12].

Both sensors (i.e., the TLS equipment and the Road Sensor) can be controlled by the TLS manager directly from the client-DAS interface. Whenever a runway risk event is detected by the MPP system, at the back-end (i.e., the MPP Server-OKM[7]), the system automatically notifies the corresponding runway manager. The format of the notification message follows the SNOWTAM format (see Sect. 4.1 for more detailed information). In the case of an unlikely lack of communication between the MPP system with the TLS equipment, the Driver using a proprietary operator mobile console will be able to access the road sensor or execute any configurations instructions requested by the TLS manager.

3.2 Characteristics of the Laser Equipment

The use of a commercial of the shelf (COTS) TLS equipment is nowadays a common practice in research projects for non-intrusive solutions, mitigating the development costs and contributing simultaneously to increase the technological maturity level, in particular for critical tasks requiring precision. The approach enabled researchers to focus their effort on what is core/innovative. After defining the specifications of the equipment, a market search for possible suppliers with equipment that best complies with the project requirements was performed. The marker survey also considered a solution with a range of flexibility by supporting external peripherals and accessories (e.g., equipment coverage for outdoor installation, power supply/consumption requirements, flexibility in operating the equipment remotely, compliance to existing 3D scanning and types of standards interfaces provided by the equipment).

---

[7] **Operational Knowledge Management (OKM)**, includes a set of software modules at the server side (i.e., system back-end) responsible to compute the raw data reported by the TLS and analyse them based on the business logic valid at the time the data were collected, which requires knowing the environmental condition (e.g., airport operational data) and traffic loads, including weather information to assess the risk of runway excursion.

Two potential types of equipment were identified (Carlson Scan2K and Riegl VZ-400i). The corresponding suppliers were contacted, and after presenting the project goals, they were mostly interested in collaborating. A set of demo sessions were scheduled to provide a quick overview of each equipment specific capabilities. Both suppliers agreed to leave the equipment for laboratory tests (during a short period). The possibility to perform laboratory tests with samples of the runway from Lisbon airport enabled us to get a better notion of the TLS capabilities. Site-tests at the Lisbon airport also provided outcomes with a very high-resolution level and topography accuracy.

The preliminary field tests were relevant to verify possible locations to position the equipment to analyze the runway pavement in specific areas, analyze the response time between the laser scan. These tests also provided concrete data to be used to configure/train the MPP system (in an early phase of the project execution) regarding the characteristics of the runway pavement, generating a 3D cloud (x, y, z) and "intensity" (the intensity i of the reflected laser signal) referred by some authors as "4D laser scanning".

During the preliminary tests, the TLS equipment was able to generate dense clouds (high-resolution). The Riegl VZ-400i equipment was more performant (complying to its specifications, which state accuracy of 5 mm, precision of 3 mm, and angular step of 0.0015° or less, depending on laser pulse rate using in a range from 250 m to 800 m). Figure 2 presented a TLS' view of a runway slice at Lisbon airport (with moving objects in the runway).

Fig. 2. Lisbon Airport Runway TLS image (runway slice).

The scan presented in Fig. 2 corresponds to a processed image, with the TLS equipment positioned in a way that allows us to analyze the details. The field tests were accomplished in a raining day with the runway wet, during a long period (over 2 h) to analyze the possible impact caused by movements at the runway during the execution of the field-tests. In Fig. 2, we can see the presence of the clutter, managed by the passing planes. However, it did not produce significant shadows to affect the image of the track. This clutter is well identified and can be easily eliminated by software.

4 Smart Airport Runway Safety Process

Automated runway inspections provide fast, accurate, and non-subjective options for manual inspections. Compared with traditional manual qualitative surveys, they can also perform a quantitative analysis of the runway pavement condition, thus providing an additional dimension [13]. The use of TLS instrumentation for monitoring the runway conditions is nowadays a state-of-the-art approach, providing reliable and precise information [14]. The technology can be used to perform inspections and to report measurements on the conditions of the runway, identifying risks related to aquaplaning, pavement deformation, and the presence of foreign objects, simultaneously allowing the visualization of the collected data in a 3D high precision [15].

Information governance provides a holistic approach for managing this type of information by implementing processes, roles, controls, and metrics that treat data as a valuable business asset. The goal is to make data assets available to those who need it while simplifying management and ensuring compliance with the types of events being monitored. Another important goal is to provide airport staff with data they can trust and easily access, while making business decisions to deal with risks associated with unmanaged or inconsistently managed information, thereby becoming more agile. The information governance framework includes defining who will specify the information workflow related to runway safety incidents and the types of data that the information governance program aims to manage. This means that information governance includes more than traditional records management. It integrates data security and protection, compliance, risk management, knowledge management, and business operations.

In addition, data governance also involves (usually a person or a specific team) the responsibility of understanding how data is collected, how it is maintained, how it is interpreted, how users use data, and why it is so valuable. If the data is inconsistent or incomplete, what steps can the organization take to change it? This means that governance needs to include management to achieve better self-service. Data stewards usually manage data catalogs, glossaries, and metadata repositories, and protect the resources required to maintain them. They promote the reuse of data and try to improve collaboration around data and analysis.

4.1 Business Scenario for Runway Contamination

The status of the runway must be regularly assessed, especially in extreme weather conditions, which may affect the runway surface. The condition of a wet runway can be measured by the depth of water in the touchdown zone. ICAO has defined standard terminology to describe the runway as dry, wet, wet, wet, or full of water [1]. In such contaminated conditions, the risk of aquaplaning is high.

When the wheels are running with water, aquaplaning may occur. This situation may also occur in some cases when water and wet snow are mixed. Aquaplaning on a runway surface with typical friction characteristics is unlikely to start at a water depth of 3 mm or less. Therefore, a depth of 3mm is used in Europe as a means to determine whether the runway surface is contaminated by water so that the assumption of aircraft performance is easily affected. When it is detected that the water depth in most areas of the runway is 3 mm (or higher), the airport operator must immediately inform all involved stakeholders of the status of the runway.

Figure 3 outlines the use case responsible for notifying the Airport Operator (with the role of RC manager) about the runway status, alerting for the risk of aquaplaning. A new notification will be issued whenever there is a significant change in the runway conditions (e.g., whenever a water-event is detected). The system infers the information at the business logic layers (i.e., by the Central Decision Management). Each time the TLS provides updated data about a runway inspection, the system will compute the data and pass the results to be analyzed. Activity five (A5) is responsible for correlating the collected data with the data about the airport operational status (provided by existing airport systems) to generate the inspection report. In case a runway event is detected, then a specific sequence flow is triggered to alert the airport operators promptly.

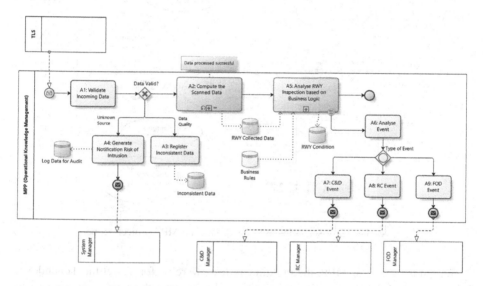

Fig. 3. The workflow associated with runway events.

The same scenario is outlined in Fig. 4 with a different viewpoint. The use case diagram highlights the system behavior from the perspective of the user. The purpose of the use case diagram is to capture the dynamic aspect of a system, meaning that when the requirements of a system are analyzed, the functionalities are captured in use cases. Business use cases should produce a result of observable value to a business actor. A key concept of use case modeling is that it can help us design a system from the perspective of the end-user. By specifying interactions with external systems (defined as actors in UML notation), this is a useful technique for communicating system behavior in the user's terms. Use case six (UC6) is responsible for notifying the RC manager about the presence of hazardous conditions due to the runway condition. Such a notification message follows the format defined by ICAO for SNOWTAM[8].

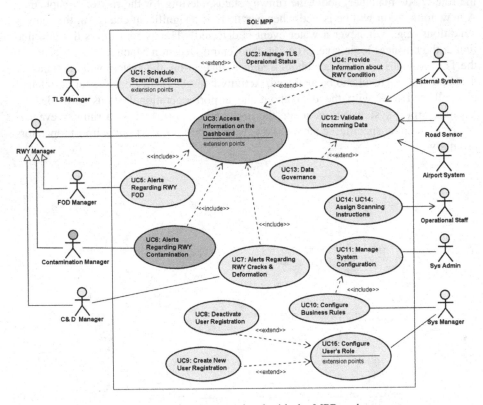

Fig. 4. Use case scenarios associated with the MPP project scope.

Within the scope of MPP, the preliminary tests were performed at the Touchdown Zone segment of the Runway in Lisbon airport. In this area, the runway condition can be affected to some degree by rubber deposits from landing aircraft. These deposits should be regularly removed to achieve a stated minimum dry friction level, mitigating the risk of viscous aquaplaning.

In most situations, raw data has no value in itself; instead, we need to extract the information contained in it. This is the first step in the discovery of knowledge to aid in decision making. End-users should be empowered to exploit the data; as such, the user experience when interacting with the system is determinant to motivate the user in

---

[8] SNOWTAM is a special series NOTAM notifying the presence, or removal, of hazardous conditions due to snow, ice, slush or standing water associated with snow, mud and ice on the movement area. A NOTAM (notice to airmen) is a notice containing information concerning the establishment, condition or change in any aeronautical facility, service, procedure or hazard, the timely knowledge of which is essential to personnel concerned with flight operations.

exploring the system capabilities to extract information from the data. The knowledge gained can be used to elaborate policies, to make decisions, or to define rules of behavior in a way that is well informed and legitimized by its fairness and transparency.

The acquisition of raw data is no longer the driving problem: it is the ability to identify methods and models, which can turn the data into reliable and comprehensible knowledge. In Visual Analytics, the central driving vision is to turn the information overload into an opportunity, making the way of processing data and information, transparent for an analytic discourse.

The big trend we see in our research is to with the need for an event-driven model were the data collected by TLS is fused with airport operational data to make the data a more significant part of decision-making. With this approach, we hope to reduce errors and in order to convert data into actionable insights and to provide the end-user with good data quality and trusted data. At the same time, the airport wants to empower more personnel to discover and share data insights to more users. This increase in self-service analytics, however, means that we must find a good balance between giving freedom to the users and providing the right oversight and data governance.

4.2   User Interface Specification

Using interactive dashboards to visualize information can create a means for end-users to be more aware of undergoing (critical) events. People normally respond better to visuals telling a clear story than a long table or description that needs interpretation. Nowadays, the combination of information visualization and visual analysis has become the medium of the semi-automated analysis process. In this process, humans and machines work together to obtain the most effective results. The user has the ultimate authority when specifying the analysis direction related to a specific task. Besides, the visual representation sketch can describe the path from data to decision, providing a reference for user group collaboration across different tasks.

Figure 5 presents a high-fidelity prototype of the proposed interactive dashboard. It relies on data visualization best practices. The interface offers a set of role-based and interactive features to support the management of runway operations and monitoring activities, promoting situational awareness to the users. Figure 5 depicts three inter-active areas of the interface: header toolbar left sidebar and a (geo)workspace container. On the right side, the notification wizard keeps the user well informed about current events, enabling the user to configure the type of events (s)he wants to keep monitoring.

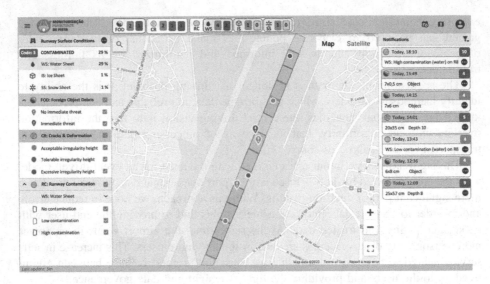

Fig. 5. The high-fidelity prototype of the runway surface conditions surveillance.

The interface supports the management of information regarding runway status, promoting situational awareness to the users. The application was designed to streamline the visualization of data related events according to three criteria:

- Foreign Object Debris (FOD)
  - Yellow, a FOD event that represents no immediate threat;
  - Red, a FOD event that represents an immediate threat that should be removed;
- Cracks & Deformation (C&D)
  - Yellow, a C&D event that represents acceptable irregularity height;
  - Orange, a C&D event that represents tolerable irregularity height;
  - Red, a C&D event that represents excessive irregularity height;
- Runway Contamination (RC), with a focus on water sheet events
  - Yellow, a runway segment classified as low contamination (between 10–25%);
  - Red, indicates the runway segment classified as high contamination (above 25%).

Runway surface conditions depend on a variety of factors, including state changes due to surface temperature effects, chemical treatment, or run-off and removal. The Runway Surface Conditions in the MPP, adopted from ICAO (see Sect. 2), are classified as:

- Dry, a runway is considered dry if its surface is free from visible moisture and not contaminated within the area intended to be used;
- Wet, a runway is considered wet when it is covered by any visible dampness or water that is above 3 mm in depth;
- Contaminated, a runway is considered contaminated when any fluid contaminant is above 3 mm, and when the contaminants represent an area above 25%. Ice and snow are not fluids; nevertheless, they are considered as contamination as well:

- Water Sheet, water depth with more than 3 mm;
- Ice Sheet, any form of ice/compacted snow, the depth is irrelevant;
- Snow Sheet, snow above 3 mm.

The information presented at the user interface in Fig. 2 is compliant to the requirements defined by ICAO for the runway condition assessment matrix (see Table 2 for a detailed list of the runway condition codes). If the runway is classified as contaminated, then the corresponding segment is marked accordingly, providing a visual context-awareness streamlining the user-perception of the risk level. The report is complemented with metadata clarifying the type of contaminator (e.g., water, ice, or snow), presenting a map-based interface for the visualization of the reported event(s). Whenever applicable, the localization of the event (e.g., FOD and C&D) is represented as a georeferenced point over the cartographic layout.

A new notification is generated if in the next cycle of the Runway inspection, new events are detected or if the existing ones persist (i.e., not solved). This is particularly relevant for FOD events. The total of unread events (or new events) is presented as an indicator to call the attention of the user. The user can configure the system to show a specific behavior for events requiring his/her immediate attention.

5 Conclusion and Future Work

To help mitigate the risk of excursion, ICAO has developed a unified method for assessing and reporting runway surface conditions. This methodology, called GRF, aims to cover requirements under all climatic conditions. GRF involves evaluating the runway through manual observation (usually done by airport operators) and using a runway condition matrix. The purpose is to establish a unified reporting system on the condition of the runway surface. In this article, we introduced the MPP project's approach to ICAO assessment of the runway surface conditions during dry/wet/contaminated conditions and the procedures/formats for reporting to all intervenient stakeholders. This project introduced an innovative method of using TLS as an automatic runway inspection. The solution applies spectrum analysis to infer the characteristics of the pavement surface, and sends the collected data to the server-side for processing, and integrates with other airport data.

Although TLS equipment monitors the runway status, other data about the airport's operating status needs to be considered when assessing the runway status. The MPP system interacts with multiple airport entities, and each entity plays a specific role in providing information. This information is used by the system to report runway status according to airport regulations, flight numbers, weather conditions, and operational status. The system accesses public services to improve the positioning accuracy of identified runway safety events. The next step in the execution of the MPP project is to implement a high-fidelity prototype and use a continuous data stream test system collected by the TLS equipment installed at Lisbon Airport. In this phase, the end-user will actively participate in verifying the information displayed for each interactive dashboard, its compliance with ICAO recommendations, and, most importantly, the usability of the system interface to handle critical runway safety-related events.

References

1. ICAO: State of Global Aviation Safety. ICAO Safety Report (2019)
2. EUROCONTROL: European Action Plan for the Prevention of Runway Incursions, ed. 1 (2017)
3. European Union Aviation Safety Agency (EASA): Easy Access Rules for Aerodromes (2019)
4. ICAO: The New Global Reporting Format for Runway Surface Conditions. https://www.icao.int/safety/Pages/GRF.aspx. Accessed 21 May 2020
5. Adamson, P.: Runway Surface Conditions: The Global Reporting Format, Uniting Aviation. https://www.unitingaviation.com/news/safety/runway-surface-conditions-the-global-reporting-format. Accessed 10 June 2020
6. European Union Aviation Safety Agency (EASA): Runway safety, Opinion No 03 (2019)
7. Vorobyeva, O., et al.: Assessing the contribution of data mining methods to avoid aircraft run-off from the runway to increase the safety and reduce the negative environmental Impacts. Int. J. Environ. Res. Public Health **17**, 796 (2020)
8. Davies, R.: Real-time runway monitoring: ICAO's new global reporting standard. Airport Technology (2019). https://www.airport-technology.com/features/real-time-runway-monitoring. Accessed 21 May 2020
9. Manzi, N.M.: The Runway Condition Report. ICAO Regional Seminar on Implementation of the New Global Reporting Format for Runway Surface Condition, 17, 796 (2019)
10. Huijbrechts, E.-J.A.M., et al.: Using Vmcg-Limited V1, controllability issues on contaminated runways and in crosswind. J. Aircr. **56**(4), 1342–1352 (2019)
11. Daidzic, N.E., Shrestha, J.: Airplane landing performance on contaminated runways in adverse conditions. J. Aircr. **45**(6), 2131–2144 (2008)
12. ICAO. Doc9981, Procedures for Air Navigation Services, Aerodromes, 2nd edn. (2016)
13. Mathavan, S., Kamal, K., Rahman, M.: A review of three-dimensional imaging technologies for pavement distress detection and measurements. IEEE Trans. Intell. Transp. Syst. **16**(5), 1524–9050 (2015). https://doi.org/10.1109/TITS.2015.2428655
14. Li, Q., et al.: Laser imaging and sparse points grouping for pavement crack detection. In: 25th European Signal Processing Conference - EUSIPCO (2017)
15. Ragnoli, A., Blasiis, M.R., Benedetto, A.: Pavement distress detection methods: a review. Infrastructures **3**, 58 (2018)
16. OutSystems, S.A.: Interface between Resource Broker and Client Systems, ANA Aeroportos de Portugal, SA, 16th July (2007)

Author Index

Printed in the United States
by Baker & Taylor Publisher Services